Being the Heart of the World

In this timely book, Nino Vallen tells the story of New Spain's gradual integration into the Pacific Basin and challenges established views about identity formation among the elites of colonial Mexico. The book examines how discussions about the establishment and desirability of transpacific connections interacted with more general debates over why some people deserved certain benefits over others. As part of these struggles, New Spain's changing place at the crossroads of transatlantic and transpacific routes became a subject of contention between actors moved by competing notions of a deserving self: the learned councillor, the veteran, the discoverer, the meritorious, the creole, and the merchant. Reassessing current historiographical narratives on creole identities and worldviews, *Being the Heart of the World* contributes to a broader understanding of the early modern self and the ways in which it was shaped by the mobilities of an increasingly globalized world.

Nino Vallen is a research fellow at the Pacific Office of the German Historical Institute Washington, University of California, Berkeley. His research focuses on the role of transpacific interactions in Latin America's social and political history. This is his first book.

CAMBRIDGE LATIN AMERICAN STUDIES

General Editors
KRIS LANE, Tulane University
MATTHEW RESTALL, Pennsylvania State University

Editor Emeritus
HERBERT S. KLEIN
Gouverneur Morris Emeritus Professor of History, Columbia University and Hoover
Research Fellow, Stanford University

Other Books in the Series

(Continued after the Index)

Being the Heart of the World

The Pacific and the Fashioning of the Self in New Spain, 1513–1641

NINO VALLEN

University of California, Berkeley

CAMBRIDGE
UNIVERSITY PRESS

CAMBRIDGE
UNIVERSITY PRESS

Shaftesbury Road, Cambridge CB2 8EA, United Kingdom

One Liberty Plaza, 20th Floor, New York, NY 10006, USA

477 Williamstown Road, Port Melbourne, VIC 3207, Australia

314–321, 3rd Floor, Plot 3, Splendor Forum, Jasola District Centre, New Delhi – 110025, India

103 Penang Road, #05-06/07, Visioncrest Commercial, Singapore 238467

Cambridge University Press is part of Cambridge University Press & Assessment, a department of the University of Cambridge.

We share the University's mission to contribute to society through the pursuit of education, learning and research at the highest international levels of excellence.

www.cambridge.org
Information on this title: www.cambridge.org/9781009322072

DOI: 10.1017/9781009322089

First published 2023

A catalogue record for this publication is available from the British Library.

Library of Congress Cataloging-in-Publication Data
NAMES: Vallen, Nino, author
TITLE: Being the heart of the world : the Pacific and the fashioning of the self in new Spain, 1513-1641 / Nino Vallen, Pacific Office of the German Historical Institute Washington, University of California, Berkeley.
DESCRIPTION: Cambridge ; New York : Cambridge University Press, 2023. | Series: CLAS Cambridge Latin American studies | Includes bibliographical references and index.
IDENTIFIERS: LCCN 2023007951 (print) | LCCN 2023007952 (ebook) | ISBN 9781009322072 (hardback) | ISBN 9781009322041 (paperback) | ISBN 9781009322089 (epub)
SUBJECTS: LCSH: Identity (Philosophical concept) | New Spain–Emigration and immigration. | New Spain–Commerce–History. | Mexico–Emigration and immigration. | Mexico–Commerce–History. | Pacific Area–Relations–New Spain. | New Spain–Relations–Pacific Area. | Pacific Area–Commerce–New Spain. | New Spain–Commerce–Pacific Area. | Spain–Colonies–History.
CLASSIFICATION: LCC DU65 .V35 2023 (print) | LCC DU65 (ebook) | DDC 304.8/20972530903–dc23/eng/20230307
LC record available at https://lccn.loc.gov/2023007951
LC ebook record available at https://lccn.loc.gov/2023007952

ISBN 978-1-009-32207-2 Hardback

For Marcela and Lea

Contents

Figures

Acknowledgments

This book would not have come into being if not for the generous help of many colleagues and friends as well as several institutions. I am especially indebted to Stefan Rinke, who has believed in this project from the moment it consisted of nothing but a vague idea. After his questions set me on my way, he supported me during every step of the slow process of writing this book. More generally, I am deeply grateful for his encouragement and guidance in the field of Latin American History.

At the Institute for Latin American Studies at the Free University of Berlin, I owe special gratitude to Marianne Braig for her spirited support and to Michael Goebel, Nikolaus Böttcher, Mónika Contreras, Lasse Hölck, Debora Gerstenberger, and Karina Kriegesmann for reading parts of the manuscript and helping me out on so many occasions. I also want to thank Peter Rietbergen, who has been a mentor and friend since I was an undergraduate student at Radboud University Nijmegen. His comments on an earlier version of the manuscript have helped me sharpen my argument. I am also indebted to colleagues in Mexico and the United States: Bernd Hausberger, Antonio Ibarra, Federico Navarrete Linares, Ana Carolina Ibarra González, and Gibran Bautista y Lugo all received me so kindly and provided valuable advice on this and other projects. I also benefited greatly from my conversations with Jeremy Adelman, Evelyn Hu-DeHart, Tatiana Seijas, and Christina Lee, who helped me to navigate the world of academic publishing. Their guidance has been crucial for making this book what it is.

This book would not have been possible if not for the financial support I received over the years. I would like to thank the International Research Training Group "Between Spaces" for bringing me to Berlin. Who would have thought that this one-year scholarship would lead to a decade-long stay at the Institute for Latin American Studies. I am especially grateful for the research grant provided by the Slicher van Bath-De Jong Fund, which allowed me to collect additional archival material and improve my writing. I am pleased to honor such a prolific historian by continuing to study the history of Latin America in his name. Grants provided by the Dahlem Research School and the Center for International Cooperation at the Free University of Berlin gave me the possibility to spend time at the University of California, Berkeley, and Princeton University. Finally, I would like to thank the German Historical Institute Washington for enabling me to finish this book while setting out on a new journey.

Two anonymous readers provided invaluable feedback on the working manuscript, and their observations and suggestions have improved it tremendously. I am much obliged to Christopher Hank, who has painstakingly read and improved my writing over the years. I also thank Cecelia A. Cancellaro at Cambridge University Press, as well as series editors Kris Lane and Matthew Restall for believing in this project.

Finally, my warmest thanks go to my family. My mother, my Mexican family, and especially my wife, Marcela, and daughter, Lea. They have brought so much light and love into my days. It took a while, but we did it. Together!

Abbreviations

Actas	*Actas de cabildo del ayuntamiento de México.* Edited by Manuel Orozco y Berra and Antonio Espinosa de los Monteros. 50 vols. Mexico: Aguilar e Hijos, 1889–1911
AGI	Archivo General de Indias (Seville)
AGN	Archivo General de la Nación (Mexico City)
AHN	Archivo Histórico Nacional (Madrid)
BNE	Biblioteca Nacional de España (Madrid)
BP	Biblioteca Palafoxiana (Puebla)
CDI	*Colección de documentos inéditos relativos al descubrimiento, conquista y organización de las antiguas posesiones españolas de América y Oceanía.* Edited by Joaquín F. Pacheco, Francisco de Cárdenas, and Luis Torres de Mendoza. 42 vols. Madrid, 1864–1884
CODOIN	*Colección de documentos inéditos para la historia de España.* Edited by Martín Fernández Navarrete et al. 112 vols. Madrid, 1842–1895
ENE	*Epistolario de Nueva España, 1505–1818.* Edited by Francisco Paso y Troncoso. 16 vols. Mexico: Antigua librería Robredo, de José Porrúa e hijos, 1939–1942
RAH	Real Academia de la Historia (Madrid)

Introduction

During the first half of the 1630s, the first Count of the Valley of Orizaba, don Rodrigo de Vivero y Aberruza, wrote a critical reflection on New Spain's pivotal position in an increasingly interconnected world. According to this creole nobleman, expanding flows of people and commodities across the Pacific were having a negative impact on life in the viceroyalty. Soldiers and friars traveling from Spain to the Philippines were deserting their companies, causing harm to Spanish and Indigenous populations alike. Transpacific trade was fueling fraud and corruption, leading to an uncontrollable hemorrhaging of wealth. Meanwhile, the exchange of valuable silver for useless vanities was excessively benefiting New Spain's merchants, enabling them to improve their social position at the cost of those whom they believed should receive the viceroyalty's benefits: the descendants of the conquistadores. These developments, Vivero warned, were having a destabilizing effect not only on New Spain but on the Spanish empire as a whole. To put an end to these threats to the colonial and imperial order, the count proposed that the monarch should "close the port of Acapulco and send aid for the Philippines from Cadiz or Lisbon."[1]

---

[1] "Discursos de d. Rodrigo de Vivero i Velasco primer conde del Valle de Orisaba," Real Academia de la Historia, Colección Muñoz, V.10 (9/4789), f. 73v. These reflections form part of a collection of documents, also including Vivero's accounts of his travels to Japan and a selection of royal grants (*mercedes*), which was prepared by his grandson, don Nicolas de Vivero Peredo y Velasco, to be presented at the court. A somewhat altered copy of this collection is also preserved in the British Library (Add MS 18287) and has been transcribed in its entirety in Rodrigo de Vivero, "Abisos y proyectos," *Du Japon et du bon*

Vivero's assessment of the negative impact of New Spain's prolifer-
ating transpacific connections was not unique at the time. Similar critiques had already been voiced both inside and outside the viceroyalty for
almost half a century. Still, the nobleman's commentary on the current
state of the empire reveals a remarkable change in his opinion about the
desirability of global interconnectedness. Earlier in his life, Vivero had
played a key role in establishing new relationships across the Pacific. With
his visits in 1609 and 1610 to the Japanese shogun, Hidetada, and his
powerful father, Ieyasu, he had made valuable contributions to the diplomatic overtures that took place between New Spain and Japan during the
following decade.[2] Vivero's experiences in the Pacific had also emerged in
the self-promoting stories he had been telling the Crown in his petitions
for rewards.[3] Yet, in his reflections from the 1630s, the count revised this
narrative, speaking now of Japanese justice and imperial politics to
reinforce his argument that New Spain would be better off acting as the
empire's outer limit rather than a pivot connecting the Iberian metropolis
to its Asian territories. The striking contrast between Vivero's writings
from the 1610s and 1620s and those from the 1630s reveals how his ideas
about the significance of the viceroyalty's connections to the world
changed as his position within ongoing struggles over royal favor shifted.
Having become a member of the landed nobility in 1627, he had
developed a new sense of entitlement, resulting in a quite different self-
image and an accordingly revised vision regarding global relationships.

This book traces the history of New Spain's gradual integration within
the Pacific Basin and the impacts of this development on the narratives that
Spaniards in the viceroyalty recounted about themselves and the changing
world around them.[4] Activities contributing to this integrative process
commenced almost immediately after the Spaniards arrived in
Mesoamerica. In 1522, only a year after the fall of Tenochtitlan, Hernán
Cortés was already building ships in the port of Zacatula, in order to
explore the secrets of the waters then known as the *Mar del Sur* (South
Sea). During the following century, expeditions sent from New Spain's
western coast established initial connections across the Pacific Basin.

---

gouvernement de l'Espagne et des Indes, ed. and trans. Juliette Monbeig (Paris: SEVPEN, 1972), 76–131.

[2] For Vivero's accounts of his time in Japan, see for example: Vivero, *Du Japon et du bon gouvernement*, 53–74.

[3] See, for example, Letter from Vivero, Jun 30, 1624, AGI, Panamá, 17, R.8, N.144.

[4] I use the term Pacific Basin to refer to the lands that border the ocean, usually called the Pacific Rim, and the islands within it.

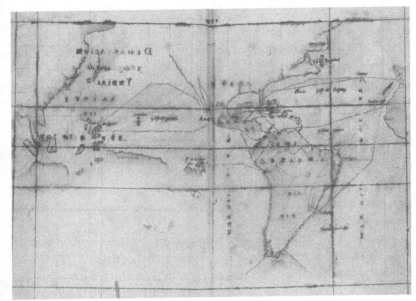

FIGURE I.I Map of the Spanish Indies. Juan López de Velasco, *Demarcación y navegación de Indias*, Madrid (ca. 1575). Courtesy of the John Carter Brown Library

Conquerors and merchants headed south, following the coast toward Panama and El Callao, in search of the treasures of the Incas and, later, the silver mined in Potosí. Others set out northward, to locate a land bridge connecting the Asian and American continents or a strait connecting the Pacific to the Atlantic. Yet others sailed west, searching for the long-desired route to Asia, especially the coveted Spice Islands. Although the Spaniards had little trouble crossing the ocean, it took them until 1565 to discover the *tornaviaje*, a sea route that allowed ships to sail east from the Philippines to California. Soon thereafter, Spanish galleons began making regular trips across the vast oceanic expanse, transporting trade goods as well as soldiers, friars, royal officials, merchants, and others from Acapulco to Manila.

With the expansion of Spanish activities in the Pacific Basin, New Spain increasingly became a point of intersection for imperial, commercial, and religious networks. Speaking to this emerging situation is a map that the royal cosmographer, Juan López de Velasco, included in his *Demarcación y división de las Indias* (Demarcation and Division of the Indies) in the mid-1570s (see Figure I.1).[5] Plotted to underline and justify

[5] Juan López de Velasco, *Demarcación y división de las Indias*, Biblioteca Nacional de España, Mss/2825. This text has been published in CDI, 15: 409–572.

Spain's territorial claims in Asia, Velasco's image depicts the Western Hemisphere as it stretches out between the line of demarcation defined by the treaty of Tordesillas (1493) and a meridian line he drew, somewhat arbitrarily, across the Malayan Peninsula to separate the Spanish from the Portuguese spheres of influence.[6] In Velasco's view of the Spanish empire, the metropolis appears in the east, hidden away on the right side of the map. The opposite side depicts the regions known today as East and Southeast Asia but which he strategically referred to as the "*Indias del Poniente*" (Indies of the West) – a region that he considered to be, after North and South America, the third component of the Spanish Indies.[7] New Spain is situated at the center of the image, its pivotal position in the imperial order highlighted by the transatlantic and transpacific routes converging on it.

Other contemporaries made similar observations about the effects of New Spain's integration into the Pacific world. Already in 1566, an anonymous account of the discovery of the return route from the Philippines concluded that "those of Mexico are mighty proud of their discovery, which gives them to believe that they will be the heart of the world."[8] Such expectations about the viceroyalty's changing position in a globalizing world became more and more a reality during the final decades of the sixteenth and first decades of the seventeenth centuries.[9] Through its western ports, New Spain extended Spain's imperial reach, providing access to the empires, kingdoms, and markets of East and Southeast Asia. The arrival of Asian migrants, objects, and plants further complicated processes of biological and cultural hybridization that had already been initiated by the transatlantic encounters between the Old World and the New.[10] Meanwhile, New Spain's capital developed into a

---

[6] For a discussion of López de Velasco's map and its relation to the imperial struggles between Spain and Portugal, see Ricardo Padrón, *The Indies of the Setting Sun: How Early Modern Spain Mapped the Far East as the Transpacific West* (Chicago: The University of Chicago Press, 2020), 161–65.

[7] CDI, 15: 410.

[8] This account has been published in Emma Helen Blair and James Alexander Robertson, eds., *The Philippine Islands, 1493–1803* (Cleveland, OH: A. H. Clark Co., 1903), 2: 230.

[9] Serge Gruzinski, *Las cuatro partes del mundo: historia de una mundialización* (Mexico City: Fondo de Cultura Económica, 2010), 124–26.

[10] During the past few decades, the role of Asian peoples and objects in these processes of hybridization and transculturation has drawn considerable attention, resulting in studies of New Spanish ceramics, *biombos*, and other types of furniture, as well as the consumption of Asian spices and beverages, such as coconut wine. See, for example, George Kuwayama, *Chinese Ceramics in Colonial Mexico* (Los Angeles: Los Angeles County Museum of Art, 1997); Donna Pierce and Ronald Y. Otsuka, eds., *Asia & Spanish*

hub for the incipient world market, where local and regional merchandise was traded next to luxury and bulk goods coming from Europe and Asia. At the beginning of the seventeenth century, New Spain's pivotal position in this incipient world of trade inspired Spanish poet Bernardo de Balbuena to exclaim in his typical hyperbolic style: "Mexico you divide the world in half, the earth bending toward it as if toward a sun, appearing to all the world as to preside over it all."[11]

Increasing connectivity and mobility in the Pacific Basin not only affected perceptions of New Spain's place in the world but also the self-perceptions of its residents and others traveling through the viceroyalty. Various projects of exploration and conquest had been influencing these notions since the early 1520s, and explorers and conquistadores spotlighted their activities in and knowledge of the Pacific Basin in the life stories they produced to obtain privileges and rewards from the Crown. Residents of New Spain continued to do so after 1565, but their narratives began to reflect another emerging reality. Movement of imperial agents, soldiers, and friars in and across the Pacific, while in many ways enriching life in the viceroyalty, led to social tensions with locals, prompting new senses of self and other.

This book studies these little-explored identity transformations by examining how the increasing mobility of people, goods, and ideas in the Pacific world converged with struggles over the distribution of New Spain's wealth, privileges, and honors to shape new concepts of the self. Discussions about the establishment and desirability of transpacific links interacted with more general debates over why some individuals or segments of the population deserved certain benefits more than others. By investigating the notions of self that were fashioned within the interstices of these disputes, I reassess existing interpretations of the emancipatory significance of the Pacific for its emerging creole population, demonstrating how the viceroyalty's place at the "heart of the world" became the

America: Trans-Pacific Artistic and Cultural Exchange, 1500–1850. Papers from the 2006 Mayer Center Symposium at the Denver Art Museum (Denver: Denver Art Museum, 2009); Thomas Calvo and Paulina Machuca, eds., *México y Filipinas: culturas y memorias sobre el Pacífico* (Zamora: El Colegio de Michoacán; Quezon City: Aleneo de Manila University Press, 2016); Paulina Machuca, *El vino de cocos en la Nueva España. Historia de una transculturación en el siglo XVII* (Zamora: El Colegio de Michoacán, 2018); Meha Priyadarshini, *Chinese Porcelain in Colonial Mexico: The Material Worlds of an Early Modern Trade* (Cham: Palgrave Macmillan, 2018).
[11] Bernardo de Balbuena, *Grandeza mexicana*, ed. Asima F.X. Saad Maura (Madrid: Cátedra, 2011), 189.

subject of contention between actors moved by diverging ideas about the distribution of its wealth and benefits.

Traditional scholarship on distributional conflicts in New Spain and the Spanish identities that emerged during these disputes has hardly considered what transpired in the terraqueous spaces west of New Spain. Studies on the distribution of land, *encomiendas*, and offices have revolved around narratives concerning European expansion in the Atlantic world and the emergence of a discourse of creole patriotism resulting from the Crown's refusal to reward the conquistadores and their descendants.[12] In turn, historians of the Spanish Pacific have contributed little to debates about colonial identities, as their studies have focused mainly on exploration and colonization in Asia, the economic dynamics of the galleon trade, as well as transcultural exchanges between New Spain and the Philippines.[13] Yet, in recent years, growing interest in the Pacific has led to new attempts to bring these distinct strands of scholarship into dialogue. On the one hand, some studies have questioned the previous tendency to separate the conquest of the American mainland from Iberian interests in Asia by demonstrating the enduring impacts that the desire to reach Asia had on the Spanish conquerors and their perceptions of American territories and Native populations.[14] On the other

[12] Marvyn Helen Bacigalupo, *A Changing Perspective: Attitudes towards Creole Society in New Spain (1521–1610)* (London: Tamesis, 1981); Anthony Pagden, "Identity Formation in Spanish America," in *Colonial Identity in the Atlantic World, 1500–1800*, eds. Nicholas Canny and Anthony Pagden, 51–93 (Princeton, NJ: Princeton University Press, 1987); David A. Brading, *The First America: The Spanish Monarchy, Creole Patriots, and the Liberal State, 1492–1967* (Cambridge: Cambridge University Press, 1991); Bernard Lavallé, *Las promesas ambiguas: ensayos sobre el criollismo colonial en los Andes* (Lima: Pontificia Universidad Católica del Perú, 1993).

[13] William Lytle Schurz, *The Manila Galleon* (New York: E. P. Dutton, 1939); Pierre Chaunu, *Les Philippines et le Pacifique des Ibériques (XVIe, XVIIe, XVIIIe, Siècles): Introduction méthodologique et indices d'activité* (Paris: SEVPEN, 1960); Rafael Bernal, *México en Filipinas: estudio de un transculturación* (Mexico City: UNAM: Instituto de Investigaciones Histróricas, 1965); O. H. K. Spate, *The Pacific since Magellan, Vol. 1: The Spanish Lake* (Canberra: Australian National University Press, 1979); Dennis O. Flynn and Arturo Giráldez. "Born with a 'Silver Spoon': The Origin of World Trade in 1571," *Journal of World History* 6, no. 2 (1995): 201–21; Marina Alfonso Mola and Carlos Martínez Shaw, eds., *El Galeón de Manila* (Madrid: Aldeasa, 2000).

[14] Richard Flint, "When East Was West: The Oriental Aim of the Coronado Expedition," in *The Latest Word from 1540: Peoples, Places, and Portrayals of the Coronado Expedition*, eds. Richard Flint and Shirley Cushing Flint, 105–16 (Albuquerque: University of New Mexico Press, 2011); Serge Gruzinski, *L'aigle et le dragon: démesure européenne et mondialisation au XVIe Siècle* (Paris: Editions Fayard, 2012); Ricardo Padrón, "(Un)Inventing America: The Transpacific Indies in Oviedo and Gómara," *Colonial Latin American Review* 25, no. 1 (2016): 16–34.

hand, historians have begun to relate mobilities in the Pacific to the formation of new identities for the Spanish residents of the viceroyalty as well as the "chino slaves" who sought to find their place as *Indios* in the colonial order.[15]

This book expands on such studies by revealing how military, religious, and trading activities in the Pacific Basin impacted the social and political negotiations that shaped the identities of those who resided in New Spain or passed through it on their way to Asia. Drawing together approaches from the fields of Mexican and Iberian social history, colonial identity studies, cosmopolitan studies, and global history, I offer an alternative framework for understanding how connectivity affected various notions of what I will refer to as the "deserving self." By applying a lens on this specific regime of self, I will demonstrate that narratives about the Pacific and New Spain's place at the heart of the world that were deployed within the context of distributional disputes can neither simply be classified as anti-metropolitan nor merely as expressions of a specific creole cultural worldview. Instead, I argue, they rather reflected the stances of actors involved in complex distributional struggles and debates over the role of global interactions in the making of colonial Mexican society and the Spanish empire as a whole.

IDENTITY AND MOBILITY IN THE EARLY MODERN SPANISH EMPIRE

The question of the relationship between identity and mobility with which this book deals has been a subject of much debate among historians and social scientists during the past three decades. Historians of the early modern period have argued over the role of migration and empire-building in the formation of (proto-)national identities, while others discussed the significance of regional, ethnic, and religious identities in the making of long-distance mercantile and information networks.[16]

---

[15] Tatiana Seijas, *Asian Slaves in Colonial Mexico: From Chinos to Indians* (Cambridge: Cambridge University Press, 2014). Also compare Edward R. Slack, "The Chinos in New Spain: A Corrective Lens for a Distorted Image," *Journal of World History* 20, no. 1 (2009): 35–67.

[16] Tamar Herzog, *Defining Nations: Immigrants and Citizens in Early Modern Spain and Spanish America* (New Haven, CT: Yale University Press, 2003). Antonio Feros, *Speaking of Spain: The Evolution of Race and Nation in the Hispanic World* (Cambridge, MA: Harvard University Press); Bernd Hausberger, "La guerra de los vicuñas contra los vascongados en Potosí y la etnización de los vascos a principios de la

More recent discussions have also focused on the role of global mobility in the formation of cosmopolitan identities among imperial and religious agents.[17] These debates have deepened our understanding of early modern processes of identity-making and the various roles that connectivity played in them. Still, historians continue to wrestle with the question of how personal identity can be adequately subsumed under general categories and what impacts movement had on both processes of self-making and identification.[18]

Illustrative of this struggle is the way in which scholars in recent years have understood the effects of transpacific connections on the development of new senses of self within the viceroyalty. Much of this scholarship has been defined by a tendency to interpret these interactions through the lens of a historiographic narrative about creolization, a process initiated by the movement of a community to a new geographic setting.[19] *Criollismo*, a well-known narrative tells us, arose in the wake of the conquest as a result of the Crown's efforts to limit the influence of an emerging local elite of *encomenderos*.[20] Growing resentment among the conquistadores and their descendants over their unequal treatment and loss of political autonomy shaped a discourse that attests, in the words of David Brading, to "a collective consciousness that separated Spaniards

---

edad moderna," in *Excluir para ser: Procesos identitarios y fronteras sociales en la América hispánica (XVII-XVIII)*, eds. Christian Büschges and Frédérique Langue, 23–57 (Madrid: Iberoamericana/Vervuert, 2005); Eberhard Crailsheim, *The Spanish Connection: French and Flemish Merchant Networks in Seville (1570–1650)* (Cologne: Böhlau, 2016).

[17] Gruzinski, *Les quatre parties du monde*; Luis Miguel Córdoba Ochoa, "Movilidad geográfica, capital cosmopolita y relaciones de méritos. Las élites del imperio entre Castilla, América y el Pacífico," in *Las redes del imperio: Élites sociales en la articulación de la monarquía hispánica, 1492–1714*, ed. Bartolomé Yun Casalilla, 359–78 (Marcial Pons historia. Madrid: Marcial Pons, 2009); José Carlos de la Puente, *Andean Cosmopolitans: Seeking Justice and Reward at the Spanish Royal Court* (Austin: University of Texas Press, 2018).

[18] Also compare John-Paul A. Ghobrial, "Moving Stories and What They Tell Us: Early Modern Mobility between Microhistory and Global History," *Past & Present* 242, Issue Supplement 14 (2019): 245–50. For a general critique of unspecified usage of "identity" as a category in the social sciences, see Rogers Brubaker and Frederick Cooper, "Beyond Identity," *Theory and Society* 29 (2000), 1–47.

[19] Ralph Bauer and José A. Mazzotti, "Introduction," in *Creole Subjects in the Colonial Americas*, ed. Ralph Bauer (Chapel Hill: University of North Carolina Press, 2009), 1.

[20] Lavallé, *Las promesas ambiguas*; Pagden, "Identity Formation in Spanish America"; José Antonio Mazzotti, "Introducción," in *Agencias criollas: la ambigüedad "colonial" en las letras hispanoamericanas*, ed. José A. Mazzotti (Pittsburgh, PA: Instituto Internacional de Literatura Iberoamericana, 2000), 12–13.

born in the New World from their European ancestors and cousins."[21] These American-born criollos began to shape new cultural formations that were not only rooted in European traditions but, due to various cultural influences and a newly emerging worldview, were also distinctively American.[22]

In their studies of New Spain's interactions with the Pacific world, historians, literary scholars, and art historians have interacted with this narrative in varying ways. The discovery of the viceroyalty's global connections and the sense of centrality voiced by people residing there have, for example, dovetailed nicely with efforts made during the past three decades to question traditional Eurocentric historiography.[23] In conventional scholarship, Latin America has generally appeared as being peripheral to the processes of global integration, its peoples presented as victims of global history rather than active participants in it.[24] The recent focus on New Spain's Pacific connections, however, has allowed scholars to overhaul this narrative, showing that in many ways the viceroyalty was much more globally connected than early modern Spain was.

Attempts to rewrite Eurocentric histories have also cohered with an idea voiced by pioneers of Pacific history, namely, that the establishment of the Manila Galleon route meant, in the words of Oscar Spate, "enhanced importance and self-esteem for New Spain" and its inhabitants.[25] Recent studies of the viceroyalty's connections to the Pacific world are inclined toward a similar idea. Economic historians have contended that transpacific commerce enriched Mexico City's creole elite, providing its members leverage to challenge restrictions forced on them by the Spanish metropolis.[26] Some have also presented the city's powerful merchant guild, the *consulado*, as the defender of creole interests against

---

[21] Brading, *The First America*, 293.

[22] Solange Alberro, *Del gachupín al criollo o de cómo los españoles de México dejaron de serlo* (Mexico City: El Colegio de México, 1992), 17.

[23] Ryan Dominic Crewe, "Connecting the Indies: The Hispano-Asian Pacific World in Early Modern Global History," *Etudos Históricos* 30, no. 60 (2017): 19.

[24] Matthew Brown, "The Global History of Latin America," *Journal of Global History* 10, no. 3 (2015): 368–69.

[25] Spate, *The Spanish Lake*, 106. Already in 1943, Mariano Cuevas considered the term *mexicanos*, as used in the 1566 account of Legazpi, Salcedo, and Urdaneta's activities in the Pacific, to reference a collective feat of Spaniards, creoles, and mestizos coming together to constitute the Mexican nation. Mariano P. Cuevas, S. J., *Monje y marino: la vida y los tiempos de Fray Andrés de Urdaneta* (México: Galatea, 1943), 202–3.

[26] Katharine Bjork, "The Link That Kept the Philippines Spanish: Mexican Merchant Interests and the Manila Trade, 1571–1815," *Journal of World History* 9, no. 1 (1998): 25–50. Concerning the importance of transpacific trade for Mexico's merchants,

royal interventions meant to protect Spanish traders.[27] Meanwhile, cultural historians have characterized celebrations of Mexico City's trade connections to the world, like the ones voiced by Balbuena, as efforts to replace Spain with the colonial metropolis as the center of the imperial order.[28]

Other scholars have even more explicitly blended a focus on global connectedness with narratives of the emergence of a creole self-consciousness. Such a tendency is particularly pronounced in studies of New Spanish material culture. Chinese–inspired Pueblan *talavera* pottery and majolica, Asian-style furniture, and popular attire, such as the China *poblana* dress, have all been interpreted as expressions of a particular creole taste.[29] According to Gustavo Curiel, components of Asian artistic traditions merged with European and Amerindian ones into distinctive creative expressions, serving "as constitutive essences of considerable weight in the discourse of creole self-affirmation."[30] Historians and art historians have especially found such self-conscious declarations of creole identity in the New Spanish *biombo*, a type of folding screen that, according to some scholars, was used by members of the creole

see also María del Carmen Yuste López, *El comercio de la Nueva España con Filipinas, 1590–1785* (Mexico City: Instituto Nacional de Antropología e Historia, 1984) and *Emporios transpacíficos. Comerciantes mexicanos en Manila, 1710–1815* (Mexico City: Universidad Nacional Autónoma de México, 2007); Mariano Ardash Bonialian, *El Pacífico hispanoamericano: política y comercio asiático en el Imperio Español (1680–1784)* (Mexico City: El Colegio de México, 2012). Yuste López and Bonialian both consider the Pacific or "Indian lake," as the latter has it, to be a space controlled by the Mexican consulado or Hispanoamerican elites.

[27] Ostwald Sales Colín, *El movimiento portuario de Acapulco: el protagonismo de Nueva España en la relación con Filipinas, 1587–1648* (Mexico City: Plaza y Valdés Editores, 2000), 18.

[28] Barbara Fuchs and Yolanda Martínez-San Miguel, "La grandeza mexicana de Balbuena y el imaginario de una 'metropolis colonial,'" *Revista Iberoamericana* 75, no. 228 (2009): 675–95; Stephanie Merrim, *The Spectacular City, Mexico, and Colonial Hispanic Literary Culture* (Austin: University of Texas Press, 2010), 121–22.

[29] Dana Leibsohn, "Made in China, Made in Mexico," in *At the Crossroads: The Arts of Spanish American and Early Global Trade, 1492–1850*, eds. Donna Pierce and Ronald Otsuka (Denver: Denver Art Museum, 2012), 11–41; José L. Gasch-Tómas, "Asian Silk, Porcelain, and Material Culture in the Definition of Mexican and Andalusian Elites, c. 1565–1630," in *Global Goods and the Spanish Empire, 1492–1824: Circulation, Resistance and Diversity*, eds. Bethany Aram and Bartolomé Yun-Casalilla (London: Palgrave Macmillan, 2014), 167.

[30] Gustavo Curiel, "Perception of the Other and the Language of 'Chinese Mimicry' in the Decorative Arts of New Spain," in *Asia & Spanish America: Trans-Pacific Artistic and Cultural Exchange, 1500–1850*, eds. Donna Pierce and Ronald Y. Otsuka (Denver: Denver Art Museum, 2009), 19.

population to challenge their marginalized position and claim royal favor by showing their worldliness and refinement.[31]

There is, however, a risk in considering the impacts of transpacific interaction on the identities of New Spain's population through the static prism of creole self-consciousness. Critical scholarship on sixteenth- and seventeenth-century creole identities has demonstrated that most creoles did not solely identify as criollo but also as "sons of the kingdom, sons of the land, sons and grandsons of the conquerors/encomenderos, [or] *beneméritos*."[32] How people related these categories to the term criollo and what significance they ascribed to the latter varied considerably according to time and place.[33] Furthermore, historians and literary scholars have pointed out that the identities of Spaniards in the Indies were determined by multiple competing loyalties and demands, with individuals seeing themselves as naturals of a municipality or as members of an extended family, religious order, or occupational guild.[34] Such observations have led some scholars to weaken the significance of creole identity as a category of analysis, characterizing it as "ambiguous," "unstable," or "a subject-in-process."[35] Others have opted for alternative analytical prisms, often defined by the political and religious dynamics of empire.[36] Exemplary of this new direction is Cornelius Conover's recent

---

[31] Alberto Baena Zapatero, "Biombos mexicanos e identidad criolla," *Revista De Indias* 80, no. 280 (2020), 651–86; Ottmar Ette, "EntreMundos o la relacionalidad transarchipiélica de Nueva España," *Iberoamericana* XII, no. 48 (2012): 162–65.

[32] Lavallé, *Las promesas ambiguas*, 17.

[33] Juan M. Vitulli and David M. Solodkow, "Ritmos diversos y secuencias plurales: hacia una periodización del concepto 'criollo,'" in *Poéticas de lo criollo: la transformación del concepto "criollo" en las letras hispanoamericanas (siglos XVI al XIX)*, eds. Juan M. Vitulli and David M. Solodkow (Buenos Aires: Ediciones Corregidor, 2009), 10–11.

[34] Richard L. Kagan and Fernando Marías, *Urban Images of the Hispanic World, 1493–1793* (London: Yale University Press, 2000), 105; Alberto Baena Zapatero, *Mujeres novohispanas e identidad criolla (siglos XVI y XVII)* (Madrid: Ayuntamiento Alcalá de Henares, 2009), 19.

[35] Yolanda Martínez-San Miguel, *Saberes americanos: Subalternidad y epistemología en los escritos de Sor Juana* (Pittsburgh: Instituto Internacional de Literatura Iberoamericana, 1999), 208; Anna More, *Baroque Sovereignty: Carlos de Sigüenza y Góngora and the Creole Archive of Colonial Mexico* (Philadelphia: University of Pennsylvania Press, 2013), 9.

[36] Anna More, for instance, uses Walter Benjamin's concept of the Baroque allegory in her book, *Baroque Sovereignty*. Empire, in turn, plays a central role in Kathryn M. Mayers, *Visions of Empire in Colonial Spanish American Ekphrastic Writing* (Lewisburg, PA: Bucknell University Press, 2012), 18; Michael J. Schreffler, *The Art of Allegiance: Visual Culture and Imperial Power in Baroque New Spain* (University Park: Pennsylvania State University Press, 2007), 3.

study of the Cult of Felipe de Jesús, in which he observes that scholars have "overemphasized matters of identity" and ignored the role of such religious cults in the constitution of empire.[37]

Although I recognize the aforementioned problems, I do not feel the need to discard the category of identity altogether. Instead, in this book I deploy the lens of the deserving self to arrive at an alternative understanding of the ways in which discoverers, conquerors, soldiers, officials, friars, and merchants in New Spain creatively revised and strategically recalibrated their own identities and those of others. Although the term criollo did shape such notions of self, it was but one among many categories that were articulated, publicized, internalized, contested, and altered by subjects of the Spanish Crown as they sought to prove that they were worthy of certain benefits or positions of authority. Heeding Lynn Hunt's recent call for new ways of explaining "how self and society expanded and how that expansion relates to globalization," I use this approach to offer a more interactive image of the multilayered identities these actors assumed and the factors strengthening their affiliations within the increasingly complex colonial society that developed at this crossroads of transoceanic networks.[38]

DISTRIBUTIVE STRUGGLE AND THE DESERVING SELF

Although the self has long been associated with authenticity, individuality, and a person's true essence, scholars today commonly consider it to be a malleable entity that is shaped by social and cultural conditions.[39] At various moments in history, different types of self have emerged or become more prominent as a result of political, economic, cultural, and technological transformations within societies.[40] The specific regime of

---

[37] Cornelius Conover, *Pious Imperialism: Spanish Rule and the Cult of Saints in Mexico City* (Albuquerque: University of New Mexico Press, 2019), 7–9. Solange Alberro, for example, has studied the significance of Felipe de Jesús – a Mexican-born Franciscan who was martyred in Nagasaki in 1597 – for the development of a creole identity. See Solange Alberro, *El águila y la cruz: orígenes religiosos de la conciencia criolla, México, Siglos XVI–XVII* (Mexico City: El Colegio de México, 1999), 115–18.

[38] Lynn Hunt, *Writing History in the Global Era* (New York: W. W. Norton & Company, 2014), 151.

[39] Anthony Elliott, *Identity Troubles: An Introduction* (New York: Routledge, 2016), 116–17.

[40] Nikolas S. Rose, *Inventing Our Selves: Psychology, Power, and Personhood* (Cambridge: Cambridge University Press, 1996), 22–25. See also Charles Taylor, *Sources of the Self: The Making of the Modern Identity* (Cambridge: Cambridge University Press, 1989).

self on which this book focuses emerged in medieval Iberian societies as a result of responses to the question of whether kings could reward the privilege of nobility.[41] Savants, clergymen, and royal officials grappling with this problem shaped a complex of knowledges, narratives, and apparatuses that impacted not only the ways in which wealth, offices, and honors were being distributed but also how contemporaries fashioned identities for themselves and others.

Selfhood moved to the center of these distributive processes as a result of two interrelated ideas that were deeply anchored in late medieval and early modern Iberian political theory. The first argued that monarchs had a moral and legal obligation to reward their vassals and subjects for the services they had rendered to God, their lord, and their patria. Such a notion of reciprocity has played an important role in recent historiography, examining ways in which power was negotiated in the polycentric Spanish monarchy.[42] This scholarship has underscored the importance of the principles of giving and gratitude for establishing the patron–client ties that simultaneously united the Spanish monarchy and contributed to the distribution of power from the center to local and regional elites.[43] Such an "economy of favor," to use the term Antonio Hespanha has coined, was especially important for the relationship between the sovereign and his subjects – the former being required to generously grant

---

[41] The debates concerning knighthood and conflicting conceptualizations of a nobility of service and nobility of blood have been studied extensively. See, for example, Jesús D. Rodríguez Velasco, "De oficio a estado. La caballería entre el Espéculo y las Siete Partidas," *Cahiers de linguistique hispanique médiévale* 17–18 (1993–94): 49–77; Jesús D. Rodríguez Velasco, *El debate sobre la caballería en el siglo XV. La tratadística caballeresca castellana en su marco europeo* (Salamanca: Junta de Castilla y León Consejería de Educación y Cultura, 1996); Georges Martin, "Control regio de la violencia nobiliaria," in *Lucha política: condena y legitimación en la España medieval*, eds. Isabel Alfonso, Julio Escalona, and Georges Martin (Lyon: ENS, 2004), 219–34.

[42] Pedro Cardim et al., introduction to *Polycentric Monarchies: How Did Early Modern Spain and Portugal Achieve and Maintain a Global Hegemony?*, eds. Pedro Cardim, Tamar Herzog, José Javier Ruis Ibáñez, and Gaetano Sabatini (Eastbourne: Sussex Academic Press, 2012), 3–8; Bartolomé Yun Casalilla, "Introducción. Entre el imperio colonial y la monarquía compuesta. Élites y territorios en la Monarquía Hispánica (ss. XVI y XVII)," in *Las redes del imperio. Élites sociales en la articulación de la Monarquía Hispánica, 1492–1714*, ed. Yun Casalilla (Madrid: Marcial Pons/Universidad Pablo Olavide, 2009), 11–13.

[43] Antonio Feros, "Clientelismo y poder monárquico en la España de los siglos XVI y XVII," *Relaciones. Estudios de Historia y Sociedad* 29, no. 73 (Winter 1998): 17–49; Christoph Rosenmüller, *Corruption and Justice in Colonial Mexico, 1650–1755* (Cambridge: Cambridge University Press, 2019), 123–52.

material benefits, social advancement, and protection in return for the latter's services.[44]

The second idea held that assessment of the social status (*calidades*), innate aptitudes (*partes* or *cualidades*), and services (*méritos*) of the kingdom's subjects constituted the foundation of an orderly or just distributive process.[45] Historians are quite familiar with the practice of rewarding being considered an act of justice. Alejandro Cañeque, for example, has pointed out how monarchs were not only supposed to punish wicked actions but also reward virtuous behavior, giving to each in accordance with their merits to meet the obligations imposed by distributive justice.[46] Although it is tempting to equate the contemporary category distributive justice with the obligation of sovereigns to reward their subjects, it is important to recognize that this scholastic concept gained salience during the sixteenth century because of the particular answer it provided to the problem of how benefit earned through merit was to be related to social status and innate qualities in the distributive process. In the strictly hierarchically organized Iberian societies, such a question was of fundamental importance, as it defined the range of social mobility produced by royal favor.[47] The Thomist notion of distributive justice provided one solution to this problem, discarding social status

[44] Antonio M. Hespanha, "La economia de la gracia," in *La gracia del derecho. Economonia de la cultura en la Edad Moderna*, ed. Antonio M. Hespanha (Madrid: Centro de estudios constitucionales, 1993), 151–76.

[45] Marco Antonio de Camos y Requeséns, *Microcosmia, y govierno universal del hombre christiano, para todos los estados y qualquiera de ellos* (Barcelona: Monasterio de Sancto Augustin, por Pablo Malo, 1592), 38–39 and 56; Antonio Pérez, *Norte de príncipes, virreyes, presidentes, consejeros, y governadores, y advertencias políticas sobre lo público y particular de una monarquía importantísimas a los tales*, ed. Martín de Riquer (Madrid: Espasa-Calpe, 1969 [1601]), 76; Juan de Santa María, *Tratado de república y policía christiana para reyes y príncipes, y para los que el gobierno tienen sus veces* (Barcelona: Por Sebastian de Cormellas, 1616), prologue, f. 11v.; Maestre Pedro, *Libro del consejo e de los consejeros*, ed. Agapito Rey (Zaragoza: Librería general, 1962), 45–47; Pedro Fernández de Navarrete, *Conservación de monarquías y discursos políticos sobre la gran consulta que el consejo hizo al señor Rey Don Felipe Tercero* (Madrid: en la Imprenta Real, 1626), 239.

[46] Alejandro Cañeque, *The King's Living Image: The Culture and Politics of Viceregal Power in Colonial Mexico* (New York: Routledge, 2004), 138–42. Compare also: Arndt Brendecke, *Imperium und Empirie: Funktionen des Wissens in der spanischen Kolonialherrschaft* (Cologne: Böhlau, 2009), 54–57.

[47] On the importance of a proportional distributive process, see for example: Antonio de León Pinelo, *Tratado de confirmaciones reales de encomiendas, oficios, i casos, en que se requieren para las Indias Occidentales* (Madrid: Juan González, 1630), 73r.

entirely.[48] Another came from the *Siete Partidas* (Seven Parts), a highly influential thirteenth-century legal codex. The authors of the *Partidas* had also sought to move around the constraints of lineage by introducing a new model of nobility, in which the absolute monarch determined whether a person deserved noble status either because of their "lineage or excellence or service."[49] At the same time, however, they defended the role of privileged lineages in society, laying the foundations for a notion that considered assessment of each of these three criteria the foundation of an orderly distributive process.

The logic of assessment that the authors of the *Partidas* deployed for this purpose originated in a body of literature commonly referred to as the sapiential tradition. Some texts belonging to this heterogeneous corpus linked the capacity of monarchs to assess people's inner nature to the crucial task of their selecting the councilors that surrounded them.[50] A constitutive component of this tradition was the pseudo-Aristotelian *Kitab sirr al-asrâr* (The Secret of Secrets).[51] Introducing the reader to the art of governance, this treatise provided a rudimentary explanation of how climes, seasons, foods, and exercise regimes impact the ways in which individuals are and how others perceive them. Subsequently, it offered an explanation on how this knowledge can be deployed to

---

[48] Christoph Rosenmüller suggests that distributive justice implied that, in the distribution of offices, the social station of recipients had to be considered. Rosenmüller, *Corruption and Justice in Colonial Mexico*, 126–33. In a strict Thomist sense, this was not the case, as there was no place for an individual's personal conditions (e.g., nationality, wealth, family, or appearance), as the "respect of persons" (*acepción de personas*) was considered a violation of distributive justice. In the tradition of the *Siete Partidas* this was correct, however. I have discussed these different notions of a just distributive process and the tensions between them elsewhere: Nino Vallen, "'What Distributive Justice Requires': Negotiating Empire and Local Orders in Sixteenth- and Seventeenth-Century New Spain," *Revista de Indias* LXXX/278 (2020): 101–29.

[49] *Las Siete Partidas del rey don Alfonso el Sabio*, Part. II, Tit. x, Law 2, 88.

[50] Texts belonging to the sapiential tradition emphasize the significance of wisdom (*sapiencia, sabiduría, seso*) as a guiding principle in a person's life. On the role of this tradition in the development of medieval political thinking, see Hugo O. Bizzarri, "Las colecciones sapienciales castellanas en el proceso de reafirmación del poder monárquico (siglos XII y XIV)," *Cahiers de linguistique hispanique médiévale* 20 (1995): 35–73; Adeline Rucquoi and Hugo O. Bizzarri, "Los espejos de príncipes en Castilla: entre Oriente y Occidente," *Cuadernos de Historia de España* 79, no. 1 (2005): 7–30.

[51] From the eleventh century, this treatise circulated in the Iberian Peninsula in two distinct translations: *Secreto de los secretos* and *Poridat de las poridades*. The two editions have been edited and published together in Pseudo-Aristóteles, *Secreto de los secretos, poridat de las poridades: Versiones castellanas del Pseudo-Aristóteles Secretum Secretorum*, ed. Hugo O. Bizzarri (Valencia: Publicaciones de la Universitat de València, 2010).

determine – through assessing the behavior, talents, and inclinations of possible candidates – who would be suitable as councilors.[52] This influential text introduced into political thinking the idea that the monarch's selection of candidates for certain offices was not simply the result of personal benevolence but, rather, the outcome of a rational act. As one popular thirteenth-century didactic guide inspired by this tradition had it, nothing in the administration of royal favor ought to be "done without order or reason."[53]

These ideas moved personhood to the center of distributive struggles. As scholars, noblemen, and social newcomers debated the nature of nobility and the monarch's ability to reward those who served him with the title of *caballero* (knight) or *hijodalgo* (untitled nobleman), they developed an increasingly sophisticated framework of cosmographical, medicinal, and sociopolitical theories to explain the origins of differences between human beings and the ways they manifested themselves in behavior and outward appearance. They also testified to a newly emerging self-consciousness, as it becomes visible, for instance, in engagements with what the medievalist Jesús Rodríguez Velasco has called the "chivalric fable." Fourteenth- and fifteenth-century legal treatises, manuals of conduct, and fictional texts written in response to the model of patronage introduced by the *Partidas* began to present the "collective hope" that, "through a series of diversely codified political and moral acts, the subject can achieve social recognition and assume jurisdictional authority."[54] The chivalric literature presented a model for readers regarding how to behave and present their actions on paper, thus demonstrating how self-images could be fashioned according to a set of socially defined criteria about knighthood and nobility that were to be assessed by the monarch or other authorities distributing favors.

Such conscious fashioning of one's behavior in the face of sociopolitical authority and beliefs existing outside of the individual remind us of Stephen Greenblatt's observations regarding the crafting of identities in sixteenth-century England.[55] According to Greenblatt, the early modern

---

[52] Ibid., 91–94, and 139–57.

[53] John K. Walsh, *El libro de los doze sabios o Tractado de la nobleza y lealtad (ca. 1237): estudio y edición* (Madrid: Aguire, 1975), 88.

[54] Jesús D. Rodríguez Velasco, *Order and Chivalry: Knighthood and Citizenship in Late Medieval Castile*, trans. Eunice Rodríguez Ferguson (Philadelphia: University of Pennsylvania Press, 2010), 5.

[55] Stephen Jay Greenblatt, *Renaissance Self-Fashioning: From More to Shakespeare* (Chicago: University of Chicago Press, 1980), 9.

period saw a change in the intellectual, social, psychological, and aesthetic structures that governed the generation of identities. Members of the upper classes began to fashion their identities according to a set of socially acceptable standards, in the process submitting themselves to an outside authority. In the Iberian Peninsula, such an outspoken awareness of the social significance of acts of self-fashioning already emerged in the late medieval struggles over the nature of nobility.[56]

The link between the logic of assessment and an emerging self-awareness can be seen even better in the administrative apparatus Iberian monarchs established during the Late Middle Ages to help them in fulfilling their duties of granting to each of their vassals and subjects what they deserved.[57] Royal institutions, such as the *Cámara de Castilla* (Chamber of Castile) and *Consejo de Órdenes* (Council of Orders), developed mechanisms by which the king could comply with his responsibility of assessing the growing number of vassals and subjects seeking royal favor. These increasingly standardized procedures turned assessment of those petitioning the monarch into a collective act involving royal councilors, local judges, and members of the petitioners' communities. As Robert Folger has demonstrated, in the petitions processed by this apparatus, a specific bureaucratic *dispositif* developed that gave shape to standardized evocations of the self.[58] Petitioners strategically adopted and appropriated various authoritative scripts in order to fashion more or less fictitious self-images of a legible and "deserving subject," highlighting their social status, professional history, services, and skills or experiences associated with the roles or positions they aspired toward, as well as

---

[56] Acts of self-fashioning between the fourteenth and sixteenth centuries are studied by contributors to Laura Delbrugge, ed. *Self-Fashioning and Assumptions of Identity in Medieval and Early Modern Iberia* (Leiden: Brill, 2015).

[57] The role of institutions such as the Chamber of Castile, also known as the *Consejo de Merced* (Council of Favors), and the Council of Orders in distributing royal favor have been studied in Salustino de Dios, *Gracia, merced y patronazgo real: la Cámara de Castilla entre 1474–1530* (Madrid: Centro de estudios constitucionales, 1993); Elena Postigo Castellanos, *Honor y privilegio en la Corona de Castilla. El Consejo de las Órdenes y los Caballero de hábito en el siglo XVII* (Valladolid: Junta de Castilla y León, 1988).

[58] Robert Folger, *Generaciones y semblanzas: Memory and Genealogy in Medieval Iberian Historiography* (Tübingen: Gunter Narr, 2003); Robert Folger, *Picaresque and Bureaucracy: Lazarillo de Tormes* (Newark, DE: Juan de la Cuesta, 2009); Robert Folger, *Writing as Poaching: Interpellation and Self-Fashioning in Colonial relaciones de méritos y servicios* (Leiden: Brill, 2011).

spotlighting other details about the qualities and services of their lineage, purity of blood, religious orthodoxy, and wealth.[59]

By the time Spaniards crossed the Atlantic at the end of the fifteenth century, negotiation over distribution of society's benefits had thus given shape to an intellectual and institutional framework that prompted the emergence of a characteristic way of addressing the world: one that impelled conquerors, officials, soldiers, friars, and others to fashion identities for themselves that would lead to their being assessed as more worthy of certain favors than others. This is what I refer to as the regime of the deserving self. Such a regime shaped people's biographies and the ways in which they presented themselves and others throughout the Iberian world. In the following chapters, I examine how a number of such identities came into being through various forms of engagement with the logic of assessment. In doing so, I move between the letters, reports, histories, and lists with which the court and its subjects sought to answer questions concerning why some deserved certain benefits more than others and the official petitions they produced within the distributive apparatus, particularly the *Real y Supremo Consejo de las Indias* (Council of the Indies).[60]

As we will see, two key aspects of these processes of the crafting of a deserving self appear to challenge traditional understandings of self-fashioning. First, fashioning a deserving self did not merely involve the aligning of one's own self-representation with desired norms of merit. Negotiation within the economy of favor always required a certain degree of submission to patrons and their ideals, as Greenblatt has suggested. Still, as Laura Delbrugge has reminded us, self-fashioning was always also an attempt to subvert or reject existing social structures.[61] Depending on the contexts in which individuals engaged the logic of assessment, the images of a deserving self that they crafted either reaffirmed existing criteria of merit, altered them, or introduced entirely new ones. Second,

---

[59] Folger, *Writing as Poaching*, 34.

[60] Scholars have long recognized the importance of self-fashioning for the *relaciones de méritos y servicios*. Compare, for example: Murdo J. MacLeod, "Self-Promotion: The *Relaciones de Méritos y Servicios* and Their Historical and Political Interpretation," *Colonial Latin American Historical Review* 7, no. 1 (1998): 28; Rosa María Gregori Roig, "Representación pública del individuo. Relaciones de méritos y servicios en el Archivo General de Indias (siglos XVII-XVIII)," in *El legado de Mnemosyne: las escrituras del yo a través del tiempo*, eds. Antonio Castillo Gómez and Verónica Sierra Blas (Gijón: Trea, 2007), 355–79.

[61] Delbrugge, ed. *Self-Fashioning*, 4

the self-images emerging in these various contexts not only concerned individuals but collectives as well. This was the direct result of the concentric perception of personhood that contemporaries held, which considered an individual's nature to be the outcome of the existential spheres in which they moved.[62] As a consequence, I argue, the assessment of individuals often involved assessments of the qualities of the people or collectives to whom they were related by blood, self-identification, or external categorization. Especially in light of negative stereotypes created and employed to try to convince the authorities why members of certain groups were unworthy of benefits or authority, assessment of the qualities of groups could become part of the self-fashioning process, thus merging individual with collective interests and forging both a sense of affiliation and belonging.

Focusing on this particular regime of self is helpful for reconsidering the relationships between mobility and processes of identity-making in the context of Spanish expansion in the Indies. The principle of reciprocity functioned as an engine, generating the mobility that fueled early global integration.[63] Explorers, conquerors, settlers, Indigenous allies, royal officials, merchants, and clergymen left their homes because they expected to receive a share of the loot, a piece of newly conquered land, or another form of exemption or privilege in return for their investment of time, energy and/or money, along with the often palpable risks associated with colonial endeavors. Speaking to the importance of this ideal are the petitions and *relaciones* that conquistadores and settlers began sending in ever larger numbers to the Council of the Indies from the 1530s.[64] Yet acts of self-fashioning also preceded their mobility, as subjects of the Spanish Crown were required to prove that they were worthy of receiving permission to travel to the Indies at all.[65] Moreover, most enterprises of exploration and conquest only materialized after their organizers had

---

[62] On the idea that people consisted of the circles or spheres integral to their very substance, see especially: Timothy J. Reiss, *Mirages of the Self: Patterns of Personhood in Ancient and Early Modern Europe* (Stanford, CA: Stanford University Press, 2003).

[63] Vitus Huber, *Beute und Conquista: Die politische Ökonomie der Eroberung Neuspaniens* (Frankfurt: Campus Verlag, 2017), 24.

[64] Córdoba Ochoa, "Movilidad geográfica, capital cosmopolita y relaciones de méritos"; Delphine Tempère, "En las fronteras del mundo iberoasiático. Discurso y vida de los agentes de la Corona española en Filipinas (Siglo XVII)," *Distributive Struggle and the Self in the Early Modern Iberian World*, eds. Nikolaus Böttcher, Stefan Rinke, and Nino Vallen, 193–218 (Stuttgart: Verlag Hans-Dieter Heinz, Akademischer Verlag).

[65] Bernhard Siegert, *Passagiere und Papiere: Schreibakte auf der Schwelle zwischen Spanien und Amerika* (Munich: Fink, 2006).

signed a *capitulación* stipulating the objectives of the expedition and the rewards the initiator would receive if successful. As this book highlights, in negotiating such contracts, aspiring organizers fashioned their own version of a deserving self that was closely linked to the imperial or religious project for which they sought to win support.

Mobility also became a preoccupation in the colonial societies examined here, especially in the context of the distributive struggles developing within them. In these conflicts, social models, characters, and categories of merit were reused or newly invented, often in relation to changing valuations of the movement of humans and things. For example, the legal identifier *descubridor* (discoverer) granted its bearer a first claim to the rewards distributed from the land to which he had been the first to arrive.[66] In a similar vein, the marker *primer conquistador* (first conqueror) or *primer poblador* (first settler) linked a person's worthiness to receive benefits to the moment that their mobility was instantiated and their role identified in the processes of the conquest or settlement of a specific region or town. Conflicts at the Spanish court and in the growing colonial societies often revolved around the question of who could take on certain identities and how these categories and subcategories of merit ought to be ordered hierarchically. As imperial expansion continued and the administration of an ever-larger empire required the mobility of officials, soldiers, and clergymen, an urgent problem arose regarding how they should fit within earlier hierarchies of merit.[67] Throughout this book, we will encounter many actors grappling with the impacts of geographical mobility on the distributive process, as well as the legal mechanisms meant either to promote or control mobility.[68]

Rather than focusing on only one of the aforementioned categories, this book takes instead the notion of the deserving self as an analytical tool to capture how actors seeking favors navigated between varying categories and norms of merit. Depending on their own social position, setting, or the

---

[66] León Pinelo, *Tratado de confirmaciones reales de encomiendas*, ff. 51–53.

[67] On these discussions, see also: Nino Vallen, "Conquista, memoria y cultura material en la Nueva España, Siglos XVI y XVII," *Iberoamericana* XIX, no. 71 (2019): 13–33.

[68] Paying attention to these changing mechanisms is important for writing histories that not only trace connections but also analyze processes of integration and fusion as well as detachment and withdrawal through the dynamics of power and violence, taking into consideration the shifting significance of such connections. Jürgen Osterhammel, "Global History and Historical Sociology," in *The Prospect of Global History*, eds. James Belich et al. (Oxford: Oxford University Press, 2016), 37–41.

kind of distributive struggle in which they found themselves, these actors relied on a diverse and idiosyncratic set of theories about human nature, social norms and roles, legal regimes, distributive theories and practices, as well as sentiments about the justness of both, to convince others of why they deserved a certain benefit or authority more than others. Using the lens of the deserving self makes it possible to capture how, at different moments in time, in a constantly evolving empire and economy of favor, Spanish endeavors in the Pacific affected the identities of people in the viceroyalty and the qualities ascribed to them.

To chart these interactions, I have relied first and foremost on the *Patronato* section of the Archivo General de Indias in Seville. Most of the documents preserved in this section were produced during the process of overseas expansion, starting with the search for a route to Asia, and the administration of royal patronage as overseen by the Council of the Indies. The travel accounts, descriptions of territories and peoples, reports from authorities in the Indies, and *relaciones de méritos y servicios* (accounts of services rendered) or *informaciones de parte y oficio* (reports on capacities and professional services) provide us with important insights into the negotiations between the Crown and its subjects over the distribution of royal favors in its overseas territories and the ways in which these evolved over time. I have combined the information found in the Patronato section with other records amassed in archives and libraries in Spain, Mexico, the United States, and England. Some of these materials resemble the Patronato documents but were written for other authorities. Other texts and artifacts that have been selected for discussion – including professional manuals, maps, and a *biombo* – were produced with the objective of influencing the outcomes of distributive processes without going through official, bureaucratic channels.

THE PACIFIC AND THE FASHIONING OF THE DESERVING SELF

The present book is structured such that each chapter focuses on a different struggle related to Spanish expansion in the Pacific Basin during the period between 1513, when Spaniards first sighted the Pacific, and 1641. The end of the timeframe for this book is determined by the convergence of two developments during the 1630s. On the one hand, this decade saw a politically induced interruption of transpacific interactions, which fueled discussions about the desirability of transpacific trade. On the other hand, during the 1630s the ways in which the descendants of New Spain's conquistadores were treated within the distributive apparatus changed. This development is reflected in the Patronato section, where there is no evidence that any more *relaciones de méritos* of these descendants were filed after 1632. When transpacific trade was resumed in 1641, the significance of the period of Spanish discovery and conquest on the distributive process and the subjectivities produced in it had forever changed.

In each of the portrayed disputes, a social character or category of merit is distinguished that linked notions of a deserving self or undeserving other to the activities in the Pacific Basin. Chapter 1 considers legal cases that developed during the 1530s and early 1540s about the question of who was entitled to the right to explore regions in the Pacific Northwest and who was to be recognized as the discoverer of this part of the world. It not only explains how the attempts of men such as Hernán Cortés and Viceroy Antonio de Mendoza to prove that they deserved to be recognized as discoverers impacted their mappings of the Pacific Northwest but also proposes that these bitter disputes had lasting effects on the distribution of privileges in the viceroyalty. Chapter 2, in turn, focuses on a group of veterans searching for a route to Asia and their quest for social advancement. I consider how these men sought to use their experiences in Asia or knowledge of the routes toward it to improve their relatively modest positions within an increasingly strict hierarchy of merit. By analyzing their interactions with the vicegeral authorities and the reports they produced during the 1550s and 1560s, I reveal how their drive for social advancement inspired interest in Spanish expansion in the Pacific, presenting in the process quite different visions of the Pacific and the possible benefits of New Spain's connections to Asia.

The remaining three chapters deal with the impacts of connections established between New Spain and Asia. Chapter 3 further deepens my exploration of the debates regarding what it meant to be a meritorious person in New Spain. It examines how during the period between 1571 and the end of the 1630s, growing tensions emerged between actors who, due to their ancestors' services, used the *Leyes Nuevas* (New Laws) of 1542–43 to claim a privileged position in the distribution of royal favor and those who traveled into the Pacific to conquer new lands or fight foreign enemies. Chapter 4 shifts the focus away from secular actors and toward the clergy in order to explore the significance of the category criollo for those dwelling along and traveling on the religious itinerary to Asia between the 1570s and early 1640s. Questioning traditional narratives about creole discourse, I highlight the various ways in which New Spain's central position and connections to Asia were thematized by both local and traveling clergymen in their efforts to prove their worthiness of the king's favors. Finally, Chapter 5 examines the effects of transpacific trade on social interaction and negotiation in New Spain, spotlighting the figure of the merchant, who became the key protagonist of interrelated debates about the sale of offices, the desirability of trade in silks and ceramics, and the impact of transpacific trade on the organization of the Spanish empire, a discussion that led to the temporary interruption of interactions across the Pacific during the late 1630s.

Being the Heart of the World primarily examines the forging of new notions of self and other; in so doing, however, it also examines stories told about the world by subjects of the Spanish Crown in their efforts to either establish new connections or to regulate or question the desirability of existing interactions. Linking these narratives to various conceptualizations of the deserving self, the book seeks to draw our attention away from a linear understanding of the making of a single world and highlights, instead, how people set in motion different narratives about the emerging world that influenced the process of global integration and – at times – disintegration.[69] The internal dynamics of the economy of favor and the logic of assessment so important to its operations shaped notions of the Pacific Basin and the links that were being established across it. Claims of entitlement, so essential to any notion of the deserving self, formed the basis of stories reflecting a particular set of presuppositions about how actors viewed the world, how it was supposed to be organized, and what their place in and rewards from it should be.

This book is an attempt to understand these interrelated processes of self- and world-making and the effects they had on both New Spain becoming the "heart of the world" and the (re)making of its own social order and that of the larger Spanish empire. But its ramifications go beyond this historical case. Precisely at a time that the sense of entitlement is fueling opposition against globalization, it is useful to dig deeper into this relationship. The use of the deserving self as a category can help us to bring to the forefront negotiations over the distribution of the resources, privileges, and recognition so crucial to the ways in which individuals and groups in different places and moments in history have positioned themselves toward the mobilities and integrative processes connecting them to a wider world.

---

[69] Sebastian Conrad, *What Is Global History?* (Princeton, NJ: Princeton University Press, 2015), 185–90; Ayesha Ramachandran, *The Worldmakers: Global Imagining in Early Modern Europe* (Chicago: The University of Chicago Press, 2015).

I

The Discoverer

Legal Struggles over the Pacific Northwest

In 1542, Spanish cosmographer Alonso de Santa Cruz produced a map of the world that graphically presented some of the geographical knowledge that had been gathered about the South Sea during the three decades since Spanish arrival on America's Pacific coast. The left side of the double hemisphere map, depicting the southern part of the globe, pictures the western seaboard from the equator to the strait through which Ferdinand Magellan had entered the Pacific in 1520 (Figure 1.1). Meanwhile, on the right side, the northern hemisphere coast, running from the equator to today's Gulf of California, is delineated. Santa Cruz stopped drawing the shoreline at around 35 degrees north, adding two annotations at this frontier of the known world. South of the tip of Baja California, which is partitioned off from the rest of the peninsula, he wrote "island discovered by the Marquis of the Valley." North of the gulf, where five houses representing the Seven Cities of Cíbola appear, he noted "land that Antonio de Mendoza ordered to be discovered." Although the glosses may appear but mere statements of fact, documenting an ongoing process of exploration, they became controversial claims in the context of a bitter conflict between two of the most powerful men in New Spain over who had discovered Tierra Nueva and, therefore, who should be given the privilege to expand Spanish rule in the Pacific Northwest.

This chapter traces the history of this conflict as part of a more general exploration of how the production of cosmographical knowledge and acts of self-fashioning interacted in negotiations over royal *capitulaciones*, a type of contract granting someone the right to carry out a maritime or

FIGURE 1.1 Alonso de Santa Cruz, *Nova verior et integra totius orbis descriptio* (1542). National Library of Sweden, KoB, AB 50 St.f

overland expedition.[1] *Capitulaciones* were of great significance to Spanish expansion. The Crown used these contracts to ensure that the leaders of expeditions recognized its political control over newly conquered territories and set apart a share of the wealth they generated. In exchange for these assurances, a *capitulación* promised expedition organizers a temporal monopoly to explore or conquer a specified geographical area, giving them time to prepare their enterprise without running the risk of others beating them to it. They also listed the rewards that contractees could expect upon successfully fulfilling their promises, including titles, offices, tax reductions, or trading monopolies, which in part determined long-term returns on their investments.[2]

Granting such contracts was no simple matter, however, as royal officials in Spain grappled with the challenge of doling out the right to conquer new land amid a dynamic process of expansion. Unfamiliar with the concrete dimensions of the territories into which the conquistadores were heading, officials usually provided only rudimentary indications regarding the limits of promised territory that, as we will see, often triggered conflicts later on. They also faced the difficulty of determining whom to entrust with the responsibility of turning unruly bands of adventurers into orderly communities that could render lasting financial contributions to the Crown. What qualities made a licensee suitable for such a complicated task? How could the competing claims of equally suitable candidates be dealt with? In the years following the fall of Tenochtitlan in 1521, these quandaries acquired increasing salience. Reports about Mesoamerica's highly developed cultures attracted wealthy and authoritative figures, capable of organizing large expeditions. Although their arrival spurred the expansion, this quickly led to conflicts and a growing need for royal intervention. Yet, the officials sent to prevent such fighting ended up becoming themselves involved in the conquest of new territories, prompting bitter disputes in New Spain and at the court.

In examining these conflicts in the context of the search for new routes to the East Indies, this chapter contributes to recent efforts to reconsider conquest in the Americas and Asia from a more integrated perspective.

---

[1] On the *capitulación* as a legal instrument for regulating conquest, see Marta Milagros de Vas Mingo, *Las capitulaciones de Indias en el siglo XVI* (Madrid: Ediciones Cultura Hispánica, 1986).

[2] Vitus Huber has recently studied the role of *capitulaciones* in the economic and risk assessments of those organizing expeditions he characterizes as "joint ventures." Huber, *Beute und Conquista*, 83–97.

Beginning with a brief discussion of prior Spanish efforts to reach Asia, it then explores how Hernán Cortés's decade-long struggle for the privilege of leading expansion in the South Sea influenced imperial policies and distributive practices between the 1520s and early 1540s. This chapter showcases how the struggles over the right to continue exploration of a region where Spaniards hoped to find a new route to Asia defined the specific meaning the category *descubridor* (discoverer) came to enjoy in negotiations over royal favor. Two factors contributed to this process. On the one hand, Cortés and his competitors helped to shape social criteria regarding what qualities a person ought to possess to lead an *entrada* (conquest). On the other hand, he and Viceroy Antonio de Mendoza also began to fashion themselves as discoverers by producing new maps and textual descriptions of the Northwestern Pacific. The dispute and the impact it had on the king's authority left deep marks on the law and turned the category of discoverer, meaning the person who "first enters the land and produces a truthful and correct account of it," into a coveted category of merit.[3] The search for a route to Asia was thus, as we shall see, hardly peripheral to the building of the Spanish empire and its distributive apparatus.

INVENTING A SEA OF OPPORTUNITIES

Already during the 1480s, encouraged by the activities of the Portuguese, explorers and merchants in Castile began fantasizing about the possibility of gaining direct access to the spices and silks that had been arriving in the Iberian Peninsula for centuries. However, there was one key obstacle that prevented Spaniards from realizing this dream. According to the terms of the Treaty of Alcáçovas (1479), they were not allowed to sail south of the Canary Islands.[4] Conceding this right had helped Queen Isabelle of Castile ward off King Afonso's claim to the Castilian throne. But once the Portuguese had reached Asia by circumnavigating the African contin-ent, her vassals were forced to look for an alternative route.

Discussion of alternatives gained momentum in 1486, when Christopher Columbus arrived at the Spanish court. The Genovese

---

[3] León Pinelo, *Tratado de confirmaciones reales*, f. 51r.
[4] Paulino Castañeda Delgado, "Las exploraciones castellanas y los problemas con Portugal antes de 1492," in *El tratado de Tordesillas y su época*, ed. Luís Antonio Ribot García (Madrid: Sociedad V Centenario del Tratado de Tordesillas; Junta de Castilla y León Consejería de Educación y Cultura, 1995), 2: 928–34.

merchant and self-taught cosmographer proposed a plan to travel to the East "by sailing West."[5] Although Columbus's project took five years to gain sufficient support, his unplanned landing in the Caribbean in October 1492 boosted Spanish hopes about their chances of beating the Portuguese in first reaching land in East and Southeast Asia. Copying from Afonso's playbook, Isabelle and Ferdinand asked the Aragonese Pope Alexander VI to draw a demarcation line through the Atlantic that prevented Portuguese ships from sailing west – terms with which Portugal grudgingly agreed by signing the Treaty of Tordesillas (1494), fixing a line of demarcation at 370 leagues west of the Azores.[6]

In the wake of Columbus's first voyage, Spaniards discussed whether he had actually already reached Asia. The admiral himself maintained that he did. During his later journeys, he continued to draw parallels between the information that classical and medieval authorities had provided about Asian geography, flora, fauna, and people, and what he had personally observed.[7] Even when he eventually recognized that the territories he had stumbled upon were not what he had been looking for, he preserved some form of link by coining it the "West Indies (*Indias Occidentales*) unbeknownst to all the World."[8] But Columbus's reluctant recognition merely confirmed what others had long maintained.[9] These lands were, indeed, something entirely new to Europeans – even if, conceptually, they could be forced to fit into a cartographical tradition

---

[5] For an exceptionally detailed study of the intellectual background of this project, see Nicolás Wey Gómez, *The Tropics of Empire: Why Columbus Sailed South to the Indies* (Cambridge, MA: The MIT Press, 2008).

[6] On the history of the Treaty of Tordesillas, see for example: Jesús Varela Marcos, ed., *El tratado de Tordesillas en la cartografía histórica* (Valladolid: Sociedad V Centenario de Tratado de Tordesillas, 1994).

[7] José Rabasa, *Inventing America: Spanish Historiography and the Formation of Eurocentrism* (Norman: University of Oklahoma Press, 1993), chapter 2; Valerie I. J. Flint, *The Imaginative Landscape of Christopher Columbus* (Princeton, NJ: Princeton University Press, 1992), 115–48.

[8] See Juan Pérez de Tudela y Bueso et al., *Colección documental del descubrimiento (1470–1506)* (Madrid: Real Academia de la Historia, Consejo Superior de Investigaciones Científicas, 1994), 3: 1391. Ricardo Padrón has explored the spreading of this geographical imaginary in "'The Indies of the West' or, the Tale of How and Imaginary Geography Circumnavigated the Globe," in *Western Visions of the Far East in a Transpacific Age, 1522–1657*, ed. Christina Hyo Jung Lee (Farnham: Ashgate, 2012), 19–42.

[9] Compare, for example, Pedro Martyr de Angleria, *Décadas del Nuevo Mundo* (Madrid: Polifemo, 1989), 11.

that had long divided Asia into a multitude of Indies.[10] Accepting that they had found something new was one thing, giving up on the search to Asia was something else. Spaniards continued to search frantically for a way to circumvent the territories onto which they had stumbled, either by locating a passageway or by determining that mainland Central America was actually a large island.[11] Yet, despite investments made in organizing new expeditions and creating a center of geographical and navigational expertise in Seville's *Casa de la contratación* (House of Trade), these efforts remained without the desired results.[12]

Meanwhile, the Portuguese were celebrating success after success. In 1498, Vasco de Gama reached India, from which he returned with a first shipment of spices the following year. Portuguese troops then conquered Goa and Malacca in 1510 and 1511, respectively, and reached the famed Spice Islands by 1512.[13] Reports about these victories and the riches that were beginning to arrive in Lisbon gave rise to Spanish envy. Rumors began to circulate that the Portuguese had reached so far east that the lands to which they had arrived legally fell within the sphere of influence of the Castilian Crown. Even King Ferdinand succumbed to these speculations, approving an impudent plan, presented to him by the Portuguese navigator Juan Díaz de Solís, to sail to Asia via the Cape of Good Hope to determine to whom the Spice Islands belonged.[14] Although the preparations for this expedition were halted for the sake of peace, his readiness to go along with it in the first place speaks to the king's growing frustrations.

By 1514, news reached the peninsula that significantly improved the king's mood. Things finally appeared to be moving forward when Vasco Núñez de Balboa, the temporary governor of Castilla de Oro, reached the western shores of Tierra Firme. In September 1513, in an attempt to

---

[10] On the meaning of "India" in pre-Columbian Europe, see Wey Gómez, *The Tropics of Empire*, chapter 3.

[11] Juan Antonio Varese, *Los viajes de Juan Díaz de Solís y el descubrimiento del Río de la Plata* (Montevideo: Ediciones de la banda oriental, 2016), 69–73.

[12] Antonio Sánchez, *La espada, la cruz y el Padrón. Soberanía, fe y representación cartográfica en el mundo ibérico bajo la monarquía hispánica, 1503–1598* (Madrid: Consejo Superior de Investigaciones Científicas, 2013), 207.

[13] Knowledge about these events also circulated in the Castilian language, for instance, in Juan Agüerro's summary edition of Martín Fernández de Figueroa's *Conquista de las indias de Persia y Ararbi que fizo la armada del rey don Manuel de Portugal y de las muchas tierras: diversas gentes: extrañas riquezas y grandes battalas que alla hubo* (Salamanca, 1512).

[14] Varese, *Los viajes de Juan Díaz de Solís*, 87–99.

escape an order for his return to the court, he had sailed together with
190 Spaniards north from San María del Darien, landing in the *cacique*
Careta's territory.[15] From there, the group, reinforced by Native warriors, traveled through rugged terrain for three weeks before reaching the
shores of a body of water that Balboa coined Mar del Sur. Detailed
reports and maps describing the voyage prompted great excitement at
the court. In a letter to the new governor of Castilla de Oro, don Pedrarias
Dávila, the king noted animatedly that "we are very grateful to our Lord
whom it seems, miraculously, to have pleased to favor us by unveiling in
our times things that have been hidden and lost for so long."[16]

Balboa's revelation of the existence of the South Sea initiated a new
phase in the Spanish search for a route to Asia. Ferdinand ordered Díaz de
Solís, who was appointed *adelantado* (provincial governor) of the South
Sea, to find a way around Tierra Firme, and Balboa to continue exploration of these unknown waters.[17] But others also hoped to benefit from
the Crown's new commitment to this endeavor, one of whom was
Pedrarias Dávila. Castilla de Oro's new governor and ambitious conqueror sported his own plans to open this oceanic space.[18] He intended
to send his confidant Diego de Albítez, and Martín Fernández de Enciso, a
royal official and adversary of Balboa, to transport ships and supplies
across the isthmus to the Gulf of San Miguel in the South Sea, where they
would establish a new settlement. In a subsequent step, Enciso would take
half of the men to explore the land and islands of the South Sea, searching
for a way to sail east to Cape Saint Augustin (Brazil), which they hoped to
reach through a passage located "beneath the equator."[19]

To obtain royal approval for this project, Pedrarias Dávila sent Enciso
to Spain in 1516. His plans to cross Balbao were thwarted, however, by

---

[15] On the events leading to the king's decision to order Balboa's return to court, see for
example: Carmen Mena García, *El oro del Darién. Entradas y cabalgadas en la conquista
de Tierra Firme (1509–1526)* (Madrid: Consejo Superior de Investigaciones Científicas,
2011), 146–49.

[16] AGI, Panama, 233, L.1, ff. 167v–168r.

[17] Capitulación with Juan Díaz de Solís, Nov 24, 1514, AGI, Patronato, 26, R. 3. AGI,
Panama, 233, L.1, ff. 170v.

[18] Memorial of Pedrarias Dávila, probably 1515, AGI, Patronato, 26, R. 4. The bitter
conflict that developed between Pedrarias and Balboa, ending with the latter's beheading
in January of 1519, has been studied extensively, including Bethany Aram's detailed
account in *Leyenda negra y leyendas doradas en la conquista de América: Pedrarias y
Balboa*, trans. Antonio J. Carasco Alvarez (Madrid: Marcial Pons Historia, 2008).

[19] Letter from Alonso de la Puente to King Ferdinand, Nov 23, 1515, AGI, Patronato, 26,
R. 5, ff. 168v–169r.

King Ferdinand's death in January of that same year. By the time Enciso arrived in Spain, the throne was vacant and the kingdom was waiting eagerly for its new king, the young Duke of Burgundy, to arrive from Flanders – which he did only in the autumn of 1517. Enciso used this time to finish the treatise for which he is best known, the *Suma de geographía* (Seville, 1519), a summation of contemporary cosmographical and geographical ideas. Having experienced on earlier occasions the challenge of securing royal favors, he appears to have written this work to impress the new monarch and his advisors and explain why his proposals for further exploration in the South Sea deserved to be taken seriously.

The relevance of these prior negotiations for Ensio's conceptualization of this treatise becomes visible in the places where he directly addresses the monarch. He explained, for example, that the king had an obligation "to determine how to discover what is still not discovered in your part, seeing that the King of Portugal, who is the lesser one, has already discovered so much."[20] The *Suma* should assist the young king in such an endeavor, helping him to understand the "things of the universe" and decide where to send his pilots to seek lands worthy of being conquered.[21] The starting point of these explorations, in Enciso's eyes, ought to have been the vast space between the Port of Higueras and Cattigara, two places then considered the extremes of the known world.[22] According to his calculations, the distance between the ports amounted to 261 longitudinal degrees or 4,350 leagues, leaving another 99 degrees or 1,650 leagues of unknown space to be explored by Charles's vassals. Exploration should not stop at Cattigara, however. With the help of another shrewd calculation, Enciso explained that the king's vassals could push west all the way to the estuary of the Ganges, where he positioned the antimeridian of the Treaty of Tordesillas that divided the world into

---

[20] Martín Fernández de Enciso, *Suma de Geografía*, ed. José Ibáñez Cerdá. Joyas bibliográficas, Vol. 1 (Madrid: Estades, Artes Gráficas, 1948 [1519]), 26.

[21] Ibid., 6.

[22] While Higueras is on the east coast of today's Honduras, Nicolás Wey Gómez proposes that Cattigara (called "Gatigaran" by Enciso) is perhaps today's Hanoi, though others believe it refers to the now lost city of Óc Eo, located in what is today the southern part of the An Giang Province of Vietnam. The city was part of the kingdom of Funan, which flourished between the first and the sixth centuries and formed an important hub between the Indian Ocean and China. Wey Gómez, *The Tropics of Empire*, 78; Granville Allen Mawer, "The Riddle of Cattigara," in *Mapping Our World: Terra Incognita to Australia*, eds. Robert Nichols and Martin Woods (Canberra: National Library of Australia, 2013), 38.

two equal halves.[23] India Ultra Ganges, that part of Asia that was "the wealthiest of all the lands mentioned in cosmography," could thus be claimed in its entirety for the Spanish Crown.[24]

Enciso's vision of the world is a perfect example of Spanish imperial world-making projects.[25] His astronomical theories, calculations, and geographical descriptions all contributed to his inventing of a space of opportunities waiting to be explored and conquered by vassals of the Spanish Crown. But producing such a summary of cosmographical and geographical knowledge served an additional purpose as well. He used it to fashion himself as a subject worthy of the Crown's attention and favor. With the *Suma*, he proved himself in the first place to be an expert in astronomy, cosmography, and geography, fields of knowledge that were crucial to those hoping to lead the search for a hidden strait. To show that he was particularly suited for such tasks, Enciso even included a table containing daily declinations for a four-year period, with an explanation on how to use them for navigating the southern hemisphere.[26]

But Enciso was not only interested in demonstrating that he possessed the skills of a pilot. He was trying to gain attention as well. To find the way to the king's ear, he relied on the well-known model of the learned councilor, to which the *Suma* refers throughout. They are a key part of Enciso's discussions of Alexander the Great, to whom Enciso liked to compare King Charles, and the lessons he provides concerning his early demise.[27] In his geographical descriptions of empires and nations, the role of philosophers and learned councilors in preserving the political and social order is underlined.[28] Undoubtedly, such allusions were part and parcel of the long

---

[23] Fernández de Enciso, *Suma de Geographía*, 24–26.   [24] Ibid., 25.

[25] Ricardo Padrón has made a similar point, arguing that Enciso placed his knowledge about the cosmos and the world in the "service of empire." Ricardo Padrón, *The Spacious Word: Cartography, Literature, and Empire in Early Modern Spain* (Chicago: The University of Chicago Press, 2004), 85.

[26] Fernández de Enciso, *Suma de Geographía*, 30–61.

[27] Enciso mentions, for example, that Charles had a unique opportunity to surpass Alexander's fame by expanding his realm in India Ultra Ganges. Fernández de Enciso, *Suma de Geographía*, 7. The most important reference to Alexander and his councilors can be found in Enciso's description of the kingdom of Macedonia, where he includes a modified version of the popular moral tale about the Macedonian king's journey to the Earthly Paradise. Fernández de Enciso, *Suma de Geographía*, 100–3. Andrés Prieto has read this story "as an allegory of the service that knowledge and knowledge professionals can offer to imperial rule and also as a cautionary tale about the risks invited by not according this knowledge its proper place in policy making." Andrés Prieto, "Alexander and the Geographer's Eye: Allegories of Knowledge in Martín Fernández de Enciso's *Suma de Geographía* (1519)," *Hispanic Review* 78, no. 2 (2010): 172.

[28] Fernández de Enciso, *Suma de Geographía*, 92–93, 153, 197, 199.

tradition of vassals reminding their lords of the importance of taking their council into consideration.[29] Yet, these reminders also provided subtle hints about the role Enciso assumed for himself. In his audience with the young king, he wanted to appear as the wise councilor, whose proposals on how to best continue exploring the Indies deserved to be taken seriously. The *Suma* proved that he possessed a crucial capacity associated with people in such a role, revealing his ability to comprehend the cosmos, the movements of the heavenly bodies, and the world in its entirety.[30]

Enciso's efforts were not in vain. On March 23, 1518, the king signed a royal order conferring to Albítez the right to create a town in the Gulf of San Blas and another south of the land of the "cacique Chepo," in what probably would be today's Veraguas province.[31] The decree chose another location for this settlement on the Pacific coast than the one Enciso had proposed, but this was likely done to respect the privileges bestowed on Balboa in 1514, which allowed him to explore the Gulf of Panama. The part of the project that Enciso himself was to oversee was stipulated in a *capitulación* signed between the king and the Portuguese explorers Ferdinand Magellan and Rui Falleiro the previous day. Magellan had arrived at the Spanish court with a proposal not unlike Enciso's but with a different goal: to finally find the route to Asia. Presenting his own world map, Magellan proposed to sail south along the American coasts, searching for a strait through which he could enter the South Sea and steer toward the Spice Islands. With ample experience in Asia and both the political and financial backing of some of the most influential men at the Spanish court, he was awarded the privilege of undertaking this journey and enjoying for ten years the benefits of the route that he discovered.[32] Still, the Crown reserved the right to send ships from Tierra Firme or the Island of San Miguel to also look for the

---

[29] Nicole Reinhardt, *Voices of Conscience: Royal Confessors and Political Counsel in Seventeenth-Century Spain and France* (Oxford: Oxford University Press, 2016).

[30] Such an ideal was grounded in Platonic and Neoplatonic traditions holding that people rise above the mundane by grasping visions of totality. On the relationship between the Neoplatonic tradition and Western globalism, see Denis Cosgrove, *Apollo's Eye: A Cartographic Genealogy of the Earth in the Western Imagination* (London: The John Hopkins University Press, 2001), 27–35.

[31] Appointment of Diego de Albítez, Mar 23, 1518, AGI, Panamá, 233, L.1, ff. 200v–201r.

[32] Christian Jostmann, *Magellan, oder, Die erste Umsegelung der Erde* (Munich: C. H. Beck, 2019), 88–93. On the role of the Consulado of Burgos in the search for the Moluccas, see also: Adelaida Sagarra Gamazo, "La empresa del pacífico o el sueño pimentero burgalés (1508–29)," *Revista de Estudios Colombinos* 9 (2013), 21–36.

said passage.[33] With this clause in the first paragraph of Magellan's *capitulación*, the Crown approved the second objective of Enciso's mission, implying that the two projects ought to contribute toward the realization of one and the same goal.

Charles's decision would, finally, bring success, with Magellan being the first to plant the Castilian flag in Asia. Yet, behind this well-known story about the first circumnavigation of the world was hidden a different one, a story that speaks to the challenges the monarch and his advisors were beginning to face. Spanish colonization of new territories not only increased the number of persons competing for the privilege of being involved in the imperial project but also compounded the difficulty of ensuring that the privileges and monopolies granted did not conflict with each other. The complexity of these negotiations would multiply even more after 1519, when Hernán Cortés opened the door, first, to the explosive expansion of Spanish presence on the American continent and, later, to new activities in the South Sea.

CORTÉS'S SEARCH FOR THE SECRETS OF THE SOUTH SEA

Like so many of the Spaniards who reached the American mainland before him, Hernán Cortés dreamt of contributing to the Spanish quest of reaching Asia. After his arrival in New Spain in November 1519, he soon sent his men out to look for a strait crossing the American mainland and to explore the Pacific coasts of the modern state of Oaxaca.[34] In May 1522, he reported to King Charles V about the results of his efforts, which he characterized shamelessly "as one of the most noteworthy services that have been rendered in the Indies."[35] Abel Martínez-Loza has contended that Cortés's delight with the discoveries made along the Pacific coasts stemmed from his belief that his men had reached the shores of the *Sinus Magnus*.[36] Yet, unlike European mapmakers, Cortés did not confuse the

---

[33] Capitulación with Fernando de Magellanes and Ruy Faleiro, Mar 22, 1518, AGI, Patronato, 34, R.1, f. 1v.

[34] Max L. Moorhead, "Hernán Cortés and the Tehuantepec Passage," *The Hispanic American Historical Review* 29, no. 3 (1949): 370–71; Hernán Cortés, Third Letter of Relation (May 15, 1522), in *Cartas y documentos*, ed. Mario H. Sanchez-Barba (Mexico: Editorial Porrúa, 1963), 191.

[35] Letter Hernán Cortés to Charles V (May 15, 1522), in ibid., 440.

[36] Abel Martínez-Loza, "Ideas geográficas de Hernán Cortés," *Anuario de Estudios Americanos* XLVII (1990): 13–17. For a similar study of notions of world geography during the era of conquest, see also: Salvador Álvarez, "Cortés, Tenochtitlan y la otra

lands he had reached with China or the Malayan Peninsula.[37] Instead, he believed that he had come closer to Asia than anyone else in Spain or Tierra Firme.

Equally important for explaining Cortés's eagerness to stress the greatness of his latest discoveries was his tense relationship with the Crown. Cortés's unauthorized embarkment on November 18, 1518, marked the beginning of a bitter conflict with the governor of Cuba, don Diego Velázquez de Cuéllar, who initiated a defamation campaign to delegitimize Cortés's feats. Velázquez blamed Cortés for rebelling against the king and usurping the rights to a conquest of the American mainland that ought to have been his, because his people had discovered the coasts of the Yucatán Peninsula.[38] Cortés, in turn, sought to counter Velázquez's reports with the help of his own *Cartas de relación*. Providing detailed descriptions of the territories and peoples he encountered after his landing in Veracruz, he sought to prove that he, rather than Velázquez, was the one who had been the discoverer of New Spain.

In Cortés's ongoing struggle for recognition, the South Sea and the route to Asia became a recurring theme. When Cortés's secretary, Juan de Ribera, arrived at the Spanish court in 1523 to present the third *Carta de relación* and inform the Crown about the fall of Tenochtitlan, he explicitly addressed both issues. On July 18, Ribera appeared before the Council of the Indies in Burgos to explain in detail how his patron intended to proceed with exploration of the South Sea. Ribera added that all costs incurred would be paid via rents earned in the region, underlining that his employer "does not want to ask nor supplicate Your Majesty for paying him, because it will be known that the said Hernán Cortés discovered the said South Sea and its lands and provinces and islands at his own expense and competence."[39]

Ribera's request came at an opportune moment. Under pressure from the bankers and merchants who had invested in Magellan's expedition, the Crown had begun to organize another expedition intended to replicate his success in reaching the Moluccas. On November 13, 1522, Charles had signed a *capitulación* with Jofre García de Loaísa, who was

---

mar: geografías y cartografías de la Conquista," *Historia y Grafía* 24, no. 47 (2016): 49–90.

[37] Compare: Salvador Álvarez, "Cortés, Tenochtitlan y la otra mar: geografías y cartografías de la Conquista," *Historia y Grafía* 24, no. 47 (2016): 49–90.

[38] Stefan Rinke, *Conquistadoren und Azteken: Cortés und die Eroberung Mexikos* (Munich: C. H. Beck, 2019), 41–56.

[39] Juan de Ribera regarding the South Sea, July 18, 1523, AGI, Patronato, 17, R.24.

instructed to retrace the route through the Strait of Magellan with the help of Sebastian Elcano .[40] Moreover, in June 1523, the king had already ordered Cortés to find a sea passage between the Atlantic and the Pacific, which was supposed to be located south of New Spain.[41] In spite of this royal order, Ribera's petition from July remained unanswered. Possibly, the councilors found his requests excessive or had a hard time aligning them with the promises made to García de Loaísa and the investors who financed his expedition.[42]

Initially, Cortés did not appear overly bothered by the Crown's failure to respond. In the subsequent two years, he continued to send expeditions to explore the west coasts of Soconusco and Guatemala, while continually making new promises to the Crown about finding a strait or a route to the Spice Islands.[43] By 1526, however, the Crown's silence concerning his requests did begin to worry him. In a letter to Charles, he wrote that he had learned that doubts had arisen at the court about his good intentions.[44] Although Cortés does not mention it, he may have been alluding to reports such as one by Diego de Ocaña, a scribe of Mexico's city council, who wrote that "some here believe that, in accordance with what they have seen in the past, if Cortés is going to [conquer the Spice Islands], he will die with [the] Crown."[45] According to Cortés, these were baseless fears. He countered that, if he actually had been driven by self-interest, he would have been better off remaining in New Spain instead of investing his time and means in a project, the sole objective of which, was to render greater service to the king.[46]

When Cortés sent this letter, word obviously had not yet reached New Spain that a few months earlier the Crown had already decided that his assistance in the South Sea was required after all. In a royal decree signed

[40] Juan Gil, *Mitos y utopías del descubrimiento*, vol. 2: *El Pacífico* (Madrid: Alianza universidad, 1989), 26–29.

[41] Instructions for Hernán Cortés, Jun 26, 1523, in *Cartas y documentos*, ed. Sánchez-Barba, 591.

[42] Mariano Cuesta Domingo, "La Casa de la Contratación de La Coruña," *Mar oceana: Revista del humanismo español e iberoamericano* 16 (2004): 60–66.

[43] Cortés, Fourth Letter of Relation (Oct 15, 1524), in *Cartas y documentos*, 233–34; Cortés, Fifth Letter of Relation (Sept 3, 1526), in *Cartas y documentos*, 320.

[44] Letter Hernán Cortés to Charles V (Sept 11, 1526), in *Cartas y relaciones de Hernán Cortés al Emperador Carlos V*, ed. Pascual de Gayangos (Paris: Imprenta central de los ferro-carriles, 1866), 375–76.

[45] Report by Diego de Ocaño to Council of the Indies, Aug 31, 1526, AGI, Patronato, 184, R.6.

[46] Letter from Hernán Cortés to Charles V, in *Cartas y relaciones*, 375.

on June 20, 1526, Charles ordered him to send several ships to the Spice Islands to find out what had happened to García de Loaísa's flotilla, which had left the port of A Coruña on July 24, 1525.[47] He was also supposed be on the lookout for the fleet of Sebastian Cabot, which had left San Lucar de Barrameda early in April 1526 to explore the islands of Tarsis and Ophir, East Cathay, and Cipango.[48] Cortés was glad about the opportunity given to him, but it took some time before his ships were ready. Only by late October 1527 did the two caravels and a brigantine he had built and outfitted weigh anchor from the port of Zihuatanejo to head toward the Spice Islands. Although Cortés harbored high expectations for the expedition that his cousin, Álvaro de Saavedra Cerón, would captain, it became an enormous disappointment. The flagship leaked and, during a severe storm, it lost sight of the other two vessels. Then, after reaching the Moluccas and locating the survivors of Loaísa's expedition in Tidore, Saavedra was unable to return to New Spain, his attempts frustrated by contrary winds and currents, which left the expedition stranded in enemy territory.[49]

A MODEL CONQUEROR AND HIS FAILED CONQUESTS

While Saavedra was struggling with the elements in the East Pacific, Cortés was fighting his own battles against fluctuating political winds. During the years leading up to the conquest of New Spain, he had been able to exercise a degree of control over the conquistadores under his command by promising them a share of the loot and punishing the disobedient. But, after the fall of Tenochtitlan, he gradually lost control. Conquerors and more recent settlers began to write the king about his authoritarian behavior and partisanship in the distribution of encomiendas and legal offices. Further resentments arose when his lieutenants used his absence from New Spain, between 1524 and 1526, to redistribute encomiendas in creating their own networks of patronage.[50]

The Spanish Crown responded to such complaints by appointing new officials. First it sent Luis Ponce de León to take over Cortés's position as

---

[47] Order for Hernán Cortés to send armada to Maluco, Jun 20, 1526, AGI, Patronato, 43, N.2, R.1.

[48] Gil, *Mitos y utopías*, 2: 29–38.

[49] Miguel León-Portilla, *Hernán Cortés y la Mar del Sur* (Madrid: Ediciones Cultura Hispánica; Instituto de Cooperación Iberoamericana, 1985), 48–53; 65–84.

[50] Francisco Manzo-Robledo, *I, Hernán Cortés: The (Second) Trial of Residency* (New York: Peter Lang, 2013), 28–32.

governor of New Spain and subject him to a *residencia* (an official performance review of his tenure). While the new governor achieved little due to his early death, Cortés's review soon thereafter became the responsibility of the *real audiencia* of Mexico, which took up its duties at the end of 1528. The first president of this royal appellate court became Nuño Beltrán de Guzmán, who had been governor of Pánuco since 1526 and was a longtime rival of Cortés. Equally troubling from Cortés's point of view was the Crown's decision to grant his old enemy, Pánfilo de Narváez, a *capitulación* making him adelantado of the region stretching from the Río de las Palmas to La Florida.[51] These changing circumstances worried Cortés so much that, after having ignored the king's requests to report to the court for years, he decided that these matters required his personal intervention.[52]

In March 1528, he departed from Mexico with an impressive retinue comprising Spaniards as well as Native nobles and ballplayers, carrying great quantities of gold, silver, and other treasures to impress the people at court and pay the bribes needed to gain support. Cortés was warmly received at the court in Toledo; he was praised and rewarded, receiving, among other favors, the title of Marquis of the Valley of Oaxaca. Despite such signs of the king's benevolence, Cortés must quickly have realized that his political relevance in New Spain was waning. This made it even more important to ensure for himself a role in the exploration of the territories that were yet to be discovered.

In line with his efforts to do so was a *parecer* (opinion statement) that Cortés wrote on the matter of granting rights for new conquests.[53] Here, he implicitly concurred with the critiques that Bartolomé de las Casas and other clergymen had articulated about conquests having already caused great damage to Native populations. To prevent this from happening again, Cortés argued that a process of careful deliberation should precede decisions to grant applicants the right to conquer further territories. He explained that the Crown should first obtain an overview of the lands that already had been conquered, who their conquerors were, what kinds

---

[51] Capitulación Narváez for discovery between Río de las Palmas and Florida, AGI, Patronato, 18, N.3, R.2.

[52] Esteban Mira Caballos, *Hernán Cortés: el fin de una leyenda* (Trujillo: Palacio de los Barrantes-Cervantes, 2010), 275–78.

[53] Pascual de Gayangos ascribes this document to 1537. But this is improbable because Cortés was not at the court at the time and does not once mention Viceroy Mendoza, which is something he always did in his letters from the late 1530s. Memorial of Hernán Cortés for Charles V, unknown date, in *Cartas y relaciones*, ed. Gayangos, 561–66.

of people were living there, what damage had been done to them during conquest, which lands had become depopulated, and why this had happened.[54] Precepts should then be created to make sure that newly discovered territories could only be entered with permission from the Crown to do so. This would mean that, when new lands or islands were found by accident, the discovers were required to describe their exact location and gather information about the kinds of people who lived there, their faith, and the whereabout of suitable ports. Subsequently, the Crown had to determine whether the Crown would be served by the conquest of these lands. Moreover, the king and his advisors had to assess the potential leader of this expedition to determine if he deserved this privilege or should, rather, be given another kind of reward for his discovery. Cortés argued that someone who could be entrusted with missions of conquest should have previous experience, have his own fortune so as not to exploit the Natives and have the intention to live in the areas that he wanted to conquer. Upon completing these steps, the selected candidate could then be instructed on how to carry out the conquest and prevent his men from bringing damage to the Indigenous population.[55]

Cortés's proposal illustrates how the production of an image of the deserving self and the (re)definition of criteria of worthiness went hand in hand. On the one hand, he reaffirmed the necessity of the Crown's initial efforts to improve decision-making processes by gathering data from the Indies and gaining a better overview of the results of the conquests it had already approved.[56] On the other hand, the qualities he singled out as most important in the selection process were those that distinguished him from his current and future competitors. Few men had as much experience and capital as he had, while those who filled positions as royal officials in New Spain's capital could not live in the conquered territories. Although it is impossible to determine how these efforts to fashion an image of himself as the ideal captain and conquistador were received, we

---

[54] Memorial of Hernán Cortés for Charles V, unknown date, in ibid., 563.

[55] Ibid., 564.

[56] The Crown did actually acquire such information in the form of two different maps of the American continent drawn around the time. In 1529, the royal cosmographer Diego Ribeiro drew a map that indicated what regions in North America the Crown had granted through *capitulaciones*. The map mentions, for example, "Land of Esteban Gómez," "Land of [Lucas Vázquez de] Ayllon," "Land of [Francisco de] Garray." In 1533, Alonso de Chavez produced a similar map, this time adding "Land of Pánfilo de Narváez" to the ones already mentioned on Ribeiro's map.

do know that Cortés was appointed as "captain general of New Spain and the provinces of the South Sea" on July 6, 1529.[57] This was an obvious demotion in comparison to his previous role as governor of New Spain, but it did allow him to continue expanding his activities in the South Sea, albeit with some clear restrictions.

The agreement that Cortés signed with the Crown in November 1529 ended up being of an entirely different nature from Ribera's proposal of 1523. None of the privileges that his agent had asked for were mentioned, while the timeframe in which Cortés was allowed to explore was reduced from six to two years.[58] Moreover, important limits were posed regarding the territories that he was allowed to explore. By no means was he to enter the demarcations of Pánfilo de Narváez and Nuño de Guzmán. This seems an odd order, considering that both had been granted territories on the east coast. But in a situation in which the limits of demarcations were mostly defined along the north–south axis, with their western frontier often being left undefined, this may have been an attempt to prevent conflicts from rising between these sworn enemies. Another limitation Cortés had to observe was posed by the Treaty of Zaragoza, which had been signed on April 27, 1529, renouncing all claims of the Spanish Crown beyond the line of demarcation drawn at 17 degrees or 297.5 leagues east of the Moluccas.[59]

The limitations specified in Cortés's *capitulación* posed a real challenge. Everyone believed that there were still plenty of opportunities for discovery in the South Sea, but this was a large space and Cortés had no concrete goal to pursue as he had had during the conquest of Tenochtitlan. During the little time given to him, it was imperative to yield results. Yet it was unclear where to start looking. To make things worse, upon his return to New Spain in 1530, he discovered that Guzmán's men had wrecked the five ships he had been building in the port of Zihuatanejo, further setting him back on an already tight

---

[57] Appointment of Hernán Cortés as captain general, Jul 6, 1529, AGI, Patronato, 16, N.2, R.15.

[58] Hernán Cortés's rights in the exploration of the South Sea, Nov 5, 1529, AGI, Patronato, 16, N.2, R.19.

[59] AGI, Patronato, 49, N.9. Mariano Cuesta Domingo, "La fijación de la linea - de Tordesillas - en el Extremo Oriente," in *El tratado de Tordesillas y su época*, ed. Luís A. Ribot García (Madrid: Sociedad V Centenario del Tratado de Tordesillas; Junta de Castilla y León Consejería de Educación y Cultura, 1995), 3: 1505–7.

schedule.[60] These growing pressures may explain his frantic pursuit of opportunities during the following years. Cortés dispatched expeditions under the command of Diego Hurtado de Mendoza (1532), Diego Becerra, and Hernando de Grijalva (both 1533) to explore the California coasts in search of Cihuatán, a mythical island the Nahua had beguiled the Spaniards about; became involved in the exploration himself when news leaked that Guzmán had impounded one of Becerra's ships; and established the Santa Cruz colony in 1535, after pearls had been discovered in Baja California.[61] The next year, Cortés also sent Grijalva, under the pretext of sending reinforcements to Franciso Pizarro in Peru, to look for an island rich in gold and silver of which people were talking and that was supposedly located off the Peruvian west coast.[62] Grijalva actually sailed so far into the ocean that he reached an island near New Guinea, where his rebellious crew was captured by the Portuguese. None of Cortés's expeditions or colonizing efforts were successful, however – even the self-proclaimed ideal conqueror first needed to discover something that was worthy of being conquered.

THE DISCOVERY OF ANOTHER "NEW WORLD"

One such target emerged on the horizon during the summer of 1536. On the eve of the Feast of Santiago, four survivors of Pánfilo de Narváez's shattered 1528 expedition to Florida reached Mexico.[63] Álvar Nuñez Cabeza de Vaca, Alonso del Castillo Maldonado, Andrés Dorantes de Carranza, and the African slave Esteban had spent eight years among the Natives, traveling with different bands and tribes from Florida through what are today the states of Louisiana and Texas into California and then

---

[60] AGI, Patronato, 16, N.1, R.2. Woodrow Borah, "Hernán Cortés y sus intereses marítimos en el Pacífico, el Perú y la Baja California," *Estudios de Historia Novohispana* 4 (1971): 4; León-Portilla, *Hernán Cortés*, 74.

[61] Michael W. Mathes, *The Conquistador in California, 1535: The Voyage of Fernando Cortés to Baja California in Chronicles and Documents* (Los Angeles: Dawson's Book Shop, 1973); Miguel León-Portilla, *Cartografía y crónicas de la California* (Mexico City, Universidad Nacional Autónoma de México, 1989), chapter 2. Paul A. Myers, *North to California: The Spanish Voyages of Discovery, 1533–1603* (Coral Springs, FL: Llumina Press, 2004), chapter 7.

[62] Borah, "Hernán Cortés, 13–18; León-Portilla, *Hernán Cortés*, 117–21.

[63] Richard Flint, *No Settlement, No Conquest: A History of the Coronado Entrada* (Albuquerque: University of New Mexico Press, 2008), 27–30; William K. Hartmann, *Searching for Golden Empires: Epic Cultural Collisions in Sixteenth-Century America* (Tucson: The University of Arizona Press, 2014), chapter 4.

south, along the Gulf of California, to New Spain. Rumors had already been circulating that the four men carried wonderful news about regions north of New Galicia that no Spaniard had ever seen before.[64] During the final stage of their journey from the Sonoran coast, the four castaways were welcomed by the most powerful men in the region. They enjoyed Nuño de Guzmán's company in Compostela as well as that of Hernán Cortés and the recently arrived viceroy, Antonio de Mendoza, in Mexico. All three hoped to learn from the survivors whether they had seen anything worth conquering in the region, which had already drawn the Spaniards' interests at an earlier time because of its role in the stories the Mexica told about their place of origin.[65]

Especially Viceroy Mendoza went to great lengths in accommodating his guests, providing them with new clothes and living quarters and promising them rewards. The viceroy had his reasons for such generosity. He belonged to a family that owed much of its status and influence to its members' contributions to the wars against the Moors and Moriscos.[66] In addition to being eager to carry on the family tradition of rendering military services to the Crown, Mendoza also had a keen interest in becoming involved in the search for a route to Asia. According to the cosmographer Alonso de Santa Cruz, whom the viceroy met before his departure to New Spain, Mendoza was well informed about recent developments in cosmography and geography and knew that there were opportunities waiting in the South Sea and in the northwestern parts of

---

[64] A vast literature exists regarding the journey of the *"náufragos"* (Sp: *naufragios*; En: shipwrecked) through the southern parts of today's United States and northern parts of Mexico. Alex D. Krieger, *We Came Naked and Barefoot: The Journey of Cabeza de Vaca across North America* (Austin: University of Texas Press, 2002); Andrés Reséndez, *Un viaje distinto: la exploración de Cabeza de Vaca por América* (Barcelona: La Vanguardia Ediciones, 2008). See also: Cabeza de Vaca's own account in Álvar de Núñez Cabeza Vaca, *Naufragios y comentarios* (Madrid: Calpe, 1922).

[65] The creole chronicler Baltasar de Obregón observes that Hernán Cortés and Viceroy Mendoza's interest in the north initially was stirred by the chronicles relating to the origins of the Mexica that were discovered among Moctezuma's papers. Baltasar de Obregón, *Historia de los descubrimientos antiguos y modernos de la Nueva España, escrita por el conquistador en el año de 1584*, ed. P. Mariano Cuevas, S. J. (Mexico City: Editorial Porrúa, 1988), 10. Mendoza also talks about this theme in a letter to the royal chronicler Gonzalo Fernández de Oviedo that is included in his *Historia general y natural de las Indias* (Madrid: Biblioteca de Autores Españoles. Recopilación de leyes de los reynos de las Indias, 1959), 4: Cap. L, 245–48; and Cap. LII, 252–53.

[66] Ciriaco Pérez Bustamante, *Don Antonio de Mendoza, primer virrey de la Nueva España (1535–1550)* (Santiago de Compostela: Tipografía de "El Eco Franciscano," 1928), 3–10; Francisco J. Escudero Buendía, *Antonio de Mendoza: comendador de la villa de Socuéllamos y primer virrey de la Nueva España* (Perea: Pedro Muñoz, 2003), chapter 3.

the continent yet to be explored by Europeans.[67] He must also have been aware that, in spite of the Treaty of Zaragoza, the Spanish Crown had not entirely abandoned its Asian project, as was illustrated by a proposal from the Council of the Indies in 1531 to dispatch two caravels to bring back the remaining survivors of the Magellan and Loaísa expeditions.[68] The return of the survivors of the Narváez expedition from the northern regions presented an excellent opportunity to determine whether these parts of the world could be worthy of further exploration.

But the reports the castaway provided did not warrant immediate action. Neither Guzmán, who controlled New Galicia and knew the region quite well, nor the viceroy acted upon the new information they received. It would take until 1539, after Guzmán had been arrested and Mendoza was able to get a confidant, don Francisco Vázquez de Coronado, appointed to the position of governor of New Galicia, before the viceroy sent a reconnoitring party to determine whether the North had anything to offer. Mendoza entrusted this mission to Marcos de Niza, a Franciscan friar who was trained in cosmography and already possessed several years of experience in Hispaniola and Peru.[69] The viceroy provided Fray Marcos with a carefully composed set of instructions. Together with Vázquez de Coronado, he first had to bring word to San Miguel de Culiacán that the viceroy would reward those serving him and punish those violating the law. Then, after traveling beyond this northernmost Spanish outpost, the friar was to come into contact with the Natives, count them, and take careful records of the "quality and fertility of the land."[70] As soon as he reached the coast of the South Sea, he was to leave signs on trees close to the water and leave information beneath them so they could be seen by the ships that were going to follow him. Finally, Fray Marcos had to take possession of any large settlements in the viceroy's name, performing ceremonies required for such cases.

---

[67] Alonso de Santa Cruz, *Libro de las longitudines y manera que hasta agora se ha tenido en el arte de navegar, con sus demostraciones y ejemplos, dirigido al muy alto y muy poderoso señor don Philipe II de este nombre rey de España*, eds. Delgado Aguilera and Antonio Blázquez (Seville: Centro oficial de estudios americanistas, 1921), 47.

[68] AGI, Indiferente general, 1092, N.25, Letter of the Council of the Indies to King, May 16, 1531. Although the councilors had proposed to charge Cortés, Alvarado in Guatemala, or Pedrarias in Nicaragua with such a task, by the time Mendoza left the Peninsula, Cristóbal de Haro was once again preparing for this supposed rescue mission. Gil, *Mitos y utopías*, 2: 45.

[69] Flint, *No Settlement, No Conquest*, 30–32.

[70] Instructions Antonio de Mendoza for Marcos de Niza, AGI, Patronato, 20, N.5, R.10, f. iv.

Fray Marcos's return to Culiacán in July 1539 inflamed an unprecedented fever for conquest. Despite the viceroy's explicit instructions not to share any information, rumors began to spread quickly about the amazing discoveries he had made in the North.[71] We learn from his official report of the three-month journey why this was the case. The friar recounts how, as he traveled north, Natives kept telling him about great cities with names like Cíbola, Marata, Acus, and Totonteac. The further north he reached, the more detailed his informants' reports became and the more they talked about "people of greater civil order (*más poleçia*) and reason."[72] He learned that the houses in Cíbola were built of mortar and stone, that some of them had up to ten stories, and that they were decorated with turquoise. Furthermore, inhabitants of the city dressed in long garments made of cotton and wool that covered them from neck to toe.[73] Although the friar acknowledged that he never entered Cíbola, due to threats from the Natives, the brief glimpse he got made it clear that it was even larger than Mexico City. To make things even better, Fray Marco claimed to have seen how the west coast "at 35 degrees, turns west," meaning that it heads toward Asia rather than simply ending at the Pacific, from which he "experienced no less joy than the good news about the land."[74]

Historians today agree that it is unlikely that the friar reached the small Zuni town in present-day New Mexico that could have been the town of Cíbola. Instead, they consider the friar's report to be the fabulated product of a fanciful mind, interpreting the information provided by local informants through a framework of preexisting perceptions about world geography. Two narratives were particularly important in shaping this geographical framework: first, the Iberian legend of the seven Christian Visigothic bishops who fled the Peninsula during the Muslim conquest to create seven cities on the island of Antilia, located somewhere in the Atlantic Ocean.[75] Such a myth harmonized well with the origin stories that the Nahua told about the place of the seven caves, known as Chicomoztoc, which also was supposed to be located in the North, all merging together in Fray Marcos' story about the Seven Cities of Cíbola.

---

[71] For a detailed account of Fray Marco's journey: Hartmann, *Searching for Golden Empires*, chapter 5.

[72] Report of Fray Marcos de Niza's journey, Sept 2, 1539, AGI, Patronato, 20, N.5, R.10, f. 2v.

[73] Ibid., ff.3v.–4r.   [74] Ibid., f. 5r.

[75] William H. Babcock, "The Island of the Seven Cities," *Geographical Review* 7, no. 2 (1919): 98–106.

Second, as Richard and Shirley Cushing Flint have pointed out, the friar relied on the idea that the American mainland was an extension of India extra Gangem.[76] A similar notion of world geography had inspired Christopher Columbus and Johannes Schöner, among others, to consider North America a part of the Asian mainland. However, such a vision was gradually replaced by one that positioned an enormous land bridge between these two parts of the world, as can be seen in Giacomo Gastaldi's *Universale Novo* from 1548 (Figure 1.2).

How significant the friar's belief that he was traveling in the direction of the lands of the Great Khan was for the stories he told after his return becomes visible, too, in the information he excluded from the official report. The bishop of Mexico, Fray Juan de Zumárraga, for example, wrote that Fray Marcos had told him that:

The people are more cultured in their wooden edifices of many stories and in their dress. They have no idols, do not worship the sun and moon. They have only one wife and if she dies do not marry another. There are partridges and cows which the father says he saw, and he heard a story of camels and dromedaries and of other cities larger than this one of Mexico.[77]

Several contemporaries repeated such observations about the intelligence of the people, the size of their houses, and the wealth of the land. But they added their own details as well. Gerónimo Ximenez de San Estéban, for example, wrote to one of his fellow friars in Burgos that the people of these lands wore silk clothing, that their temples were covered with emeralds, and that camels and elephants could be found further north.[78] Others spoke of gold and silver, of people who spoke a language resembling that of the Mexica and rode unknown animals. Some of these captivating stories were so wonderful that one Bocanegra considered the lands that contemporaries came to refer to as *Tierra Nueva* to be an actual "new world."[79]

---

[76] Richard Flint and Shirley Cushing Flint, *A Most Splendid Company: The Coronado Expedition in Global Perspective* (Albuquerque: University of New Mexico Press, 2019), 21–23.

[77] Juan de Zumárraga, "Letter to an Unknown Religious from Juan de Zumárraga, México, April 4, 1537," in Henry R. Wagner; "Fray Marcos de Niza," *New Mexico Historical Review* 9 (Apr 1934): 198–99.

[78] Joaquín García Icazbalceta, *Nueva colección de documentos para la historia de México* (Mexico City: Antigua Librería de Andrade y Morales, Sucesores, 1886), 1: 194–95.

[79] Trial of the Marquis of the Valley [of Oaxaca] and Nuño de Guzmán and the adelantados Soto and Alvarado, about the discovery of Tierra Nueva. 1541, in CDI, 15: 397.

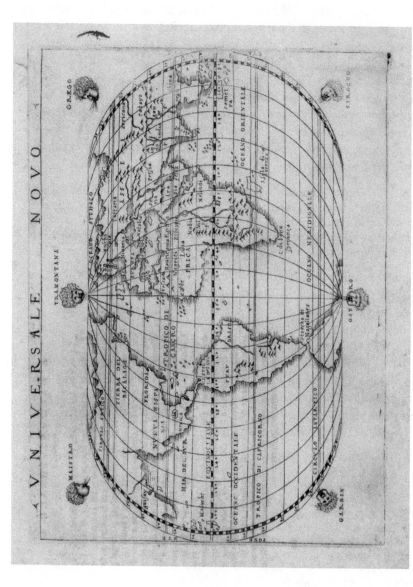

FIGURE 1.2 Giacomo Gastaldi, *Universale Novo* in *La geografia di Claudio Ptolemeo alessandrino*, Venice (1548). Courtesy of The Barry Lawrence Ruderman Map Collection, David Rumsey Map Center, Stanford Libraries

As excitement in the viceroyalty grew based on such rumors, the friendly relationship that Cortés and Viceroy Mendoza had maintained quickly went sour. As captain general of New Spain and the coasts of the South Sea, Cortés believed that the territories the friar had discovered fell within the boundaries of his *capitulación*. In fact, after learning in November 1538 that the viceroy was planning to send explorers to the region, Cortés began preparing his own expedition to explore the waters between the "island" of Santa Cruz and the mainland. On July 8, 1539, only a few days before Fray Marcos returned to Culiacán, a flotilla of three ships commanded by Francisco de Ulloa sailed from Acapulco to realize Cortés's plan.[80] When news of Fray Marco's findings reached Cortés later that month, he wrote to the viceroy that he had always believed that "good lands" would be found in the north but, also, that he did not expect them to be so near. "God," he wrote in an attempt to let Mendoza know that he was ready to take over the endeavor, "desires that we shall not be idle but otherwise, because he placed us in these parts for each to use his talents."[81] To his chagrin, however, Mendoza had no intention of making use of Cortés's talents and experience. Instead, after having interviewed Fray Marcos in private, the viceroy himself took the lead in preparing the entrada of Tierra Nueva of Cíbola. This decision led to a bitter conflict with important consequences for the development of the Spanish empire.

DISPUTING DISCOVERERS

From the moment Mendoza began to plan his activities in the Pacific Northwest, he and Cortés became involved in a contest over who ought to be recognized as the discoverer of this unknown territory. Mendoza sought to bolster his claim to this status by having Fray Marcos appear before Mexico's audiencia on September 2, 1539. Here, the friar presented the instructions that the viceroy had given him together with the report he produced of his journey to testify to the veracity of both.[82] This ceremony and the file that was produced from it helped the viceroy to establish a chain of responsibility in the process of the discovery of Tierra Nueva. The instructions foregrounded his leading role in sending the reconnoitering party, while the friar's report provided what was

[80] León-Portilla, *Hernán Cortés*, 137–45; Myers, *North to California*, 102–62.
[81] Contract Hernán Cortés with Charles, RAH, 9-5825, f. 51v. This letter is dated July 26.
[82] AGI, Patronato, 20, N.5, R.10.

considered a precise and truthful account of what had been discovered in his name. By fashioning himself as the person responsible for the discovery of Cíbola, Mendoza underlined his claim to the right of undertaking any future conquests. Only after he had dealt with these legal procedures, he shifted his attention to logistics. To verify Fray Marco's account and gather additional information about the route and availably of provisions, he ordered Melchor Díaz to take fifteen horsemen from Culiacán to retrace the friar's steps. In the meanwhile, he began preparing the expeditions that Francisco Vázquez de Coronado would lead over land and Hernando de Alarcón by sea.[83]

Mendoza's efforts to prove his leading role in the discovery of Tierra Nueva were closely related to Cortés's own legal maneuvering. In September 1538, the Marquis had already written the Council of the Indies, reminding the councilors of the rights he had received to explore the islands and coast of the South Sea, while also noting that he had nine ships at his disposal but not enough pilots to navigate them all.[84] He further explained that, since the viceroy had sent the Crown a detailed report describing the qualities of the land and its inhabitants, he saw no need to speak about the matter. Yet, so as not to remain silent – and to more subtly give the king a chance to assess his services – Cortés added a map depicting what he had discovered to this point.[85] One year later, he wrote a similar petition to Charles, pointing out that in accordance with royal orders he had sent Diego Hurtado de Mendoza to explore as far north as 27 degrees, of which there existed perpetual proof (*"ad perpetum rei memoriam"*) in the form of a royal certification or *probanza*. Because of these and other efforts, he believed it to be a grave injustice to be banned from the islands and coasts of the South Sea that were rightfully his to explore.[86] Cortés made a similar argument before the audiencia, asking the judges to see to it that his royally given rights were protected.[87]

Cortés's pleas to the king and the audiencia provoked a strongly worded response from the *fiscal* (king's attorney) of Mexico's audiencia,

[83] Flint and Cushing Flint, *A Most Splendid Company*, 81–87.

[84] Letter from Hernán Cortés to Council of the Indies, Sept 20, 1538, AGI, Patronato, 16, N.1, R.18.

[85] The map Cortés speaks of here may have been one depicting a part of the coast of New Galicia, the region north of Culiacán, Santa Cruz, and several other islands in the southern part of the Gulf of California, which can be found in AGI, Mapas y planos, México, 6.

[86] Memorial of Hernan Cortés to Charles V. Undated, in CODOIN, 4: 201–6.

[87] RAH, 9-5825, f. 43.

Cristóbal Benavente. On September 11, 1539, Benavente presented to the audiencia a petition in which he made the case for prohibiting Cortés from continuing his explorations in the South Sea.[88] He noted that Cortés had had his chances but, again and again, had proven unable to act in accordance with the king's orders. It had taken him four years to send a first expedition, thus exceeding the timeframe of two years agreed upon in his *capitulación*. His men's exploitation of the Natives had caused much turmoil, and, contrary to all royal commands, Cortés had been recruiting participants in New Spain who were already or were about to get married. The fiscal cynically observed that these disruptions of both Native and Spanish republics made it look as if Cortés had set out "to depopulate the populated and peaceful, [rather] than to discover and settle new lands."[89] Benavente continued that the only land the Marquis had discovered was an island that had turned out to be utterly useless. Referring to Cortés's attempts to establish the colony of Santa Cruz, the lawyer argued that the land was inhabited by some kind of wild "Caribs" who live only on raw fish and meat, go around dressed in animal hides, and are in no way inclined to serve the king.[90] Cortés himself had been aware of the futility of his colony, for he had himself abandoned it after two years, leaving the island "unoccupied (*pro derelictam*)" for more than a year and half. As a consequence, he lost all claims to which he would have been entitled as "first discoverer."[91] Benavente also argued that Cortés had only ordered Ulloa to return to Santa Cruz when Fray Marcos arrived from his journey with news of a rich and well-populated land, but this was actually only a pretext to reach Tierra Nueva before the viceroy did.[92] As Cortés had violated the terms of his contract, Benavente contended that he should by no means be allowed to enter the new territory.

During the following months, it must have dawned on Cortés that he was not going to win this battle. Mendoza's grip over the audiencia was too strong, and the viceroy's allies proved a threat to any expedition Cortés might send. As he later reported, not only did they prevent his men from buying supplies but also persecuted and eventually burned one of Ulloa's vessels, the *Santa Agueda*, which had been sent to report to

---

[88] Ibid., ff. 45v–49v.   [89] Ibid., f. 47r.
[90] One day later, Francisco Vázquez de Coronado reaffirmed this perspective on the worthlessness of the island for colonization. As there was nothing to eat, and the Natives were unwilling to serve the monarch, Cortés would only have risked causing a rebellion. Ibid., ff. 53v–55r.
[91] Ibid., f. 48r.   [92] Ibid., f. 49r.

Cortés about new discoveries.[93] Faced with such opposition, Cortés saw
no other option than to return to Spain. Briefly before his departure, he
wrote to his attorneys at the court to remind the Council of the Indies of
the four expeditions he had already dispatched at his own expense and to
warn them not to provide any kind of information to Mendoza's agents.[94]
They were also to inform the Council that the viceroy was already sending
men without waiting for permission, distracting the viceroy from his
political responsibilities.

Cortés's return to Spain early in 1540 coincided with the beginning of
a legal process in the Council regarding distribution of rights to conquer
Tierra Nueva.[95] By this time not only were Cortés and Mendoza making
such a claim but also representatives of Pedro de Alvarado, Hernando de
Soto, and Nuño de Guzmán. Each believed that the newly discovered land
fell within the demarcations stipulated in the respective *capitulaciones*
these men had signed with the Crown. Alvarado relied on the contracts he
had signed in the summer of 1538 that granted him within fifteen
months permission to dispatch two galleons and a vessel to explore the
West ("*el poniente*") and two ships to explore the westward bend of
New Spain "to learn about all the secrets that are there on the coast."[96]
Nuño de Guzmán's claim was based on his entitlements as governor and
adelantado of New Galicia – of which Tierra Nueva was a part, his
attorneys argued. Hernando de Soto, who was governor of Cuba at the
time but had also received rights over the lands that had once been
promised to Pánfilo de Narváez and Lucas Vázquez de Ayllon before
him, made the claim that the limits of his governorate in Florida extended
all the way to the opposite coast.

In spite of the heated arguments taking place before the Council of the
Indies, the Crown did not want the expansion to come to a halt. On April
15, 1540, royal officials dispatched an order to Mendoza granting him
permission to proceed with organization of the *entrada*, seeing that he

[93] Memorandum by Hernán Cortés for the king, Jun 25, 1540, in *Cartas y documentos*, ed.
Sánchez-Barba, 408–9.
[94] Instructions to Juan de Avellaneda, Jorge Cerón, and Juan Galvarro, in CODOIN, 4:
206–12.
[95] Among the materials presented, we find a description of the journey that Pedro de
Guzmán made in the name of Nuño de Guzmán to the island of Nuestra Señora in
1532 and a description of what Diego de Guzmán discovered on the coasts of the Mar del
Sur in 1533. Lawsuit: Marquis of the Valley and others against the royal prosecutor,
1540, AGI, Patronato, 21, N.2, R.4.
[96] Appointments and concessions to Pedro de Alvarado, AGI, Patronato, 28, R.63.

had been the one who sent Fray Marcos.[97] In the meantime, the Council would look for a solution. This decision was taken in agreement with the royal attorney, Juan de Villalobos, who on May 25, 1540, wrote in his recommendations to the Council that it should ignore the baseless arguments of those claiming any rights over Tierra Nueva. According to Villalobos, Viceroy Mendoza had discovered these lands for the Spanish Crown, and there was no one who merited them either because of an older *capitulación* or having been the first to describe them. Therefore, he suggested that the Crown simply keep this territory for itself, which meant that Mendoza would oversee its conquest.[98]

On June 25, 1540, Cortés responded to these developments in a memorandum addressed to Charles, who had left Spain to suppress the Revolt of Ghent in the autumn of the previous year. He accused Mendoza of preventing him from conquering the lands that fell within the demarcation established by the *capitulación* he had signed with the Crown in October 1529. To prove that he deserved to be in charge of this enterprise, he pointed out that he had done everything in his power to comply with the terms of the contract, spending 200,000 ducats to organize four expeditions. His efforts had brought him to Santa Cruz, where he had learned from the Natives about the areas that Fray Marcos had reported on. According to Cortés, the friar had only become aware of them because Cortés had already told him what he knew, blaming the friar for "feigning and recounting something he did not see or know."[99] Thus, even though Cortés himself had been busy provisioning his colony and could not himself explore these territories, it was his information that had led to their discovery. Cortés also shared his worries about the inexperienced Vázquez de Coronado being unable to subdue regions of such great quality and quantity, where the people are "bellicose, and of more understanding and knowledge than any other [nation] that has been discovered in the Indies until today."[100] Additionally, he believed it to be a great risk to have the viceroy involved in the conquest. Failure on his part could create an impression among the Natives of the already conquered territories that he was weak, giving them reason to rebel.[101] Finally, he contended that the king did not have the right to grant the

---

[97] Pérez Bustamante, *Don Antonio de Mendoza*, 58.   [98] CDI, 15: 376–79.

[99] Memorial Hernán Cortés, Jun 25, 1540, AGI, Patronato, 21, N.2, R.4, second block, ff. 3–5r.

[100] Ibid., f. 3v.   [101] Ibid., f. 4r.

title and provision to Mendoza, as it violated the terms of an earlier agreement. He therefore urged Charles to look at the papers he had prepared and to ask his "cosmographers and experts in the art of navigation and cosmography" for their opinions.[102]

Cortés's plea was repeated more than once by his lawyers before the Council. But it appears that at least some of the royal officials had already made up their minds. On July 10, 1540, the king's secretaries prepared two royal decrees that were meant to end the conflict. The first was addressed to Viceroy Mendoza, directing him to stop preventing Cortés from sending his ships to explore the islands in the South Sea.[103] The second decree was also addressed to the viceroy but, this time, to the other persons involved in the lawsuit as well. It first summarized the entire conflict, naming all the stakeholders and their claims. Then it repeated the instructions that Cortés had a right to the islands in the South Sea and to the coasts of Tierra Firme that had been unknown at the time of signing the *capitulación* of 1529 and that lay outside the demarcations reserved for Guzmán and Narváez. Alvarado had received the right to explore west in the Pacific and the bend of New Spain in the direction of Asia, while De Soto had inherited the claims over La Florida that had once belonged to Narváez as well as the land that had been discovered by Ayllon. Still, as it was Mendoza who had sent Fray Marcos to explore lands north of New Galicia, the councilors concurred with the fiscal that this land fell outside any of their *capitulaciones* and, therefore, belonged to the viceroy.

The royal decrees demonstrate that little doubt existed within the Council about distribution of the privilege of conquest. They possibly considered exploration of Tierra Nueva to be part of the search for the still unknown parts of Asia and, therefore, they may have wanted to ensure the Crown's control over the endeavor. Mendoza being a scion of the powerful Mendoza clan could also have played a role, allowing him to enjoy more political support at the court. For Cortés, it would have been disastrous if he would have been deprived here of a role in what he described to his lawyers as the "greatest and most important thing discovered in these parts."[104] But as the king was not in Spain, he did not sign any of the documents, which left the case wide open.

---

[102] Ibid., f. 4v.
[103] Royal decree for Antonio de Mendoza, Jul 10, 1540, AGI, Patronato, 16, N.2, R.49.
[104] CODOIN, 4: 207.

THE MAPS OF THE DISCOVERERS

While litigants wrestled in the courts of Mexico and Madrid, maps acquired an increasingly important role. On both sides of the Atlantic, navigators and cosmographers drew charts that were used as evidence supporting Cortés's and Mendoza's opposing claims of being the discoverer of Tierra Nueva. Maps were also destroyed and manipulated to control the narratives each of the parties tried to convey. In Mexico, supporters of the viceroy engaged in such manipulation after Francisco de Ulloa's expedition returned in May 1540. Some of the expedition's participants carried the captain's account of the journey. This report described how his ships had sailed north along the Pacific coast to the estuary of the Colorado River at 34 degrees north, from which they turned south again to round Cape San Lucas and continued their journey west of Baja California, at least as far as the Cedros Islands and Cabo de Engaño.[105] In addition to this description of the itinerary and people they had encountered, Ulloa's men also brought a map and seven acts of possession produced by the fleet's notary, Pedro de Palencia. Upon receiving these papers, Cortés's *mayordomo* (steward) in Mexico, Francisco Sánchez de Toledo, immediately asked the *alcalde ordinario* (first-instance judge) and a public scribe of the city of Mexico to make copies of them, because he feared that they could be "torn apart or get wet or burned" when sending them to Cortés.[106]

As the certified copies of these documents were being prepared, Benavente, the fiscal of the audiencia, also got wind of the return of Ulloa's men. On July 28, 1540, he wrote the king that he had not been able to get the men to serve as witnesses in the trial, and he requested the king to order Juan de Castellón, one of Ulloa's navigators, to draw a map that could be introduced as evidence.[107] Benavente's request seems odd, considering that Ulloa had already sent a map drawn by the other navigator of the flotilla, Pedro de Bermes. Yet efforts seem to have been made to keep this map from appearing during the trial. Not only was the

---

[105] Contemporaries located this cape in different places. Domingo de Castillo places it only a short distance north of Cedros Island, at 27.5 degrees North, while Francisco López de Gómara notes that the cape was located at the same altitude as the Ancón de San Andrés, closer to 32 degrees North, that is. Francisco López de Gómara, *La conquista de México*, ed. José Luis de Rojas (Las Rozas: Dastin, 2003), 421.

[106] Henry Raup Wagner, *Spanish Voyages to the Northwest Coast of America in the Sixteenth Century* (San Francisco: California Historical Society, 1929), 15.

[107] RAH, 9-5825, f. 70r.

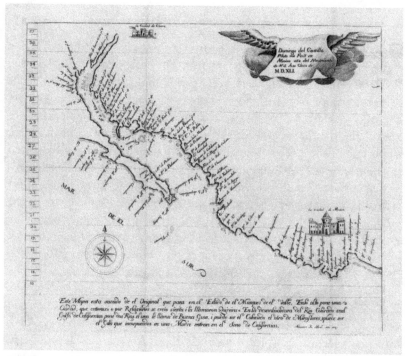

FIGURE 1.3 Domingo del Castillo, Map of the Pacific Coast (1541). From a copy in *Historia de la Nueva España* by Fernando Antonio Lorenzana (1770). The Rare Books Division of the Library of Congress

part of Ulloa's report in which he spoke about the map mutilated but, by asking Castellón to draw a new map, Benavente had also picked a person who held a strong grudge against Cortés and disagreed with Bermes on the latitudes they had sailed.[108] Eventually, not Castellón but rather, Domingo de Castillo, drew a map that the fiscal used to make his case against Cortés (Figure 1.3).

Domingo de Castillo had been a navigator on the ship that Hernando de Alarcón captained at Viceroy Mendoza's behest along the east coast of the Gulf of California at the end of 1540. The map he drew combined data gathered during the voyages of both Ulloa and Alarcón. The latter explained the objective of this map and accompanying acts of possession in his account of the journey. According to Mendoza's captain, Ulloa had exaggerated by two degrees when claiming that he had reached 34 degrees

[108] Henry Raup Wagner, "Francisco de Ulloa Returned," *California Historical Society Quarterly* 19, no. 3 (1940): 240–44.

north while sailing upward on the Colorado River and emphasized that "we have travelled farther than they did by more than four degrees."[109] With the help of the measure of parallel degrees on the left side of the map, Domingo del Castillo and Alarcón reinforced their claim that they had reached 36 degrees when sailing up a branch of the Colorado river they called Brazo de Miraflores, apparently bringing him very close to the sought-after Cíbola.[110] When Benavente presented this material to the audiencia, Cortés's lawyer Álvaro Ruiz tried to downplay its significance, noting that "as the lands and the river that the said Alarcón entered are all one and the same thing, being all so close to each other, it suffices for the said Marquis to have taken possession of and conquer them as he did."[111] The conflict about the status of discoverer had thus become one about degrees.

Around the same time that these developments were taking place in the viceroyalty, in Spain, Cortés's lawyer Íñigo López de Mondragón was arguing that the Crown should consult its "cosmographers, pilots, and experts."[112] The Council seems to have done so but only in response to an unexpected turn in the dispute. On February 5, 1541, Charles wrote from the German town of Speyer that he had been informed of Mendoza having confiscated all the "reports and charts" of one of Cortés's captains.[113] He considered this a great disservice, as it had brought the process of discovery and conquest to an undesired halt. He ordered that Mendoza should no longer prevent Cortés from further exploration; meanwhile, a decision about whose conquest it was had to be taken within fifteen to twenty days, without losing valuable time via a regular lawsuit. Around this time, Charles also wrote Cortés, ordering him to nominate the navigators and cosmographers who should determine

---

[109] Alarcón's report is preserved only in an Italian translation by Giovanni Battista Ramusio. A transcript and English translation can be found in Richard Flint and Shirley Cushing Flint, eds., *Documents of the Coronado Expedition, 1539–1542* (Dallas: Southern Methodist University Press, 2005), 182–222.

[110] The name Quivira that appears on the map is incorrect, since that name only became known after the return of Coronado to Mexico. This alteration was probably made when the map was copied in 1769. W. Michael Mathes, "Spanish Maritime Charting of the Gulf of Mexico and the California Coast," in *Mapping and Empire: Soldier-Engineers on the Southwestern Frontier*, eds. Dennis Reinhartz and Gerald D. Saxon (Austin: University of Texas Press, 2005), 23.

[111] RAH, 9-5825, f. 363.

[112] Response from Íñigo López de Mondragón to petition of Juan de Barrutia, Aug 8, 1540, in CODOIN, 15: 389.

[113] CDI, 15: 398–99.

whether the province of Cíbola fell within the territories granted to him by the 1529 *capitulación*. Cortés responded to these royal orders by saying that there were many excellent pilots and cosmographers in Seville who could help with this, including "Pero Mexía and Francisco Facelo and Sebastian Cabot."[114] The Council, in turn, appears to have turned to another expert, Alonso de Santa Cruz, who had been a cosmographer of the House of Trade since 1533 and in whom the emperor had long confided.

Two maps both coming from his hand reveal that Santa Cruz was of the same opinion as the Council when it came to Mendoza's claims of being the discover of Tierra Nueva. One of these maps appeared in his *Islario general de todas las islas del mundo* (General Atlas of All the Islands of the World, 1541). On a map depicting North and Middle America, California appears as an island and the Gulf of California as a circular bay. Santa Cruz added a description specifying that the island had been discovered by Cortés, whereas the inhabited land to the north had been discovered under the orders of Viceroy Mendoza (Figure 1.4). Almost the same image appears on the map that we examined in the introduction to this chapter, bearing the title *Nova verior et integra totius orbis descriptio* (A New, More True and Complete Description of the Whole World, 1542: Figure 1.5). The true novelty of this later map was the way in which it presented both hemispheres separately, to achieve a less distorted image of distances and proportions (Figure 1.1). Santa Cruz had already produced an earlier version of such a map in 1540, which probably served as the model for the 1542 drawing.[115] Although by 1542 the data that had been gathered by Ulloa and Alarcón had arrived on the Peninsula, Santa Cruz did not use any of it. It is, of course, possible that he had not seen this new information or was simply not interested in redrawing his own maps. Yet, more likely is that his omission had something to do with the reasons for which the 1542 map seems to have been drawn.

Santa Cruz's 1542 double hemispheric map stands in direct relation to earlier maps that had alluded to the distribution of *capitulaciones*, including the world maps drawn by Diego Ribeiro in 1529 and Alonso de Chavez in 1533. Both maps had been produced during a period when

---

[114] AGI, Patronato, 21, N.2, R.4.
[115] E. W. Dahlgren, *Map of the World by Alonso de Santa Cruz, 1542* (Stockholm: P. A. Norstedt & Söner, 1892), 13.

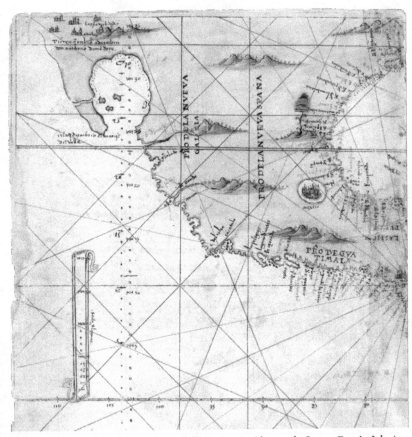

FIGURE 1.4 Detail of map of North America in Alonso de Santa Cruz's *Islario general* (1541). Folio 19v. Image taken from the holdings of the Biblioteca Nacional de España, Madrid

the Crown was trying to concretely pin down which North American territories it had granted, showing what land had been given to whom. Santa Cruz's map does the same by delimiting the various provinces and specifying who had discovered certain regions. On the East Coast, for example, appear glosses indicating "Land of Esteban Gómez," "Land of Lic. Ayllon," and "Pánfilo de Narváez, named La Florida." The map also separates New Spain from New Galicia, indicating what so-called island Cortés had discovered and what part of the mainland Mendoza had sent Fray Marcos to. In so doing, Santa Cruz's map provided a new instrument in the dispute over the claims to Tierra Firme. With its grid made up of crossing parallels and meridians, the map made it even easier to set

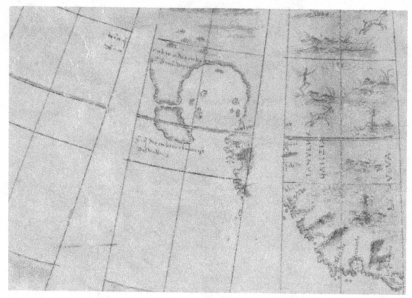

FIGURE 1.5 Detail of *Nova verior et integra totivs descriptio* depicting the Gulf of California and the lands discovered by Antonio de Mendoza and Hernán Cortés. National Library of Sweden, Sweden

limits between the grants, helping to justify the position of the royal fiscal and others at the court that Mendoza deserved to lead further discovery and conquest of this territory and, perhaps, serving to convince Charles to revise his position on the matter.

The map was not, however, very successful in achieving this goal. After Charles's return to Spain at the end of 1541, forces challenging the position of Viceroy Mendoza were gaining momentum. As awareness grew that everything Fray Marcos had recounted was a lie and, consequently, it became clear that Vázquez de Coronado had departed on an expedition that was fated to be doomed, Charles increasingly came to believe that this case had not been handled well. Proof was piling up confirming Cortés's repeated accusations of Mendoza abusing his power and neglecting his administrative tasks. Particularly damning was the news that the viceroy's explorative activities had led to an uprising in Nueva Galicia – the Mixton rebellion of 1540–42 – which had put the entire colony at risk. To prevent such a situation from reoccurring, the Crown decided to include a series of rules in the *Leyes Nuevas* (New Laws) promulgated in November 1542. Drawing on or at least in agreement with Cortés's proposal of 1529, these laws formulated a revised set of procedures regarding how new territories were to be discovered and how Spanish discoverers should inform the Crown that they possessed the required qualities to receive the privilege of conquering a particular area. These laws also made clear that the Crown's appointed governors, including the viceroy, were no longer allowed to receive this right.[116] As if this were not enough, things got even better for Cortés the following year, when the councilors concurred that the viceroy's actions warranted a closer investigation and decided to subject him to a painful *residencia*.[117] Upon his return to Spain, Charles also recognized Cortés as the "first discoverer of New Spain," which was a tremendous victory for the marquis in his enduring battle against the descendants of Velázquez.[118]

Vindication for Cortés also came in the form of a map that Sebastian Cabot published in Nuremberg in 1544. Like Cortés, Cabot had long played a somewhat unfortunate role in the discovery of a route to Asia. His father, John, had discovered Newfoundland for the English King Henry VII, and Sebastian had followed in his father's steps as he continued to search for a northwest passage.[119] In the service of the Spanish Crown, he had led his own expedition in 1526, with the Moluccas as its original objective; but Cabot ended up exploring the Rio de la Plata in search of silver and gold, instead. After having been financially punished for his incompetence in this near-disastrous expedition – which included a suppressed mutiny – he managed to acquire a position as a cosmographer at the House of Trade in Seville. Although Cabot's influence at the House was considerable, his years in Seville were marked by financial lawsuits and conflicts with the other cosmographers, some of whom blamed him for being a terrible sailor and navigator. Like Cortés, Cabot was also an opportunist and excellent self-promoter. With this goal, he produced and had printed on his own account a new kind of map with his 1544 planisphere (Figure 1.6). Several scholars have pointed out that Cabot neglected to include the latest geographical information available to the House of Trade. In fact, Harry Kelsey has argued that, due to his

---

[116] Icazbalceta, *Colección de documentos para la historia de México*, 2: 217.

[117] "Memorial of Hernán Cortés for Charles, presenting his services. Undated," in CODOIN, 4: 219–31, esp. 229. See also Accusation of Hernán Cortés against Antonio de Mendoza, 1543, AGI, Patronato, 16, N.2, R.52.

[118] *Recopilación de Leyes de los Reinos de las Indias*, Vol. 3, Tit. 6, Law 1, 104.

[119] Heather Dalton, *Merchants and Explorers: Roger Barlow, Sebastian Cabot, and Networks of Atlantic Exchange, 1500–1560* (Oxford: Oxford University Press, 2016), esp. chapters 5 and 6; Alison Sandman and Eric H. Ash, "Trading Expertise: Sebastian Cabot between Spain and England," *Renaissance Quarterly* 57, no. 3 (2004): 816–27.

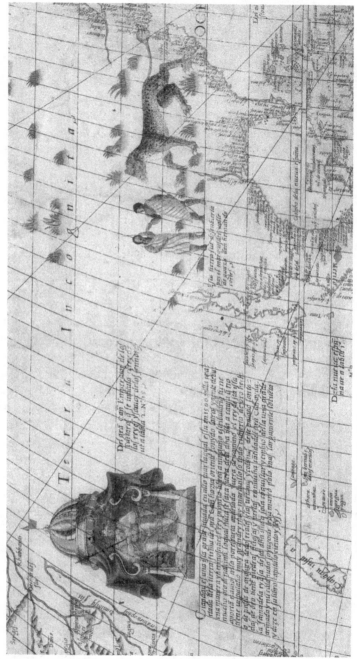

FIGURE 1.6 Detail of world map by Sebastian Cabot, Nuremberg (1544). Bibliothèque nationale de France, Paris

many problems and conflicts, Cabot may have been cut off from the flow of new information.[120] What he did have at his disposal when he drew this chart, however, was a map of Ulloa's expedition.

Cabot depicted an open-ended Pacific Northwest. But, in comparison to Santa Cruz, he drew a much more accurate picture of the Gulf of California and the California Peninsula, by and large articulating its topography in correspondence with Ulloa's. More importantly, the map made an unequivocal statement about who had discovered Tierra Nueva. Under the two stereotyped Indians representing the halfway-developed cultures inhabiting Tierra Nueva was written "[t]his land was discovered by the Marquis of the Valley of Oaxaca don Fernándo Cortés." What makes this map so interesting is not just this attribution, which was diametrically opposed to the Council's position but also the fact that it identifies the discoverers of the different parts of the Spanish Indies. By positioning himself and his father, John, as the discoverers of Newfoundland, listed among discoverers such as Columbus, Pizarro, Magellan, and Cortés, Cabot clearly had the intention of heightening his own prestige. Why he would name Cortés so explicitly as the discover of *Terra Incognita* is not clear, however. One possibility is that he drew a logical conclusion based on the New Laws' prohibition of governors being recognized as discoverers. Another possibility is that Cortés may have struck a deal with Cabot to offer him access to the material he had or even a financial contribution in return for an attribution of this kind. Whatever the case, Cabot's printed map, which circulated more widely than any of the Spanish maps, performed a valuable service for Cortés, unambiguously naming him as the discoverer of *Terra Incognita*, a region that on Cabot's map seems to lead directly to the lands of the Great Khan.

By the time Cabot published his map, the question of whether Cortés had discovered Tierra Nueva was quickly losing its relevance. The failure to discover people in the North who were equally or even more technologically or socially "developed" than the Natives of Mexico left many demotivated and disinterested in what would happen next. The bitter dispute between Cortés and Mendoza about who deserved the status of discoverer was won by the former. In spite of the viceroy's efforts to control the flow of information, or maybe precisely because of it, Cortés gained his sought-after recognition from the Crown and, eventually, the wider public. As this chapter has revealed, in the decades-long process of

---

[120] Harry Kelsey, "The Planispheres of Sebastian Cabot and Sancho Gutierrez," *Terrae Incognitae* 19 (1987): 58.

achieving this goal, Cortés fashioned himself again and again as the "discoverer" who first saw and described New Spain and Tierra Firme. Such claims never went uncontested, however, and the disputes fought between those claiming the sole right to enter newly discovered territory reverberated widely across both sides of the Atlantic. Not only did these conflicts have profound impacts on the production of geographical and cartographical knowledge of the Pacific Northwest, in particular, and the world in general; they also had legal implications affecting people and knowledge production throughout the Spanish empire. Cabot's planisphere reflects such an impact, illustrating how the honorary status given by the New Laws to the discoverers of the Indies prompted him to fashion himself as one of them, underscoring his own claims to favor from the Crown. Chapter 2 delves deeper into such impacts generated by the New Laws, further exploring their effects on territorial expansion, the distributive process in New Spain, and the relationship between the two.

2

The Veteran

Capitalizing on Knowledge of the Routes between the Indies

As we have already gotten hints of in the previous chapter, the years between 1540 and 1542 stand as a period of unprecedented activity in the process of Spanish expansion in the Pacific. With Cortés mired in legal battles in Spain, Viceroy Mendoza assumed the leading role in what developed into a three-tiered search for new routes to Asia.[1] One of these routes passed through Tierra Nueva, for which Francisco Vázquez de Coronado set out in late February 1540.[2] The two other routes were the ones Pedro de Alvarado had agreed to explore in 1538: one leading to the Islas del Poniente, the other running northward along the American west coast, purportedly toward East Asia. Under pressure of the Crown, Mendoza and Alvarado became partners in these endeavors at the end of 1540.[3] Yet, when Alvarado died in New Galicia in July 1541, Mendoza used his ships to proceed with the explorations on his own. He ordered Francisco de Bolaños to sail north of Cedros Island, and one year later he instructed the Portuguese navigator Juan Rodríguez de Cabrillo to push in this direction even further.[4] At the end of 1542, he also dispatched a flotilla under the command of Ruy López de Villalobos to sail west from the port of Navidad (current-day Jalisco) to discover the

---

[1] Flint and Cushing Flint, *A Most Splendid Company*, 87–89.
[2] Flint and Cushing Flint, *Documents*, 135–36.
[3] *Capitulación* between Antonio de Mendoza and Pedro de Alvarado, Nov 29, 1540, AGI, Patronato, 21, N.3, R.2.
[4] Harry Kelsey, *Juan Rodríguez Cabrillo* (San Marino, CA: Huntington Library, 1986), 123–63.

unknown Islands of the West, which were supposed to be located within the Spanish demarcation, as well as a return route to New Spain.[5]

The tremendous mobilization of people and capital during the first three years of the 1540s was largely in vain, however. Cíbola proved to be nothing like the impressive city Fray Marcos had made it appear. The same held true for Quivira, a town located in central Kansas, to which Vázquez de Coronado traveled at the suggestion of a Native guide in the late summer of 1541.[6] By March of the next year, the disillusioned expedition leaders decided to end their fruitless wanderings and commence their forlorn return journey. Things did not fare any better for the naval expeditions. Cabrillo's flotilla returned after a ten-month journey in April 1543 with more news about "excellent lands" but nothing that could make up for mounting losses.[7] Even worse was the outcome of the Villalobos expedition. After having discovered several unknown islands en route, the expedition arrived in Mindanao in February 1543 and called at Antonia Island (Sarangani) and Isla Filipina (Leyte or Samar) during the following months. But just like Saavedra a decade and a half earlier, Villalobos and his crew struggled to find supplies in these hostile environments and were unable to make their way back to the Americas. Forced to surrender to the Portuguese, Villalobos failed to comply with Mendoza's orders and violated the terms of the Agreement of Zaragoza, angering both Iberian monarchs.

The massive loss of lives, capital, and dreams during this short period fueled already mounting social tensions in New Spanish society. Spaniards had been arriving in the Indies with expectations of a better life – a collective hope Steve Stern has called the "utopia of social precedence."[8] Yet the realities often turned out to be different. Among the conquistadores involved in the conquest, loot was distributed according to status and services, leaving many with barely enough profit to repay the debts they took on. Frustration about the lack of recognition of the feats

---

[5] Consuelo Varela, *El viaje de don Ruy López de Villalobos a las islas del Poniente, 1542–1548* (Milan: Cisalpini-Goliardica, 1983); García de Escalante Alvarado, *Viaje a las Islas del Poniente*, ed. Carlos Martínez Shaw (Santander: Servicio de Publicaciones de la Universidad de Cantabria, 1999); José María Ortuño Sánchez-Pedreño, "La expedición de Ruy López de Villalobos a las Islas del Mar del Sur y de Poniente. Estudio histórico-jurídico," *Anales de derecho* 23 (2005): 249–92.

[6] Hartmann, *Searching for Golden Empires*, 327–28.

[7] Account by Juan Páez regarding the discoveries made by Juan Rodríguez, 1543, AGI, Patronato, 20, N.5, R.13.

[8] Steve J. Stern, "Paradigms of Conquest: History, Historiography, and Politics," *Journal of Latin American Studies* 24 (1992): 8–9.

of some conquistadores had been soaring since the late 1530s, and the ranks of the dissatisfied grew further when disappointed expedition members returned to Mexico and other cities without immediate object-ives or income.[9] After March 1544, the unrest reached an apex when *encomenderos*, the group that until this moment had benefited the most from the distributive practices of the previous decades, were confronted with the New Laws.[10] They were furious about the Crown's plan to gradually abolish the encomienda system and redistribute the limited sources of income and status among even more conquistadores. The struggles that followed upon the pronouncement of these laws in Mexico's audiencia had great impacts on New Spanish society as well as the processes and debates that shaped integration of New Spain into the Pacific world.

This chapter examines the interplay between these two distinct devel-opments from the perspective of a group of veterans who had been part of the search for a route to Asia, exploring their efforts to capitalize on their knowledge of Asia or how to get there while grappling with their rela-tively modest position within a hierarchy of merit. In contrast to the common tendency to think of all Spaniards as conquistadores, the chapter argues that a multilayered hierarchy of *beneméritos* (meritorious or deserving subjects) became increasingly clear by the end of the 1540s, as a result of the efforts of viceregal authorities to identify and hierarchically order New Spain's conquistadores, first settlers, and others who had served the Crown. Men like Andrés de Urdaneta, Guido de Lavezaris, García de Escalante Alvarado, Castaneda de Nájera, and Juan Pablo de Carrión, who all belonged to this third category, sought to stand out among the ranks of the meritorious by fashioning themselves as veterans of the strenuous search for a route to Asia. In analyzing their interactions with the viceregal authorities and reviewing the reports they produced, this chapter reveals how the drive of these veterans for social advance-ment fueled interest in Spanish expansion in the Pacific, generating in the process various visions of the Pacific and the possible benefits of strengthening New Spain's connections to Asia. As we will see, several of these veterans played a crucial role in the endeavors that, in 1565, finally led to the first successful journey from the Philippines to New

---

[9] Huber, *Beute und Conquista*, 344–47.
[10] Lesley Byrd Simpson, *The Encomienda in New Spain: The Beginning of Spanish Mexico* (Berkeley: University of California Press, 1950), 145–58.

Spain, completing a seven-decade-long quest for a Spanish-controlled
route to Southeast Asia.

ROYAL INTERVENTION IN COLONIAL POLITICS

Crown intervention in New Spanish politics at the end of 1542 produced
a sphere of negativity around the exploratory endeavors of the previous
years. The decision to intervene was the result of a convergence of distinct
calls for action. Bartolomé de las Casas's lobby in defense of the Native
population of the Indies, for example, convinced the king and his councilors that more radical reforms were required. At the same time, however, the increasing number of conquistadores, their widows, and children
complaining about the poverty in which they lived worried the Crown
and led to a search for measures to address their needs. Finally, as we have
already seen in the previous chapter, Hernán Cortés's defamation campaign against Mendoza persuaded royal authorities to subject the king's
representatives in New Spain to stricter control. Far-reaching political
reforms addressing each of these issues were gathered in the New Laws,
promulgated on November 20, 1542, and amended on July 4, 1543. The
Spanish Crown also appointed Francisco Tello de Sandoval *visitador*
(investigative judge) of the viceroy and the audiencia as well as inquisitor
of New Spain and ordered Lorenzo de Tejada, *oidor* (civil judge) of
Mexico's audiencia, to investigate allegations against Francisco Vázquez
de Coronado and his men about having mistreated the Natives of the
northern plains.[11]

Sandoval's arrival to the viceroyalty in February 1544 marked the
beginning of a three-year period during which he and Tejada heard
witnesses to determine if and what kinds of crimes had been committed
in preparation for and during the expeditions to Tierra Nueva and the
South Sea. Mendoza and Vázquez de Coronado had to defend themselves
against accusations of having caused the Natives in Jalisco to revolt and
illicitly using royal funds to finance their expeditions.[12] In the midst of
these investigations, King Charles sent Mendoza an angry letter from

[11] Arthur Scott Aiton, *Antonio de Mendoza, First Viceroy of New Spain* (Durham: Duke
University Press, 1927), 137–71; Pérez Bustamante, *Don Antonio de Mendoza*, 99–106.
[12] In the royal *visitador*'s list of 44 accusations of June 21, 1546, accusations 35, 41, and
42 explicitly mention the journey to the "new land of Cibola." Lewis Hanke, *Los
Virreyes españoles en America durante el Gobierno de la casa de Austria* (Madrid:
Ediciones Atlas, 1976), 1: 110–20. On the case that Lorenzo de Tejada brought against
Francisco Vázquez de Coronado, see Richard Flint, *Great Cruelties Have Been Reported:*

Bruges. Having learned about Ruy López de Villalobos's activities in Asia, Portugal's king, João III (1521–57), had complained about the flotilla the viceroy had sent to explore the Islas del Poniente. According to the Portuguese, Villalobos had knowingly violated the Treaty of Zaragoza when he refused to leave when ordered by the governor of the Moluccas, Jorge de Castro. Charles instructed Mendoza to demonstratively reprimand and punish those who were on the expedition, "so that it is known that what we have sent concerning this matter has to be accomplished and carried out in a way that the Most Serene King [of Portugal] and those who have requested this in his name can be content."[13]

Although Charles later informed the viceroy that he had only written the letter to please the Portuguese king, Mendoza responded bitterly to the sudden challenges he was facing. To his longtime confidant at the court, Juan de Aguilar, he wrote that he wanted the Council of the Indies to be informed that all he had done was comply with the terms of the *capitulaciones* that he and Alvarado had signed with the Crown.[14] He questioned the veracity of João's accusations, pointing out that they had not been verified by any other accounts. The viceroy further explained that Villalobos had publicly sworn to obey his orders to avoid the Portuguese at all costs and that he had no reason to question his actions. In his opinion, it would actually be a grave mistake to give up on any of the rich and wealthy islands at the first objection by the Portuguese, as they were undoubtedly situated west of the line of demarcation and therefore could be claimed by the Spanish Crown. Echoing the message Martín Fernández de Enciso conveyed in the *Suma de geographía*, the viceroy confided that Charles could still extend his realm 1,500 leagues west, giving him the opportunity to acquire the perpetual fame of having discovered "what is remaining of the world and place this under his rule."[15] In fact, Mendoza explained, he already had had two ships and 450 ready men to follow Villalobos but had been unable to dispatch them because of Sandoval's arrival.

Mendoza continued his rant by alleging that, from the moment of his disembarkation in New Spain, the royal *visitador* had done everything in his power to tarnish his good name. To questions regarding what would happen to him, Sandoval had replied that Mendoza would "be sent on a

The 1544 Investigation of the Coronado Expedition (Dallas: Southern Methodist University Press, 2002).

[13] Letter from Charles to Antonio de Mendoza, Nov 9, 1545, AGI, Patronato, 23, R.12.

[14] Letter from Viceroy Mendoza to Juan de Aguilar, undated, AGI, Patronato, 23, R.11.

[15] Ibid., image 3.

ship" to Spain. Moreover, the *visitador*'s public pronouncements about the residencia had made the viceroy appear like "the most deplorable *corregidor*" (judicial official). Adding further shame to this humiliating treatment was the clause in the New Laws prohibiting him from being involved in any new discoveries, which completely deprived him of the credit and reputation that were required to proceed with the exploration in Asia. Mendoza ended his letter to Augilar denouncing the mistreatment that he and the inhabitants of New Spain had received:

I do not know how vain hypocrisy, especially of the Christian religion, can blind His Majesty in such a way that he believes that persons can understand affairs even when they have never dealt with them and that his servants and those who serve him in these parts are so heartless and conscienceless that we defer from the service to God and to him, without there being anyone defying this general opinion. It would please God that, as His Majesty has set his eyes on the Oriental empire, he would have one eye, too, in the back of his head with which he looks west, where it would see things of no less grandeur that are not less worthy of his great mind and thoughts.[16]

Mendoza's letter reveals not only the immediate impacts on the expansion project that he saw resulting from the Crown's interventions but also exhibits a remarkable critique of Charles's decision to approve the New Laws. Mendoza, who was familiar with the king's fascination with Asia, blamed him for ignoring his American affairs, relying on partial information provided by the clergy – read Las Casas – rather than taking the time to request the opinions of those involved in the daily government of the Indies. Because of this lack of attention, a set of laws had been promulgated that could have disastrous outcomes for New Spain, while throwing sand in the engine that had been driving the expansion.

Mendoza had several reasons for being disappointed about the New Laws. Besides banning governors from becoming involved in new discoveries, they also undermined the colonial order he had been trying to create, foremost by proposing measures to eradicate the excesses of the encomienda system.[17] The laws dictated that under no condition could Indigenous people be enslaved, used to carry loads, or work in circumstances that could create risks to their life or health. They also prohibited the creation of new encomiendas, or the inheriting of existing ones, and the granting of encomiendas to royal officials and prelates. Although

---

[16] Ibid.
[17] Lewis Hanke, *The Spanish Struggle for Justice in the Conquest of America* (Boston: Little Brown, 1965), 87–88.

Mendoza was not blind to the problems of the encomienda system, which he had sought to resolve by creating *corregimientos*, he considered the pace with which the Crown sought to implement these reforms a recipe for disaster.[18] Too many Spaniards at once saw their livelihoods and status being threatened by a far-off king, who had benefited from their sufferings and now sought to deprive them of their just rewards. Yet this was not the only problem Mendoza saw. Another less often observed danger lay in the redistributive program included in the New Laws.

For years, the Crown had been trying to take away some of Cortés's excessive possessions and, with the promulgation of the New Laws, it now also aimed its arrows at other *encomenderos* who were deemed to have received too much.[19] This initiative to redistribute New Spain's wealth and benefits among its conquistadores was triggered by petitions from Francisco Tellez and eighty-four other conquistadores and first settlers, who blamed the king for not having gratified their services with an appropriate number of Indians, as was laid down by "use and custom."[20] In 1539, the Crown had already responded to these complaints by ordering Mendoza to see to it that these men received what they were due. By 1542, the viceroy had prepared a list containing the names of seventy-nine verified conquistadores, describing for each their qualities and economic situation accompanied by a recommendation following the assessment of both.[21] Some men had the right qualities and had already received Indians or a *corregimiento*, so the Crown did not need to bother about them. In other cases, Mendoza suggested granting a full or half *corregimiento* to a conquistador or his descendants. For others, however,

---

[18] *Corregimientos* were encomiendas or other jurisdictions held directly by the Crown and administered by an appointed royal official, a *corregidor*. Ethelia Ruíz Medrano, *Gobierno y Sociedad en Nueva España: Segunda Audiencia y Antonio de Mendoza* (Zamora: El Colegio de Michoacán y el Gobierno del Estado de Michoacán, 1991), 141–85.

[19] Specifically, the names mentioned by the New Laws of persons whom the Crown believed to possess excessive amounts of Indians were Gil González de Ávila, Gil González de Benavides, Juan Infante, Juan Jaramillo, Francisco Maldonado, Diego de Ordaz, Martín Vázquez, Francisco Vázquez de Coronado, and Bernaldino Vázquez de Tapia. Joaquín G. Icazbalceta, *Colección de documentos para la historia de México* (Mexico City: Biblioteca Porrua, 1858), 2: 214.

[20] Letter about the merits and services of various conquistadores, Feb 28, 1541, AGI, Patronato, 56, N.2, R.1.

[21] Mariano González-Leal, *Relación secreta de conquistadores: informes del archivo personal del emperador Carlos I que se conserva en la Biblioteca del Escorial, años de 1539–1542* (Guanajuato: Universidad de Guanajuato, Taller de Investigaciones Humanísticas, 1979), 29–37.

he advised the king to deprive them of their benefits because of a lack of certain qualities.

In the New Laws, the needs of this group of supplicants for royal favor were addressed once more. The original set of laws of November 1542 mandated that all persons of the "quality" of first conquistador were, for their "moderate subsistence and honest diversion," to be given a share of the tribute paid by Indians to the Crown. Even more significant promises were made, however, in the 1543 annex, stipulating that in the distribution of *corregimientos* and other benefits "first conquistadores," followed by "married settlers," should always be preferred over other candidates. No benefit was to be provided to any other person until all able men of that quality had been rewarded. "Sons of the first conquistadores" who did not possess an encomienda and were born from legitimate marriages were to be assessed and rewarded "as their fathers would have been if they had been alive."[22]

The promises the Crown made in the New Laws, to see to it that each first conquistador and settler received what he deserved, followed a proven logic. By vowing to redistribute the tribute paid by the now-liberated Natives, the Crown complied with an ideal of distributive justice that was crucial to early modern ideas about a king's obligations to his vassals.[23] But it also used this promise to drive a wedge between the conquistadores and settlers who would win from these laws and those who had the most to lose: the *encomenderos*. By turning the category conquistador into a quasi-quality, similar in function though not in dignity to the *hidalgo* (nobleman without a hereditary title), the Crown established new privileged lineages, providing their members honorable status and claims to benefits.[24] Creation of this hereditary service elite offered an alternative to the encomienda and a chance for less-fortunate conquistadores to earn favor. At the same time, struggles concerning the identification and recognition of members of this group would help to strengthen the Crown's position, even when no actual financial investment was required.[25]

---

[22] Icazbalceta, *Colección*, 2: 221.

[23] Vallen, "'What Distributive Justice Requires,'" 104–7.

[24] Precedents for this decision were the unfulfilled promise of a perpetual repartimiento in 1528, a royal cédula from 1534 promising the widow and the oldest son of an *encomendero* that they would inherit his encomienda, and the *Ley de Sucesión* of 1536, which promised to grant encomiendas for two lifetimes to those who joined the conquest of Peru.

[25] Michael J. Crawford has argued that the Spanish Crown constantly sought to protect its role as the ultimate arbiter in decisions about the granting of the hidalgo status in order to exploit legal disputes toward its own ends. On the other hand, it did little toward enforcement of its decisions or even encouraged municipal resistance against people

The viceregal authorities were not opposed to the Crown's wish to ensure that each conquistador received what he was due. They, too, believed that distributive justice played a crucial role in preserving the hierarchical colonial order.[26] Yet, as some saw it, the promises made in the New Laws could have grave consequences for the distributive process. In 1544, Mendoza and the *oidores* (judges) of the audiencia gave anecdotal insight into one such undesirable effect, reporting on a conquistador who had come looking for a reward for himself and his eight legitimate sons. Because the man "was not even of half a quality," he received a small annual pension of 200 pesos. Unsatisfied with this decision, the recipient replied that "his children would have been better served with him being dead than alive."[27] The royal officials explained that dealing with precisely this group of conquistadores of low quality and their descendants had become extremely tedious. With the New Laws reaffirming a sense of entitlement among such men, it was to be expected that even more of them would seek some form of remuneration, further pressuring the distributive process. Although the Crown's decision to revise its strategy in 1546 temporarily delayed this effect, the repercussions became, as we will see in Chapter 3, very much an issue during the final three decades of the sixteenth century.

The Crown's decision to revise its redistributive policy was the result of mounting pressures throughout the Indies. After an almost unequivocally negative response to the New Laws, Prince Philip wrote to the viceregal authorities in April 1546 to tell them that parts of them would be retracted. Instead, he ordered initiation of a general and perpetual redistribution of Indians that would "keep everyone content and quiet."[28] Philip's order triggered an outburst of public happiness on the streets of Mexico.[29] Yet, not everyone joined in the joyful mood. Although the viceregal elite welcomed the Crown's decision to preserve the encomienda, they opposed its intention to execute the long desired

---

claiming hidalgo status, thereby keeping the cost of such favors – in this case, in the form of loss of tax revenues – in check. Michael J. Crawford, *The Fight for Status and Privilege in Late Medieval and Early Modern Castile, 1465–1598* (University Park: The Pennsylvania State University Press, 2014), 41–42.

[26] Letter from the Bishop of Mexico, Fray Juan de Zumárraga, and Fray Martin de Hojacastro and Fray Francisco de Soto to the king, Oct 4, 1543, BNE, Mss. 20285/3, f. 15.

[27] ENE, 4: 119.

[28] Cédula for Viceroy Mendoza, Apr 14, 1546, in Diego de Encinas, *Cedulario indiano*, ed. Alfonso García Gallo (Madrid: Ediciones Cultura Hispánica, 1945), 2: 189–90.

[29] Letter from Jerónimo López to king, Mar 1, 1547, in ENE, 5: 7.

repartimiento general (the fulfilment of the promise to grant to each of the first conquistadores and first settlers or their offspring a share of the wealth that the Natives produced). In the following years, Mendoza refrained from taking any drastic measures, but he did begin gathering information that could be used for executing the prince's distributive project.[30] This time, however, not only the conquistadores who came to New Spain with Cortés or Narváez but all settlers and residents who had rendered some form of service were contemplated as beneficiaries, including those in Tierra Nueva and the South Sea.

VETERANS AND THE *REPARTIMIENTO GENERAL*

The early years of the 1540s were difficult ones for all who had been involved, either in person or as investors, in the discoveries in the South Sea or Tierra Nueva. Without having conquered anything, there was little loot to be divided. Moreover, the negative sentiments surrounding the expeditions had made it almost impossible to ask for royal remuneration. Rather than filing petitions about their feats and sufferings, the veterans who shared their stories during these years did so mostly during the trials against Mendoza or Vázquez de Coronado. This situation changed with Prince Philip's order concerning the *repartimiento general*. Residents of New Spain who believed that they deserved some form of royal grace or favor were now invited to present themselves and their services to the viceregal authorities. By the end of 1549, or early in 1550, the results of this request had been recorded in a massive register containing the names of 1,386 *beneméritos*. Preparing this catalogue of the meritorious had been a time-consuming matter, as each of the petitioners was presented with a brief but detailed description that was subsequently ordered into an elaborate hierarchy of merit.[31]

In presenting the deserving subject, most of the entries in the register follow a similar pattern. First listed are the city or town the petitioner enjoyed citizenship rights in, where he or she was born, and who his or her parents were. Then petitioners' qualities, whether they were hidalgos

---

[30] On November 27, 1548, the Crown sent detailed instructions on what information it required to initiate the *repartimiento*. Francisco de Solano, ed. *Cuestionarios para la formación de las relaciones geográficas de Indias, siglos XVI/XIX* (Madrid: CSIC, 1988), 5–7.

[31] AGI, México, 1064, L.1. This document has also been published by Francisco A. de Icaza, ed., *Conquistadores y pobladores de Nueva España: diccionario autobiográfico.* 2 vols. (Madrid: El adelanto de Segovia, 1923).

or caballeros, the services they or, sometimes, a family member had rendered, and during which phase of the conquest and settlement of the land are listed. Finally, whether the person had already received remuneration for services or losses is noted and, if so, what the compensation consisted of. All 1,386 petitions were then divided into three main groups: first, the *relaciones* of the persons who came to New Spain with Hernán Cortés and Pánfilo de Narváez; second, the *memoriales* (autobiographical statements) of the wives and sons of conquistadores; and, third, the declarations of all others. The distinction between the first (entry 1–210) and second (entries 211–588) groups seems to be that those belonging to the former were officially recognized as conquistadores, whereas those appearing in the latter claimed to be descendants of the conquistadores but were not necessarily recognized as such. The three groups were subsequently subdivided into eight, three, and five subcategories, respectively – including "wives and children of the conquistadores who came with Narvaéz" or "bachelors who say they have their wives in Spain" – each of which were further defined by moment of arrival, possession of Natives, marital status, family situation, and place of residence.

Veterans of the Tierra Nueva and South Sea expeditions appear mostly among the groups that had arrived to New Spain after Córtes and Narváez.[32] Most of them had traveled with Hernán Cortés to California (24 entries) or with Francisco Vázquez de Coronado to Cíbola (28 entries), but some also stated that they were veterans of the expeditions of Diego Hurtado de Mendoza, Diego Becerra, and Francisco de Ulloa. The one veteran of Jofre García de Loaísa's expedition who appears in the register is Andrés de Urdaneta, who would later be involved in the discovery of the return route from Asia to the Americas.

Although Urdaneta was one of few residents of New Spain who had circumvented the world, his service record (no. 1362) was rather discreet. It states that he was a native from the Basque province of Gipuzkoa, where he had been born to Juan Ochoa de Urdaneta and doña Gracia de Cerain, both inhabitants of the town of Villafranca. The most important

---

[32] Within the category of recognized conquistadores who came to New Spain with either Cortés or Narváez, only Alonso Pérez (no. 63) stated that his son went with Francisco Vázquez de Coronado, and Mari Hernández (no. 209) declared that her husband went with Cortés to the island of California. Among those who claimed to be conquistadores but whose status was not definitely proven, there were others with similar claims.

services he had rendered were during an eleven-year stay in the Moluccas, where he fought against the Portuguese as a soldier and captain and served as royal treasurer. A second service mentioned in the entry was his investment in Francisco de Camargo's expedition to Chile, which left him broke when its departure was delayed. He further served the king in a variety of military and administrative positions after he had traveled to the Indies in the company of Pedro de Alvarado and ended up in New Galicia. For the services rendered over the course of more than two decades and the costs incurred, Urdaneta "asks and appeals that they will favor him in the repartimiento."[33]

Urdaneta's record offers a glimpse into the life of a *benemérito* who possessed years of experience in the East Indies. Such knowledge had come in handy when he enlisted for the expedition that Alvarado was planning to send to the Islas del Poniente in 1538.[34] After Alvarado's unfortunate death, it also served to persuade Viceroy Mendoza to give Urdaneta a leading role in the expedition that was supposed to follow Ruy López de Villalobos.[35] To occupy Urdaneta while waiting for news to arrive from Asia, Mendoza granted him the office of *corregidor* in Ávalos, in the province of Michoacán, and later that of *visitador* of Zapotán and the Port of Navidad. In 1544, the viceroy even appointed him admiral of the fleet that was to transport 600 men to Peru to subdue Gonzalo Pizarro's rebellion.[36] Yet, as the prospect of a new expedition faded and Urdaneta's achievements as *corregidor* turned out to be nothing but mediocre, he lost the confidence of the viceregal authorities.[37] This waning status is reflected in his entry to the register prepared for the *repartimiento general*, which not only makes Urdaneta's feats look unremarkable but, worse, classified him as one of the "bachelors, [and] widowers who say they have their wives in Spain," a group that had little chance of receiving encomiendas and the more stable existence that came with it. Such bleak prospects may well have played a role in Urdaneta's

---

[33] Icaza, *Diccionario autobiográfico*, 2: 345–46.

[34] Luis A. Barandica Martínez, "Andrés de Urdaneta en la Nueva España (1538–1568)," in *Urdaneta novohispano: la inserción del mundo hispano en Asia*, ed. María Cristina E. Barrón Soto (Mexico City: Universidad Iberoamericana, 2012), 37–41.

[35] Gil, *Mitos y utopías*, 57.

[36] Thomas Hillerkuss Finn, "Andrés de Urdaneta y sus años de funcionario en el occidente novohispano," in *Andrés de Urdaneta: un hombre modern*, ed. Truchuelo García (Ordizia: Ayuntamiento de Ordizia), 433.

[37] Thomas Hillerkuss, "Tasaciones y tributos de los pueblos de indios de la Provincia de Ávalos, 1535 hasta 1555," *Estudios de historia novohispana* 16 (1996): 22–23.

decision to enter the Convent of San Augustin in Mexico in 1552 and take his vows at the beginning of the following year.[38]

Chances of being granted rewards were not much better for the survivors of the Villalobos expedition who also appear in the register.[39] In addition to Villalobos himself, whose children asked for rewards for their deceased father's services, six men who had traveled with him to the Philippines are identifiable: Gonzalo de Ávalos, Alonso de Torres, Guido de Lavezaris, Alonso Manríque, Iñigo Ortiz de Retes, and Tomás de Bracamonte. They had been among the 144 survivors of this disastrous mission who had arrived in Spain in the late summer of 1548. Instead of punishing the men, the Crown had paid their wages and even granted permission to several of them to bring African slaves with them as they returned to New Spain.[40] While a dozen of these survivors arrived in the viceroyalty in October or November of that same year, only the six aforementioned men were deemed worthy of inclusion in this register because of the services they had rendered and hardships they had suffered.[41] Others were not so lucky. Either they lacked the required qualities or were considered to have done a poor job in the office they had occupied, for which they had already been punished in Spain or received punishment in the viceroyalty.[42]

Standing out among the six men who were included was Guido de Lavezaris. A native of Genoa, Lavezaris had been a bookseller for the Crombergers in Mexico before serving as the royal treasurer of the Villalobos expedition.[43] When he returned to the viceroyalty, he brought along samples of ginger and pepper and "an extensive account of these

[38] José Manuel Pereira Fernández, "Andrés de Urdaneta: In memoriam en el quinto centenario de su nacimiento," *Revista de historia naval* 26, no. 102 (2008): 12.

[39] Barandica Martínez, "Andrés de Urdaneta en la Nueva España," 44–54.

[40] AGI, Indiferente general, 424, L.21, f. 258; AGI, Indiferente general, 1964, L.11, f. 106.

[41] Gonzalo de Ávalos (no. 514), Alonso de Torres (no. 861), Guido de Lavezaris (no. 1158), Don Alonso Manríque (no. 1370), Iñigo Ortiz de Retes (no. 1374), and Tomás de Bracamonte (no. 1381).

[42] During the investigation of the royal fiscal, Francisco de Benavente, regarding whether Villalobos had knowingly led his men to the Moluccas, Juan Martel, Pero Pacheco, Pero Pérez, Diego de Hartacho, Francisco Giralta, and Antonio Corso appeared as eyewitnesses. Their names are not, however, mentioned in the register of the meritorious. A transcription of this case can be found in Varela, *El viaje de don Ruy López de Villalobos*, 185–91.

[43] Klaus Wagner, "Guido de Lavezaris, genovés (1512–1582), de librero a gobernador de Filipinas," in *Tra Siviglia e Genova: Notaio, documento e commercio nell'età colombiana*, ed. Vito Piergiovanni, 378–91 (Milan: Giuffrè, 1992).

parts and their hydrography."[44] In 1550, Viceroy Mendoza rewarded him for his services with the position of *corregidor* of "half the town of Taymeo," in the province of Michoacán.[45] At some point during this year, Lavezaris also became part of plans that the viceroy and his son had devised for the latter's future. The two men had attempted to pass the position of viceroy on to Francisco, which inflamed the king's wrath, leading to Mendoza's forced departure to Peru.[46] Facing these new circumstances, father and son settled on the cultivation of Asian spices. To present this plan to Charles, Lavezaris joined Francisco on a journey to the Spanish court at the end of July 1552, with the latter presenting his father's final reflections on the Crown's colonial policy together with data that had been gathered for the *repartimiento general*, including the register of *beneméritos* and a register of all the towns of New Spain that could be granted as encomiendas or *corregimientos*.[47] As Lavezaris would later explain, he had come along on this mission to report to the king about "the islands and province [of the East Indies], the quality and quantity of the people, [and] their businesses."[48] To this end, he brought from the viceroyalty a globe on which all the Spanish discoveries in the Indies had been drawn.[49]

Lavezaris saw in his journey to the court an opportunity to present himself as a deserving subject. He carried a letter of recommendation written by the Flemish Augustinian Nicolas de Witte, who praised his services in Asia and his knowledge of these lands.[50] During a meeting with the Council of the Indies, he also had the chance to exhibit his

---

[44] Letter from Fray Nicolás de Witte to the Emperor, Jul 15, 1552, AHN, Diversos-colecciones, 23, N.64.

[45] Luis F. Muro, "La expedición Legazpi-Urdaneta a las Filipinas. Organización, 1557–1564," in *Historia y sociedad en el mundo de habla española. Homenaje a José Miranda*, ed. Bernardo García (Mexico City: El Colegio de México, 1970), 204. Pressed to find resources to reward loyal subjects, Viceroy Mendoza often estimated how much tribute a town could raise and, if sufficient, then split it between two *corregidores*.

[46] Francisco Javier Escudero Buendía, *Francisco de Mendoza, "El Indio" (1524–1563): Protomonarca de México y Perú, Comendador de Socuéllamos y Capitán General de las Galeras de España* (Guadalajara: Aache Ediciones, 2006), 69–84.

[47] Nino Vallen, "Healing Power: Land Surveying Politics and the Archive of Mendoza's America (1535–1552)," in *Las agencias de lo indígena en la larga era de globalización. Microperspectivas de su producción y represetación desde la época colonial temprana hasta el presente*, eds. Romy Köhler and Anne Ebert (Berlin: Gebr. Mann Verlag, 2015), 89–93.

[48] Letter from Lavezaris, May 30, 1565, AGI, Filipinas, 34, N.2, f. 4.

[49] Barandica Martínez, "Andrés de Urdaneta en la Nueva España," 48.

[50] AHN, Diversos-colecciones, 23, N.64.

familiarity with the Philippine Islands and Portuguese businesses in the Moluccas. In this context, the councilors are likely to have interrogated him about Viceroy Mendoza's remarkable ideas about a group of Portuguese sailors who sought to find their way from Southeast Asia to New Spain.[51] Lavezaris benefited little from his four-year-long stay in Spain. Just before his departure at the end of 1556, he received an annual pension of 400 pesos as a reward for his "reconnaissance of the Islas del Poniente."[52] Yet, to his great frustration, not much later the monopoly to cultivate ginger and pepper in the viceroyalty was given to Francisco de Mendoza, cutting him, the one who had delivered these spices to New Spain, out of the agreement.[53]

Another veteran of the Villalobos expedition with a unique experience related to the *beneméritos* register was García de Escalante Alvarado. A cousin of Pedro de Alvarado, Escalante had served as captain and royal factor, responsible for the flotilla's finances. He did not immediately return to New Spain, as some of his former companions had, but did so only after he had had the opportunity to update Charles.[54] During his audience with the emperor, he discussed a detailed report that he had finished in Lisbon in August 1548, which not only provided valuable details about the route the expedition took and the events that took place during the journey but also about New Guinea, China, and Japan as well. In his account of the voyage, Escalante stressed the enormous profits to be gained from establishing trade relations between Southeast Asia and New Spain. While most of such gains would benefit the viceroyalty, he esti-mated that, without even taking into consideration the *quinto real* (royal

---

[51] Hanke, *Los virreyes españoles*, 1: 58. The councilors found the idea sufficiently convin-cing to write Luis de Velasco, telling him to make sure that these persons were well received. In case the rumors turned out to be true, the Council apparently wanted to ensure that everything was done to convince these Portuguese to share their knowledge about the route they had sailed. Parecer of the Counil of the Indies, 1552, AGI, Patronato, 46, R.7.

[52] Flint and Cushing Flint, *A Most Splendid Company*, 315. In comparison, the annual salary of a *corregidor* ranged from 100 to 380 pesos.

[53] AGI, Filipinas, 34, N.2, f. 4r. On Francisco de Mendoza's efforts to produce ginger and black pepper in the Americas, see also: Escudero Buendía, *Francisco de Mendoza*, especially chapter 12. Compare also Paula De Vos, "The Science of Spices: Empiricism and Economic Botany in the Early Spanish Empire," *Journal of World History* 17, no. 4 (2006): 417–20.

[54] Letter from García de Escalante to Charles V, Mar 24, 1552, in ENE, 6: 153–56.

fifth) and other benefits, the treasury could at least make an annual profit of "one million in gold."[55]

A series of royal orders promulgated during the autumn of 1549 reveal that Escalante had left an excellent impression at the court. He was promised a habit of the Order of Santiago and received permission to ship a hundred African slaves to New Spain without paying the obligatory export and import duties.[56] In addition, the king recommended him to New Spain's new viceroy, don Luis de Velasco (1549–64), in a letter that highlighted his hard work in the journey to the Islas del Poniente.[57] Because of his late arrival back to the viceroyalty in Velasco's retinue, Escalante did not appear in the original register produced for the *repartimiento*. This fact clearly bothered him because he asked the departing Viceroy Mendoza to produce an annex to the register for him. Mendoza actually wrote a short text with the same structure as the other petitions, listing Escalante's services in New Galicia and the islands.[58] Even after Velasco had appointed him *alcalde mayor* (district judge) of Vera Cruz, Escalante wrote Charles, just before Francisco de Mendoza's departure from New Spain, to make sure he was being considered for the *repartimiento general*.[59] He reminded the king of their meeting four years earlier, during which they had discussed Spanish expansion in Asia. Pointing out the fraud that the Portuguese were committing by making the journey from Portugal to the Moluccas via the Cape of Good Hope appear shorter than it was, Escalante requested that Charles order the viceroy make a careful description of the Pacific route to Asia. Although he did not mention it explicitly, Escalante probably saw for himself a role in this project, after having produced one of the most detailed accounts of the journey to date.

Each of the men discussed here hoped to personally benefit from the *repartimiento general*. For the veterans of the expeditions to Tierra Nueva and the South Sea, this clearly was a way to be recognized among the meritorious subjects of New Spain and receive a share of the wealth of a territory they had not actually conquered themselves. But just like so

---

[55] Escalante Alvarado, *Viaje a las Islas del Poniente*, 153. The original report is preserved as AGI, Patronato, 23, R.10.

[56] ENE, 6: 155; AGI, Indiferente, 424, L.22, ff. 13r–14r.

[57] King Charles recommending Garcia de Escalante Alvarado, Sept 28, 1549, AGI, México, 1089, L.4, f. 104r.

[58] Letter from Viceroy Mendoza recommending Garcia de Escalante Alvarado, Nov 12, 1550, AGI, México, 19, N.10.

[59] ENE, 6: 153–56.

many others who had had high hopes tied to their decision to venture into the New World, for these veterans the project would turn out to be a great disappointment. Viceroy Mendoza did not take Natives away from the *encomenderos* to redistribute them among the other *beneméritos* included in this register, nor would his successor do so later on.[60] Although the authorities complied with the king's orders to prepare the list, they actually urged him to refrain from taking any more drastic interventions.[61] The vast number of petitioners listed in the register certainly could have helped Francisco de Mendoza to make an argument about the enormous disruption that the redistribution of New Spain's limited number of remaining Natives would cause.

Although the veterans had hoped to benefit from being included in the register of the meritorious, the production of this hierarchically ordered list actually seemed to have moved them further away from receiving the king's favor. As most of the veterans belonged to groups whose degree of worthiness of remuneration was deemed lower than that of the conquistadores, they were forced to look for alternative livelihoods or become once again engaged in new conquering enterprises. Not without reason were veterans among the first to offer to the authorities their knowledge about the expeditions they had been part of, as such knowledge was highly valued and considered crucial to the success of new expeditions. Urdaneta, Lavezaris, and Escalante Alvarado all benefited in one way or another from the information they brought before the royal authorities. But their successes were fragile and depended on concrete possibilities for organizing new expeditions. The advice that the Council of the Indies gave Charles in 1552 to stop exploration of the South Sea affected the veterans' chances to negotiate with the royal authorities over their involvement in new projects from which new benefits could result.[62] This interruption would not last long, however. The need for an outlet for the idle and the restless quickly led to new efforts to connect New Spain to Asia.

REVISITING THE ASIAN DREAM

After the arrival of Viceroy Velasco, interest in the regions that had been left uncolonized during the previous three decades gradually began to

---

[60] Letter from Jerónimo López to Emperor Charles, Jan 20, 1548, in ENE, 5: 75.
[61] Instructions from Viceroy Mendoza for Viceroy Velasco, undated, in Hanke, *Los virreyes españoles*, 1: 54–55.
[62] AGI, Patronato, 46, R.7.

increase. Reports of silver-rich lands northwest of Zacatecas led to a new generation of discoverers and conquerors wanting to return to the regions Vázquez de Coronado had merely passed through. Men such as Gínez Vázquez del Mercado, Juanes de Tolosa, Francisco and Diego de Ibarra, and Luis Cortés began organizing small expeditions to the provinces of Copala, New Biscay, and Chiametla in the modern-day states of Durango, Chihuahua, Coahuila, Sinaloa, and Sonora.[63] They were followed by bands of Franciscan friars who hoped to bring the Christian faith to the *Chichimecas*, as the nomadic tribes residing in these regions were known.[64] La Florida also reverted back into the center of attention due to a series of shipwrecks and pirate attacks from French corsairs. The disaster of 1553, especially, prompted calls for new efforts to settle the region between Pánuco and the Florida peninsula.[65]

In 1557, the Spanish Crown resolved that it was indeed desirable to instigate new colonizing projects. On September 21, in the name of the new king, Philip II (1556–98), royal officials promulgated a provision assigning to Viceroy Velasco the task of finding a sea route "to the Islas del Poniente, in the direction of the Moluccas."[66] This surprising initiative may have been triggered by Francisco de Mendoza, who presented his plan to cultivate Asian spices in the Americas in January 1557, shortly after Lavezaris had returned to New Spain.[67] Mendoza's proposal, which came at a time when the royal treasury urgently needed to develop new revenue streams to fill its empty coffers, could have once more aroused interest in the search for a route to Asia. Another factor playing a role in this decision were the French ambitions of expanding their presence in the

---

[63] Carlos Sempat Assadourian, *Zacatecas, conquista y transformacion de la frontera en el siglo XVI: minas de plata, guerra y evangelización* (Mexico City: El Colegio de México, Centro de Estudios Históricos, 2008), 57–68; María Justina Sarabia Viejo, *Don Luis de Velasco: virrey de Nueva España, 1550–1564* (Seville: Escuela de Estudios Hispano-Americans, 1978), 453–60.

[64] Sempat Assadourian, *Zacatecas*, 54.

[65] Particularly influential was the ambitious plan articulated by Pedro de Santander, an official in New Spain, which piqued Philip II's interest. The proposal has been printed in CODOIN, 26: 340–65.

[66] The royal provision has been printed in Luis Felipe Muro, *La expedición Legazpi-Urdaneta a las Filipinas* (Mexico City: Secretaría de Educación Pública, 1975), 132–35.

[67] AGS, Camara de Castile, Sección diversos, 46, 23, Francisco de Mendoza's proposal and conditions for the cultivation of pepper, clove, cinnamon, ginger, and sandal wood in Spain or New Spain and agreement with the king, f. 203r. Compare also: Asiento with Francisco de Mendoza about the cultivation of spices in the Indies, Mar 21, 1559, AGI, Indiferente, 738, N.47. Lavezaris received permission to take eight slaves with him to New Spain on May 22, 1556. AGI, Indiferente, 425, L.23, f. 230v.

Americas and Asia, as well as in the still unexplored Tierra Australis in the South Pacific.[68] In response to the growing threat of a French presence in the Caribbean and North America, where the existence of a strait leading to the Pacific was still suspected, the regency government also decided to initiate the conquest of La Florida. On December 29, 1557, it ordered Velasco to settle there and place the region under orderly government, "in spite of the prohibition which has been issued ordering that he shall make no new discoveries or settlements."[69] Under these changing circumstances, new opportunities opened up for the veterans in New Spain. To gain the attention of those involved in planning and organizing new expeditions, they used their knowledge and experience to produce geographies of the regions Spaniards had visited before. In the process, New Spain's connections to Asia were revived as well.

One self-proclaimed veteran who jumped at this chance was Pedro Castañeda de Nájera. Although he had joined Vázquez de Coronado's expedition to Cíbola in 1540, this native of Baeza (b. 1515) would never play any actual role in it. When the company reached San Miguel de Culiacán – the last Spanish outpost in these northern regions – sudden illness had forced him to stay behind.[70] As he had not officially participated in the expedition in any meaningful way, Nájera was unable to present himself to the authorities in the investigation for the *repartimiento general* like his townsman Juan Panyagua did.[71] Yet, as the years passed and people's memories of the expedition faded, Castañeda de Nájera likely saw a chance to prove being worthy of some responsibility in a new project that Alonso de Zorita, who was *oidor* of the audiencia of Mexico, was trying to realize. Its goal was to take twenty friars and a small military force to commence peaceful conversion of the Natives of Culiacán, New Mexico, and Florida.[72] At some point during the second

---

[68] Paul E. Hoffman, *A New Andalucia and a Way to the Orient: The American Southeast during the Sixteenth Century* (Baton Rouge: Louisiana State University Press, 1990), 125–43.

[69] Herbert Ingram Priestley, *The Luna Papers: Documents relating to the Expedition of Don Tristan de Luna y Arellano for the Conquest of la Florida in 1559–1561. Volumes 1 & 2* (Tuscaloosa: The University of Alabama Press, 2010 [1928]), 44.

[70] Flint and Cushing Flint, *Documents*, 378.

[71] Icaza, *Diccionario autobiográfico*, 2: 353.

[72] Flint and Cushing Flint, *Documents*, 378–80. See also: Alonso de Zorita, *Relación de la Nueva España: relación de algunas de las muchas cosas notables que hay en la Nueva España y de su conquista y pacificación y de la conversión de los naturales de ella*, eds. Ethelia Ruiz Medrano, Wiebke Ahrndt, and José M. Leyva (Mexico City: Conaculta, 1999), 1: 29–31.

half of the 1550s, Castañeda de Nájera wrote for the judge an extensive report of the Coronado expedition, known today as the *Relación de la Jornada de Cíbola* (Account of the Journey to Cíbola), probably in the hope of Zorita taking him along on the new expedition.[73]

Like the other veterans appearing in this chapter, Castañeda de Nájera displays in the *Relación* a strong preoccupation with the routes that future expeditions could take. In the first part of his account, he presented the route that the Coronado expedition followed to reach Cíbola and the events that occurred during this journey. The third part does the same for the return from the kingdom of Quivira to Mexico in the spring of 1542. In both, the author indicated where errors were made, who had made them, and how others could avoid repeating the same mistakes. The second part differs from these two sections in that it contains a discursive map of the northern part of the regions between La Florida and the coasts of the South Sea, describing all the things Castañeda de Nájera had seen with his own eyes or of which he had learned from reports.[74] Here he outlined the quality of the land and its inhabitants, and, using the little "modicum of cosmography and geometry" at his disposal, gave distances between the cardinal points of his itinerary.[75] One objective of these descriptions was to inform readers about the conditions and peoples that members of a new expedition could await in the North. Another aim was to address the false rumors that had been circulating about these regions being uninhabitable or contiguous with either La Florida or India Mayor.[76] Consequently, he presented several routes to different destinations within Tierra Nueva, offering various possibilities for the distinct groups that currently had set their eyes on the region.

Although Castañeda de Nájera explicitly refuted the idea that India Mayor started in Tierra Nueva, the connection between the two parts of the Indies nonetheless played a role in his proposal for future expeditions. The possibility for humans to be able to travel over land from New Spain to India Mayor or China forms the basis of what Maureen Ahern has identified as a "spatial and cultural order" that Castañeda de Nájera projected onto Tierra Nueva.[77] Within this space, he identified two main

---

[73] The original text written by Pedro Castañeda de Nájera is not known to exist; the version used here is the transcript of a handwritten copy made by *licenciado* Bartolomé Niño Velázquez in Seville in 1596. The report is transcribed and translated in Flint and Cushing Flint, *Documents*, 384–493.

[74] Flint and Cushing Flint, *Documents*, 385.   [75] Ibid., 433.   [76] Ibid., 384–85.

[77] Maureen Ahern, "Mapping, Measuring, and Naming Cultural Spaces in Castañeda's *Relación de la jornada de Cíbola*," in *The Coronado Expedition from the Distance of*

foci deserving attention. One was the Tiguex region, situated in the Rio Grande Valley in modern central New Mexico, the other, the region of Quivira, located on the eastern extreme of the Great Plains. In the introduction to the second part of the *Relación*, Castañeda de Nájera explained that one of these regions was worth being settled by Spaniards while the other was not. Yet, he continued, the reverse applied to the missionaries, because "in the one land there is human civilization and in the other the barbarity of animals and, more than that, of brutish men."[78]

Tiguex was where civilization was to be found. According to the *Relación*, the town of Tiguex formed the center of a conglomerate of sixty-six pueblos, including the Seven Cities, that lay scattered on the two banks of a river carrying the same name (now called the Rio Grande). The people in this sparsely inhabited region all shared similar qualities. According to Castañeda de Nájera they were very intelligent, wore large ponchos to conceal their sex, and the men only had one wife.[79] They lived in multistoried houses that were well built, organized, and clean. A council made up of elder citizens and priests governed them and instructed them on how to live. Finally, Castañeda de Nájera noted that traces could be found of a kind of Christian awareness, for the people made a cross as a sign of peace. This latter observation led him to conclude that,

[b]ecause they are a people of small numbers and are so different in behavior, government, and civilization from all the peoples which have been seen and discovered in these western regions, it is understood that they are foreigners from that part of Greater India, the coast of which lies toward the west of this land. They may have descended through that region, crossing those mountain ranges, coming downstream along that river [Río del Tizón: Colorado River], and settling in the place that seemed best to them.[80]

In Castañeda de Nájera's opinion, the small groups of descendants of Asian migrants that inhabited the Tiguex region had little to offer Spanish conquistadores.[81] Still, the high degree of civilization of these people made them a perfect target for the friars, who would have little difficulty converting them. Men-at-arms should only take this trajectory to "go in search of the land the Marquis del Valle, don Hernando Cortés, was

---

460 *years*, eds. Richard Flint and Shirley Cushing Flint (Albuquerque: University of New Mexico Press, 2003), 282.
[78] Flint and Cushing Flint, *Documents*, 415.   [79] Ibid., 418–20.   [80] Ibid., 421.
[81] Ibid., 433.

searching for."[82] Traveling northwest, they could head to the Río del Tizón to travel all the way to Asia.

Quivira, on the other hand, offered perfect conditions for a conquest similar to those in New Spain. Densely populated by people whose qualities oscillated between those of the settled communities of Middle America and the nomadic purported barbarians from Tartary, there was a legitimate need to create encomiendas. Castañeda de Nájera's assessment of the qualities of the residents of this region was largely based on a comparison with the Teya – one of two nomadic nations roaming the Great Plains. The Teya, Castañeda explained, came from the interior regions of East Asia and traveled around like "Arabs (*alarabes*) with their tents and droves of dogs equipped with packsaddles, and chin[es]," eating raw bison meat.[83] People in Quivira resembled the Teyas in nature and dress but were more intelligent, better warriors, and inhabited the same sort of towns as the Native inhabitants of New Spain. Even though the people of Quivira displayed more signs of civilization than the Teyas, this still was no place for missionaries to go without military support. To underline this presumed fact, Castañeda de Nájera related the story of the murder of Fray Juan de Padilla, a Franciscan friar who had stayed in the province after Coronado departed from it.[84]

In his efforts to present himself as a veteran whose experiences and knowledge could be of use to Zorita, Castañeda de Nájera produced an elaborate cartography of Tierra Nueva, illustrating how, even on the fringes of the empire, people were aware that the figure of the veteran could be useful for fashioning a deserving self. Even though he never got very far with the original expedition in search of Cibola, Castañeda de Nájera managed to organize some information he had gathered from others and much that he probably made up himself into a carefully styled report proving his familiarity with the land and its people as well as a rudimentary knowledge of current cosmographical and geographical learning. In addition, Castañeda de Nájera also manifested a keen awareness that Tierra Nueva was not the only destination that was being considered for new imperial and religious projects. He explicitly discarded La Florida as an option, arguing that nothing had ever been found beyond the Río de Espíritu Santo (Mississippi) but hot, barren lands and swamps.[85] He left open the possibility of reaching Asia via an overland route but makes clear that the Villalobos expedition had proven that the

---

[82] Ibid., 493.   [83] Ibid., 423.   [84] Ibid., 433.   [85] Ibid., 434.

distance to these lands was much greater than had once been believed and that there was a possibility of a strait cutting into the continuous landmass between the continents.[86] Castañeda de Nájera concluded that in the end, Tierra Nueva, the land he supposedly knew best, should be the focus of new expeditions.

CONTROVERSY FLARES AMONG VETERANS

While Castañeda de Nájera exacerbated growing controversies regarding the future of the northern territories, others returned their focus to Asia. Already in 1550, Viceroy Velasco had discussed with Mendoza the importance of the spice trade. Following royal instructions, however, he had refrained from undertaking anything in this area until further notice from the Crown.[87] When orders to try one final time to locate a return route from Asia to the American mainland arrived early in 1558, Velasco immediately began consulting veterans of earlier expeditions. Putting his trust in two of them, he soon found himself confronted by yet another conflict over routes.

One of the first veterans whom Velasco talked to as he started the preparations for a new expedition was Juan Pablo de Carrión. Like the viceroy, Carrión was a native of Carrión de los Condes, a city in the province of Palencia in northern Spain. He had served as a helmsman during the Villalobos expedition, but upon his return to the Iberian Peninsula in 1548 he decided to stay in Castile. Little is known about his activities during this period, although it seems that he became involved in the trade with the Indies.[88] Sometime between 1555 and 1558, he returned to New Spain, where he had the chance to recount his experiences in the Philippines and ideas on how to continue Spanish exploration in the region to the viceroy. Velasco was impressed by what he had heard and decided to send Carrión to the court to acquire support for the expedition that he, as King Philip II understood it, would also be leading.[89] This decision was of enormous importance for Carrión, as it opened a unique opportunity for him to settle in New Spain and be in charge of an expedition that could open trade with Asia.

---

[86] Ibid., 414.   [87] Sarabia Viejo, *Don Luis de Velasco*, 464.
[88] AGI, Indiferente, 1965, L.12, f. 98; AGI, Indiferente, 1965, L.12, f. 220; AGI Indiferente, 1965, L.12, f. 285.
[89] Letter from King Philip II to Viceroy Velasco, Sept 24, 1559, AGI, Patronato, 23, R.12, f. 5v.

Carrión's approach to presenting himself as a person worthy of leading such an enterprise was a familiar one. In a *parecer* he presented during his stay at the court, he underlined his firsthand knowledge about the geography and hydrography as well as the political constellations of Southeast Asia.[90] Yet, as Carrión was well aware, after five failed attempts to return from the Philippines to the American continent, any new proposal for a naval expedition to Asia would have to include a convincing solution to this vexing problem. Carrión believed he had one. He argued that two ships should leave the port of Acapulco in November or December to sail to the Moluccas or the Philippines via the Islas Ladrones (modern-day Mariana Islands), following exactly the same course as Villalobos had in 1542.[91] After having provided ideas on how the Spaniards could in all secrecy explore as far as the Moluccas without drawing the attention of the Portuguese, he shifted his attention to the *tornaviaje*, the eastern-bound return route from the Philippines to the American continent, which, it appears, he had drawn out on a now lost map that he carried with him.[92]

Carrión proposed that the flotilla should leave the Philippines in April in order to benefit from the eastern winds blowing in "all of India" until the end of August.[93] The ships should sail in the direction of "the Lequios Islands or Japan" to about 40 degrees north. Once the ships reached this latitude, they should shift course on their journey in the direction of New Spain. It was of great importance that the ships leave the "mainland of Miaco" no later than the beginning of July to arrive on the American coast that same month or, at the latest, the next.[94] From there, the ships would only have to follow the coast southward, taking the same route Cabrillo had been exploring in 1542 and 1543. Following these instructions, the text noted, could finally lead to realization of

that which Your Majesty has desired for so many years and for which in these realms so many persons have died and so many thousands of ducats have been spent. It is thus that our Lord will be served and his holy Faith exalted, the

---

[90] AHN, Diversos-Colecciones, 34, N.2.

[91] In the text, the following islands of this group are mentioned: Islas de los Reyes, Corales, Matalotes, Arrecifes, and Ladrones. Ibid., f. 2.

[92] Ibid., f.6r.   [93] Ibid., f. 5v.

[94] Carrión provides his own ideas regarding the dimensions of the Pacific, stating the distance between La Navidad and the Philippines to be 1,500 leagues and estimating the distance between Japan and the coast of New Spain at no more than 500 leagues, "which is a journey of fifteen or twenty days." Ibid., f. 9r. In reality, it usually took the Spanish galleons between three and five months to sail from the Philippines to New Spain.

patrimony of Your Majesty further augmented, and those in New Spain, Nicaragua, Panama, Peru, Chile, and all the other provinces of the Indies will be given great benefits. For a way will be opened to get rid of the lost folks and vagabonds that inhabit the Indies, and those who stay in these parts will live more peacefully, with more options, and less disturbances and rebellions as have taken place and take place continuously due to the necessities that become greater every day as a result of the constantly increasing population.[95]

Carrión concluded his proposal by mentioning that, in case the king did not want the ships to cross the South Sea, they could also take Cabrillo's route. Sailing along the west coast, the ships had to head north until they reached a bend of the coast, which they should then follow all the way to Miaco or the "Islands of Japan."

Carrión's elaborate proposal was well received at the court. Philip II sent him back to New Spain with instructions for Velasco to prepare two ships for the expedition, providing royal provisions and guarantees that the materials and weapons Carrión requested would be dispatched to the viceroyalty as soon as possible.[96] Velasco, too, was pleased with the outcome of this visit. After Carrión returned to the viceroyalty, he granted him the responsibility of overseeing the activities of the shipyard in La Navidad. Work here had already started in December 1557, but, to Velasco's frustration, things were progressing much slower than expected. Earlier he had appointed Guido de Lavezaris to assist Hernando Botello, the *alcalde mayor* of the Valley of Autlán, with the administration, but at this point Carrión was supposed to replace them both.[97] Under his supervision, things got even worse, however. Ignorance and malice, as well as diseases and natural disasters, resulted in the costs of the operation quickly spinning out of control.[98] As the preparations for the expedition dragged on, the relationship between Velasco and Carrión gradually began to deteriorate.

Contributing to these tensions was the other veteran in whom the viceroy had put his trust: the now Augustinian friar, Andrés de Urdaneta. As Carrión was not a trained pilot, it had been clear to Velasco from the outset that an experienced navigator had to be involved in the project as well. When he sent Carrión to the court, he gave him a petition asking the king to urge Urdaneta to join the expedition. King Philip II had sent the requested letter, and the friar reluctantly accepted

[95] Ibid., f. 6v.   [96] AGI, Patronato, 23, R.12, f. 5.
[97] AGN, Mercedes, 5–6, ff. 52v–53v.
[98] Muro, *La expedición Legazpi-Urdaneta a las Filipinas*, 31–36.

the royal orders – in part, due to the pressures exercised by his prior and brothers of the Augustinian Order.[99] In May 1560, Urdaneta discussed with Velasco the expedition that he and Carrión had been planning to this point. In a letter he wrote to Philip after the meeting, the friar argued that the decision to return to Isla Filipina was opposed to the royal orders of 1557. The island was located along the same longitude as or even west of the Moluccas and, therefore, unequivocally belonged to the Portuguese.[100] Instead, he proposed a plan to send an expedition to investigate the position of the Philippine Islands, "so that it will be known how far the 180 longitudinal degrees of His Royal Majesty's demarcation reaches."[101]

After having expressed his objections to Velasco and Carrión's plans, in 1561 Urdaneta prepared another extensive memorandum to explain his plans for the expedition to the king.[102] Here, the friar demonstrated how his decade-long experiences in New Spain, and New Galicia in particular, as well as in preparing Alvarado and Mendoza's fleets, could be of use. He identified some of the problems that were plaguing the current preparations and offered detailed solutions concerning the location of the shipyard, supply routes, and recruitment of crew members in Spain. In comparison to Carrión, Urdaneta was less worried about demonstrating his supposedly exceptional knowledge of Asia. He described the same two routes Carrión had proposed but added one alternative. According to the friar, the armada could leave the port of Acapulco between November 10, 1561, and January 20, 1562, to sail in a southwestern direction to 25–30 degrees south, at which point they should veer west to reach New Guinea. After exploring this unknown land, the ships ought to then sail north to the Philippines, where they should arrive no later than November 1562. While Carrión in his 1558 proposal had carefully discussed interactions between the Spaniards and the Natives that they would likely encounter, Urdaneta mostly stuck to mapping out the routes. He demonstrated some understanding of the *vendavales*, winds blowing from the sea to the land that changed direction in Southeast Asia with the seasonal monsoons, but remained vague on

---

[99] Royal cédula for Fray Andrés de Urdaneta, Sept 24, 1559, AGI, Patronato, 23, R.12, f. 6r.

[100] Fray Urdaneta's answer to the king, May 28, 1560, AGI, Patronato, 23, R.12, f 21.

[101] Parecer Fray Urdaneta about the journey to the Philippines, undated, AGI, Patronato, 23, R.12, f. 22v.

[102] Memorandum by Fray Urdaneta about the journey to the Philippines, undated, AGI, Patronato, 23, R.15.

how these could help the armada's ships return to the Americas.[103]
Urdaneta may have considered the question of the return route to have
already been sufficiently answered or, possibly, did not have such a clear
solution as Carrión did.

Although two of his proposed routes were the same as Carrión's,
Urdaneta was convinced that New Guinea should be the primary destination of the expedition. Intrigued by the way in which the maps he had
recently received from Europe depicted the New Guinean coastline, the
friar joined European cartographers, most notably those of the French
Dieppe school, in speculating about the nature of these unknown territories in the Southern Pacific.[104] He argued that New Guinea was part of a
much larger landmass that stretched all the way down to the Arctic Pole
or the Strait of Magellan (Figure 2.1).[105] Following Urdaneta's recommendation, Velasco instructed the expedition's general, Miguel López de
Legazpi, to "navigate to the southwest in search of the coast of New
Guinea."[106] To Carrión, this change of plan was an enormous disappointment, and tensions between him and Urdaneta ran so high that, at
one point, the latter threatened the viceroy not to go with the expedition if
Carrión did as well.[107] Velasco responded by forbidding Carrión to be
part of the enterprise, depriving him of any possible rewards that could be
earned in new conquests or due to the discovery of the *tornaviaje*.[108]

Carrión fiercely disputed the viceroy's decision, writing to the king that
he and Urdaneta held opposing ideas about the objectives of the voyage to
the Islas del Poniente. To explain why his proposal was worth being taken
seriously, he presented Urdaneta and himself as veterans of two distinct
expeditions. The "more than sixty-year-old" friar had traveled to the
Moluccas in the company of Loaísa and had never seen the Philippines.

---

[103] The question of whether Andrés de Urdaneta did or did not have a plan for the return to
New Spain is discussed in Patricio Hidalgo Nuchera, "La embajada de Juan Pablo de
Carrión a la Corte en 1558 y el conocimiento colectivo del tornaviaje," in *Anais de
história de além-mar* XV (2014): 59–66; Juan Gil, *Legazpi. El Tornaviaje: navegantes
olvidados por el Pacífico norte* (Madrid: Fundación José Antonio de Castro, 2019),
lxxxiv–v.

[104] Concerning Tierra Australis, see for example: Thomas Suárez, *Early Mappings of
Southeast Asia* (Singapore: Periplus Editions (HK) Ltd., 1999), 158–63.

[105] AGI, Patronato, 23, R.12, f. 2v.

[106] Copy of Luis de Velasco's instructions for Miguel López de Legazpi regarding the
discovery of the Islas de Poniente and the coasts of New Guinea, undated, AGI,
Patronato, 23, R.12, f. 31v., item xxv.

[107] Report by Juan Pablo de Carrión for the president of the Council of the Indies, undated,
AGI, Patronato, 263, N.1, R.1.

[108] AGI, Patronato, 23, R.12, f. 29v., item xi.

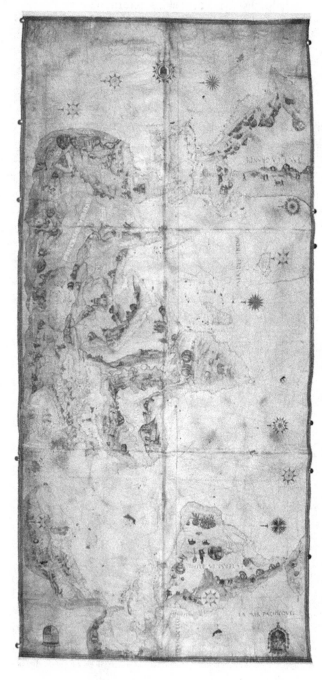

FIGURE 2.1 "Jave le Grande" on the Dauphin or Harleian world map (ca. 1547). The British Library Board, British Library, Mss. Add. 5413

He himself, on the other hand, knew from firsthand experience that these islands were a much better destination than New Guinea was. As he continued to explain why the expedition should sail directly to the Philippines, he related how members of the Villalobos expedition had traveled along the New Guinean coasts for three and a half months, covering 380 leagues "without ever seeing anything else but nude Blacks" living on "miserable foods." In the Philippines, however, the situation was much better. The land was rich in foods and provisions, and there were ample opportunities for trade. The Natives with whom the Spaniards had been on friendly terms and with whom they could communicate were "of much reason and order." The islands were also located in the best region of the entire archipelago, as mainland China lay to the north and the Moluccas 200 leagues to the south. Moreover, their northern position would make them a perfect point of departure for the return journey. With this knowledge already available, Carrión implored, why set out on a "new journey with so much uncertainty and risk."[109]

As he was claiming a voice in the debate about the destination of Legazpi's expedition, and with it a role in the enterprise itself, Carrión's self-image as a veteran was crucial to presenting himself as the worthiest of the two expert voices involved in this debate. For some of his critiques he found a receptive but critical ear in the person of the royal *visitador*, Jerónimo de Valderama, who became the highest royal authority in New Spain after Viceroy Velasco's sudden death at the end of July 1564. On the one hand, Valderama held Carríon in low esteem, describing him as an opportunist who had "delayed the enterprise for his own interests" and did not deserve his protection. On the other hand, Valderama and the judges of Mexico's audiencia nevertheless concurred that, after the enormous investments that had been made, the outcome of Urdaneta's project seemed too uncertain. It would lead the expedition in the opposite direction of the area where the return route would supposedly be found, increasing the risk of failure. For this reason, in all secrecy and without Urdaneta's knowledge, they altered the viceroy's original instructions, changing the voyage's main destination to the Philippines. Valderama legitimized this decision by arguing that the friar was wrong to believe that the Philippines belonged to the Portuguese, for the king had written that "by no means they should enter the Moluccas, only other islands in its surroundings, like the Philippines and others that are outside the said

---

[109] Letter from Juan Pablo de Carrión to King Philip, undated, A.G.I., Patronato, 263, N.2, R.1.

treaty."[110] In light of what happened later, this interpretation and the trick played on Urdaneta probably saved the expedition from yet another disastrous outcome.

DISCOVERY OF THE *TORNAVIAJE*

During the early hours of November 21, 1564, Miguel López de Legazpi's flotilla left the port of La Navidad. Without Carrión but with several other South Sea exploration veterans among the crew of 380, including Urdaneta and Lavezaris, the ships set out in the direction of New Guinea. After four days of sailing, Legazpi organized a meeting on the capital ship – attended by all the captains, clergymen, and pilots of the armada – to open the audiencia's instructions. The change of destination greatly surprised the attendants and infuriated the five Augustinians.[111] A few days after this shocking event, on December 1, another disturbing incident took place, when the patache *San Lucas* disappeared in the middle of the night.[112] In spite of this rocky start, the remainder of the journey was uneventful. The ships reached the Marshal Islands on January 9, 1565, Guam two weeks later, and Samar on February 13. During the course of the following two months, Spaniards disembarked on Leyte, Limasawa, Bohol, and Mindanao to search for provisions and a suitable location to create a permanent base. Eventually they settled on Cebu, which was densely inhabited and provided ample food supplies. On the last day of May 1565, expedition members established the settlement of San Miguel there.

Soon after their arrival in Cebu, preparations were initiated to outfit the capital ship, the *San Pedro*, for its return to New Spain. With a capacity of 500 tons, the ship offered more space than the others to stow provisions for its crew of 200, comprising mostly sailors as well as 10 soldiers and the Augustinian friars Andrés de Urdaneta and Andrés de Aguirre. Legazpi appointed his grandson, Felipe de Salcedo, as the

---

[110] Letter of the licenciado Valderrama, Aug 18, 1564, AGI, Mexico, 97.

[111] Gil, *Legazpi*, xciv.

[112] Although the crew of the *San Lucas* would later claim that they lost sight of the rest of the fleet, some historians suspect that its pilot, Alonso de Arellano, led a mutiny and began his own search for the Island of Bartolomé, where the biblical King Solomon had supposedly brought his gold. The story of the ship's journey and the judicial inquiry that followed upon its return to New Spain is told in Charles E. Nowell, "Arellano versus Urdaneta," in *Pacific Historical Review* 31, no. 2 (1962): 111–20; Gil, *Mitos y utopías*, 61–64.

frigate's captain, while Esteban Rodriguez and Rodrigo de Espinosa were chosen as pilots. On June 1, the *San Pedro* lifted anchor and sailed – as Carrión had proposed seven years earlier – in a northerly direction until it reached 39.5 degrees north. From here the ship was steered due east and managed to reach the California coast, then sailing southward and eventually arriving in the ports of La Navidad on October 1 and Acapulco on October 8, where the crew, exhausted after having spent 130 days at sea, was received with great excitement.

Successful completion of an eastern-bound route crossing the Pacific was a major achievement. Finally, after almost seven decades of exploration, Spaniards would have direct access to the wealthy and densely populated regions of East and Southeast Asia. This discovery, which was more the result of a predetermined plan than Urdaneta's abilities as a pilot and cosmographer, had important consequences for the Spanish empire.[113] One key outcome was the creation of a Spanish colony in the Philippines. In October 1566, a galleon from New Spain arrived in Cebu. Although the news that a return route had been found must have boosted the moral of the conquerors, after months at sea the ship had few supplies left and the crew was practically starved to death.[114] Things improved considerably in July of the next year, when three ships arrived that had brought along ample supplies and men. Finding sufficient provisions continued to be a problem, however, which led Legazpi to organize an expedition to Panay in 1569 and in 1570 to Luzon, the northernmost of the Philippine islands, conveniently located in the vicinity of China. After having received the king's instructions to create a permanent colony, Legazpi transformed San Miguel into the city named Santo Nombre de Jesús, which he placed under the command of Guido de Lavezaris. Thereafter, Legazpi traveled to Luzon, where he established the city of Manila along the estuary of the river Pasig, after having negotiated a peace treaty with Rajah Sulayman and Lakan Dula. The Bay of Manila not only provided a secure port for the city but also served as a direct gateway for its residents to the centuries-old trading networks of the

---

[113] In his study of Urdaneta's role as a pilot and navigator during the two crossings of the Pacific, Juan Gil reveals that extant sources actually have very little positive things to say about the friar. Not only does it appear that the other pilots ridiculed him, but not a single source mentions his contribution to the discovery of the *tornaviaje*. This only changed when members of the Augustinian order began to celebrate his feat. Gil, *Legazpi*, cii–xvi.

[114] Junald Dawa Ango, "The Cebu-Acapulco Galleon Trade," *Philippine Quarterly of Culture and Society* 38, no. 2 (2010): 149–52.

South China and Philippine Sea. The city would remain the center of the Spanish presence in Asia for more than three centuries.

The developments in the South Sea also impacted the lives of those residing in New Spain. As the anonymous author of the 1566 account of the Legazpi expedition underlined, people in Mexico felt great excitement about the discovery and the new situation this created, which made them "believe that they will be the heart of the world."[115] As this chapter has argued, in the process of the viceroyalty acquiring this pivotal position between the metropolis and its Asian possessions, veterans of earlier expeditions in the search for a route to Asia played a leading role. Grappling with a distributive system that had not rewarded their earlier feats, they used their own firsthand experiences and knowledge of unconquered territories and the people inhabiting them to create new opportunities. Consciously fashioning themselves as veterans of prior expeditions, they not only promoted new expeditions to lands left unconquered but also helped to pass on knowledge gathered during those earlier journeys that became crucial for Spanish survival in the Philippines and the eventual discovery of the *tornaviaje*.

Although the veterans that we have met in this chapter proposed different, even conflicting, projects and argued about directions and destinations, they all agreed that benefits would come from expanding the Spanish empire all the way to Asia. This sentiment was not shared by everyone, however. Already during the preparations for the Legazpi expedition, the conquistador Pedro de Ledesma wondered whether all the money that was being spent on such a journey would not be better invested in the viceroyalty. "If Your Majesty were to spend one part of these costs on New Spain," he groused to Philip, "this would be the best land in the world, and Your treasury greatly augmented."[116] Along with growing activity in the Pacific Ocean, such questions rose increasingly frequently during the following decades. With integration processes accelerating, some began to ask if this development was desired and whether measures ought to be taken toward the control of mobility. In these discussions, notions of a deserving self were no longer automatically related to the ideal of a more connected world, which we have seen in the previous two chapters. Instead, new notions of a deserving self and undeserving others emerged as people grappled with the movements of

---

[115] Blair and Robertson, *The Philippine Islands*, 2: 230.
[116] Letter from Pedro de Ledesma to King, May 22, 1563, in *ENE*, 15: 78.

soldiers, friars, and burgeoning trade in the viceroyalty as well as the effects these had on distributional conflicts therein. The following three chapters examine these struggles, beginning with ongoing quarrels between the conquistadores of Mexico and the *beneméritos* who had earned their stripes by serving the Crown in the South Sea.

3

The Meritorious

Rootedness and Mobility in the Pacific Basin

The discovery of a route between the Philippines and New Spain prompted new forms of mobility in the Pacific and created new opportunities for subjects of the Spanish Crown to gain their place among the meritorious and, hopefully, some form of reward. The Spanish wars in East and Southeast Asia required officers and soldiers, while officials were needed to administer the newly conquered territories.[1] New possibilities also emerged closer to the viceroyalty. Rumors about treasures being transported across the Pacific attracted English and Dutch corsairs, giving inhabitants of New Spain a chance to fight against the Crown's European enemies and a clear reason to explore the California coast. Processes like these, driving New Spain's integration into a Hispano–Asian Pacific world, changed the region's role in struggles over the viceregal order. Explorers, conquistadores, officers, and royal officials continued using their experiences in the region to fashion themselves as deserving subjects, but new forms of mobility in this oceanic space also became the subject of more general disputes concerning distribution of the king's favor. Such

---

[1] On Spanish military expansion in East and Southeast Asia, see Rafael Valladares, *Castilla y Portugal en Asia (1580–1680). Declive imperial y adaptación* (Louvain: Leuven University Press, 2001); Tonio Andrade, *How Taiwan Became Chinese: Dutch, Spanish, and Han Colonization in the Seventeenth Century* (New York: Columbia University Press, 2008); Ostwald Sales-Colín Kortajarena, "Intentos de fortalecimiento español allende Filipinas: Moluco, Matheo e Isla del Norte, 1605–1653," *Estudios de Asia y África* 50, no. 2 (2015): 355–94; Manel Ollé, "Portugueses y castellanos en Asia Oriental," in *Portugal na Monarquia Hispânica. Dinâmicas de integração e conflito*, eds. Pedro Cardim, Leonor Freire Costa, and Mafalda Soares da Cunha (Lisboa: CHAM, 2013), 253–76.

discussions were never solely about mobility in the Pacific. Rather, they were fundamentally shaped by a question that was gaining salience in New Spain during the second half of the sixteenth century: What was the significance of movement in defining the category *benemérito* (meritorious subject) and the hierarchy of the meritorious?

As the previous chapters have underscored, contemporaries closely associated movement with merit. Still, not every kind of movement was valued equally, nor was it a given how this particular criterion of worthiness ought to be valued in relation to others. This chapter focuses on one conundrum raised by the latter question concerning the compatibility of movement and rootedness as metrics of merit.[2] The principal reason such a problem arose was changing royal policy. During the first three decades after the fall of Tenochtitlan, the Crown had pledged the benefits of the new territories to the first conquerors and settlers and their descendants. By making the merit of the first Europeans in New Spain inheritable, royal officials had hoped to reduce mobility and secure population growth. This worked for a while but, over time, reduced the incentive for the descendants of the first conquistadors and settlers to serve the interests of the Crown. Entitled to a reward due to blood and their status as natives of the colony, they felt justified in petitioning royal authorities without first rendering their own services. By the 1560s, however, the Crown was looking for ways to mobilize capable men for the administration and defense of its ever-growing empire. Continuous relocation of these imperial agents was key to ensuring that royal authority reached even the most far-flung territories and prevented its agents from becoming too close with local elites.[3] Yet the promises of rewards and promotions made to mobilize these men were not always compatible with the earlier ones, occasioning time and again controversies over who the real *beneméritos* were.

In examining the services that men-at-arms and officials rendered in the Pacific against the background of this conundrum, this chapter takes another look at the role of mobility in shaping the identities of New Spain's residents. In broad strokes, two general tendencies in how

[2] Insightful reflection on this vexing question can be found in León Pinelo, *Tratado de confirmaciones reales*, Part I, Cap. 9, ff. 50v.–53v, 72–73.

[3] Serge Gruzinski, "Les élites de la monarchie catholique au carrefour des empires (fin XVIe-début XVIIe siècle)," in *L'Empire portugais face aux autres Empires*, eds. Francisco Bethencourt and Luiz Felipe de Alencastro (Paris: Maisonneuve & Larose, 2007), 273–87; Córdoba Ochoa, "Movilidad geográfica," 359–78; Adolfo Polo y La Borda, "Don Mauro's Letters: The Marquis of Villagarcía and the Imperial Networks of Patronage in Spain," *The Americas* 76, no. 4 (2019): 555–83.

historians have usually interpreted this relationship can be distinguished. On the one hand, traditional scholarship has argued that the arrival of Peninsulars and their appropriating of positions in the viceroyalty contributed to the formation of a rooted population, sharing a collective creole identity.[4] On the other hand, more recent studies have explored the role that movement played in *relaciones de méritos y servicios* (accounts of services rendered) or *informaciones de oficio y parte* (reports on capacities and professional services).[5] These "moving stories," as John-Paul Ghobrial has called the mobility narratives of the early modern world, have often been studied as evocations of merit, with the sacrifices and risks to health, family, and property of which these representations told, spotlighting each supplicant's worthiness of royal favor.[6] Yet, neither one of these perspectives, I argue, properly grasps the developments that were taking place within the distributive apparatus, nor do they address the challenges that those looking for royal favor faced as they sought to balance mobility and rootedness in the process of fashioning deserving selves.

The chapter explores this transformation and the responses it prompted through the writings of a heterogenous group of imperial agents about the Spanish expansion in the Pacific world. The texts they produced reveal how mobility acquired meaning in relation to the distributive struggles taking place within the viceroyalty as well as how their authors dealt with movement, immobility, and rootedness as they crafted notions of a deserving self or undeserving others. In examining the dynamics of the struggles that New Spain's global integration produced, this chapter, ultimately, seeks to deepen our understanding of the ways in which they affected perceptions of the viceroyalty's place in the world.

DESCENDANTS OF THE CONQUISTADORES AND THE PLAN TO CONQUER CHINA

Felipe de Salcedo's return to New Spain in the autumn of 1565 came at an opportune moment. Social pressures had been rising in the viceroyalty as a result of ongoing struggles over the extension of encomienda grants and

---

[4] Baltasar Dorantes de Carranza, *Sumaria relación de las cosas de la Nueva España*, ed. Ernesto Torre de la Villar (Editorial Porrúa, S.A., Mexico City, 1987), xxvii; Bacigalupo, *A Changing Perspective*, 109–40; Brading, *The First America*, 225, 295–96.

[5] Córdoba Ochoa, "Movilidad geográfica," 359–78; Tempère, "En las fronteras del mundo iberoasiático, 193–214.

[6] Ghobrial, "Moving Stories," 245–50.

lack of opportunities.[7] A new conquest could alleviate some of these tensions, providing those lacking means of sustenance, including some of the children and grandchildren of the first conquistadores and settlers, with an opportunity to improve their social and economic status. The first reports coming from the islands were promising. Salcedo arrived in New Spain with samples of gold, cinnamon and ginger, as well as rich silks, revealing a possible route for economic exploitation.[8] In addition, there still existed the possibility that, by becoming involved in the conquest of unclaimed land, adventurers could gain the status of first conquistador, which would allow them to claim an encomienda or *corregimiento* in the territory they helped to subjugate.[9]

The effect of these pull factors was short-lived, however. When Salcedo returned to the Philippines in 1567, he managed to recruit 300 sailors and soldiers as reinforcements – a substantial part of whom died during the crossing as a result of mutiny, provoking Legazpi to lament the lack of support he had received.[10] In the following years, the number of recruits gradually decreased. In 1570, Juan de la Isla, another of Legazpi's confidants charged with bringing supplies and reinforcements, departed from Acapulco with only 180 passengers, including merchants, men-at-arms, married settlers, and clergymen.[11] In 1573 and 1574, Viceroy Martín Enriquez de Almansa (1568–80) sent one ship each year, each carrying 130 soldiers.[12] Finally, in 1575, Francisco de Sande, the new governor of the Philippines, rallied 350 recruits, 180 of whom were soldiers and only 36 of whom came from New Spain.[13] Reports about de Sande's recruitment process show that 146 consecutive days of public announcements only yielded meager results, with many of the enlisted having been

---

[7] María Alba Pastor, *Crisis y recomposición social: Nueva España en el tránsito del siglo XVI al XVII* (Mexico City: Universidad Nacional Autónoma de México; Fondo de Cultura Económica, 1999), 43–48.

[8] Blair and Robertson, *Philippine Islands*, 2: 220–32, esp. 226.

[9] Royal decrees and laws on various matters, Biblioteca Nacional de México, UNAM, Mexico City. Ms. Ms. 1284ff. 7r.–7v; ff.18v.–19r; f. 26.

[10] Letter from Legazpi about discoveries and lack of help, Jul 23, 1567, AGI, Filipinas 6, R.1, N.7.

[11] Letter from Juan de la Isla to Viceroy Enríquez, Mar 8, 1570, AGI, Patronato 24, R.4, N.9.

[12] Antonio Francisco García-Abásolo, "La expansión mexicana hacia el Pacífico: La primera colonización de Filipinas (1570-1580)," *Historia Mexicana* 32, no. 1 (1982): 55–88.

[13] Luis Muro, "Soldados de Nueva España a Filipinas, 1575," *Historia Mexicana* 19, no. 4 (1970): 479–91.

deemed unfit, either because they were physically impaired or simply too young to be of any use.[14]

The difficulties of Spanish authorities in finding appropriate men were a result of the growing awareness among New Spain's residents of the risks and hardships awaiting in Asia. In the years after Salcedo's return from the Philippines, negative accounts began circulating about the long journey across the Pacific, the constant food shortages, the region's inhospitable climate, and the violent resistance of Native populations. Rumors also spread that the islands offered far fewer riches than had been expected, an image that was confirmed by the lack of success stories and encomiendas providing lucrative tributes to reward those taking great risks there.[15] Politically and militarily ambitious men in New Spain found attractive opportunities closer to home, especially in the Bajío region, where wars against the semi-nomadic Chichimeca tribes allowed men-at-arms to demonstrate their military prowess and return home with loot or enslaved Natives.[16] Those who traveled to the Philippines mostly belonged to the lower classes. They really needed the wages the Crown promised them, belonged to families happy about having one less mouth to feed, or were forced by the viceregal authorities, eager to get rid of criminals and vagabonds who presented a threat to public order.[17]

This situation did not change noticeably after the Spaniards shifted their focus from the Philippines toward the Asian mainland. From the second half of the 1570s, the Islas del Poniente increasingly came to be seen as a steppingstone for what was supposed to be the true goal of

---

[14] Ibid., 471.

[15] Miguel López de Legazpi created encomiendas, but his men soon complained that the number of Natives stipulated in the grant did not correspond to the population actually inhabiting these territories. The conflicts that followed underscore that the encomienda system of the Philippines was still a long way from providing stable incomes to grant holders. Patricio Hidalgo Nuchera, *Encomienda, tributo y trabajo en Filipinas, 1570–1608* (Madrid: Universidad Autónoma de Madrid; Ediciones Polifemo, 1995), 41–49.

[16] Alberto Carrillo Cázares, *El debate sobre la Guerra Chichimeca, 1531–1585: derecho y política en la Nueva España* (Zamora: El Colegio de Michoacán and Colegio de San Luis, 2000), 71.

[17] Stephanie J. Mawson, "Convicts or Conquistadores? Spanish Soldiers in the Seventeenth-Century Pacific," *Past & Present* 232, no. 1 (2016): 96–104. Mawson has noted that during the seventeenth century, on average a soldier's wage equaled 96 pesos a year. There were always difficulties in paying these salaries, however. Difficulties in the recruitment of soldiers for the Philippines have also been studied for a later period by Eva Maria Mehl, *Forced Migration in the Spanish Pacific World: From Mexico to the Philippines, 1765–1811* (Cambridge: Cambridge University Press, 2016).

Spanish expansion in Asia: the conquest of China.[18] Spaniards had learned new things about this kingdom during the previous two decades, both from Portuguese sources and interactions with Fujianese traders in Manila.[19] Information about China's wealth, the size of its population, and its highly structured society rekindled dreams of conquering it. López de Velasco's map of the Spanish empire of 1575, which we already saw in the Introduction (Figure I.1), captures these sentiments, presenting, as Ricardo Padrón has noted, an ideological fantasy that shaped the picture of the empire and the transpacific space along the lines of Spanish conquests in the region and vague imperial ambitions that included the conquest of China.[20]

Nevertheless, in New Spain, enthusiasm for the project remained limited to a small circle. As Viceroy Enríquez wrote to the King in 1576, Spaniards born in the viceroyalty had little interest in heading out to the Philippines or fighting the Chinese. Although there were enough "vagrant persons and of little use," as Enríquez noted, he could not convince them to travel across the Pacific. Ironically, some of these men justified their refusal by referring to the friars' arguments about it being illegal to take Native tributes for maintaining the troops. "They are so rooted," the viceroy concluded, that to move them "more will be needed than only nice words."[21]

The unwillingness of residents of New Spain to cross the Pacific became notorious. For Diego García de Palacio (1540–95), an *oidor* (civil judge) from Guatemala's audiencia, it was one of the reasons to propose to the Council of the Indies his own plan for the conquest of China.[22]

---

[18] The Spanish plans to conquer China have been studied in detail in: Manel Ollé, *La empresa de China. De la Armada Invencible al Galeon de Manila* (Barcelona: Acantilado, 2002); Gruzinski, *L'Aigle*, 359–403; Padrón, *Indies of the Setting Sun*, 169–77.

[19] On the history of the image that Iberians had of China, see: Manel Ollé, *La invención de China. Percepciones y estrategias filipinas respecto a China durante el siglo XVI* (Wiesbaden: Harrasowitz Verlag, 2000), 11–51; Birgit Tremml-Werner, *Spain, China, and Japan in Manila, 1571–1644: Local Comparisons and Global Connections* (Amsterdam: Amsterdam University Press, 2015), 139–40.

[20] Padrón, *Indies of the Setting Sun*, 151–66.

[21] Letter of Viceroy Enríquez to Philip II, Oct 31, 1576, in *Cartas de Indias* (Madrid: Ministerio de Fomento, 1877), 328–29.

[22] Letter from García de Palacio to Philip II, Mar 8, 1578, AGI, Patronato, 24, R. 44; Memorial of García de Palacios in which he petitions for the conquest of the kingdom of Taibin in China, AGI, Patronato, 24, R.47, doc. 3. For a more detailed discussion of these plans, see: José Antonio Cervera Jiménez, "Los planes españoles para conquistar China a través de Nueva España y Centroamérica en el siglo XVI," *Cuadernos Inter.c.a.mbio sobre Centroamérica y el Caribe* 10, no. 12 (2013): 218–24.

Between 1574 and 1578, he lamented on multiple occasions the lack of progress that had been made in the pacification and conversion of this kingdom. One of the reasons for this undesirable situation, he noted, was the bad reputation that both the Philippines and China enjoyed in New Spain, which had led to "few [persons] of good quality" being willing to go to the islands.[23] To solve this problem, he believed it was more feasible to recruit soldiers in Spain and have them travel to Asia via Panama rather than by means of the usual route through New Spain. By keeping the soldiers out of these parts, they would likely experience fewer temptations to desert, as they would not learn of the many negative stories circulating there.

A decade later, Dr. Sancho Sánchez de Muñón, then *maestrescuela* (schoolmaster) of Mexico's cathedral, was even more critical of the aversion of New Spain's inhabitants toward expansion in Asia. Like Viceroy Enríquez, Sánchez de Muñón argued that it would be in the Crown's interest to induce recruits to travel to the Philippines. He argued, however, that the current royal policy was not producing the desired result.[24] Instead of sending men of "higher quality" to the islands, the Crown had relied on officials and workers who could contribute to viceregal society but were unfit for conquest. Most were "miserable" persons without honor, for whom the Crown had to provide everything "from their shirt to their sword." Meanwhile, he noted in a letter written two years later,

[m]any honorable and respectable men, sons and grandsons of the conquistadores and other naturals of these kingdoms live in idleness without having the means to sustain themselves, of whom, as I have brought to Your Majesty's attention on other occasions, many could leave from here well-armed and with little cost to Your Majesty's royal treasury. Even if no other good comes from it, it will remove from this kingdom persons that are redundant, as demonstrated by the damages that they have caused.[25]

Referring in both of his letters to the unrest the descendants of the conquistadores had generated in Peru and New Spain, Sánchez de Muñón clearly sought to tap into lingering fears about the American elite rebelling against the Crown. Such a tactic was fitting for a man who liked to highlight his role in uncovering the alleged conspiracy to overthrow the Crown in 1566, which had involved, among others, the Ávila brothers, Alonso and Gil; the second Marquis of the Valley of

---

[23] AGI, Patronato, 24, R.44, image 2.
[24] Letter from Doctor Sánchez de Muñón to King Philip II, Apr 20, 1581, AGI, México, 105.
[25] Letter from Doctor Sánchez de Muñón, Jan 18, 1583, AGI, México, 70, R.6, N.90.

Oaxaca, don Martín Cortés; and the dean of the cathedral chapter, Alonso Chico de Molina.[26] Yet Sánchez de Muñón's recurrent allusions to the social disorder caused by the conquistadores' descendants was also grounded in the everyday experience of the viceregal capital as well.

Reports written by New Spain's viceroys provide a better picture of what was going on, revealing the problems entailed by the sheer and seemingly endless number of petitions for remuneration that these descendants brought before the viceregal authorities.[27] As Viceroy Enríquez observed in 1580, many of these petitioners possessed the "quality (*partes*) of being born in this land and son of a conquistador," but most of them were so incapable that he "would not even trust them with the staff of the inspector of weights and measurements."[28] Dealing with such cases was not just time consuming; the fact that so many had to be disappointed actually posed a threat to the social order. Viceroys described how they had been yelled at, their reputations tarnished by disgruntled petitioners, or had to grapple with protests outside the viceregal palace organized by those who felt they had been treated unjustly.[29]

---

[26] Sanchez de Muñón regularly sent reports to the court to advise the monarch and the Council of the Indies on matters of good governance. See for example: Doctor Sancho Sánchez de Muñón: Good governance of Nueva España, Jan 10, 1569, AGI, Patronato, 182, R.36. Whether the accused conspirators actually had been planning to rebel against the Crown or had become themselves victims of an abuse of legal powers remains unclear. Debates about this question date back to the months after the tumultuous arrest of ninety-eight persons and the hasty conviction of some, prompting procedural and moral critiques of their defenders. In subsequent decades, authors like Juan Suárez de Peralta and Fray Juan de Torquemada continued to discuss the actions of those involved in the alleged conspiracy and the Crown's response. For an overview of these discussions, see for example: Shirley Cushing Flint, "Treason or Travesty: The Martín Cortés Conspiracy Reexamined," *The Sixteenth Century Journal* 39, no. 1 (2008): 23–44; Covadonga Lamar Prieto, "La conjuración de Martín Cortés en la monarquía indiana de Fray Juan de Torquemada," *Archivum* LVII, no. 57 (2007): 91–122.

[27] Illustrative of this growing demand for royal grace and favor is the fact that during the 1570s, 110 *relaciones de méritos y servicios* confirming the petitioners' status as a descendant of a conquistador entered the royal archives, a number considerable higher than the 76 petitions filed during the first two decades after the conquest. This number reflects not all the cases that appeared before the viceregal authorities during the 1570s but the ones that were approved by them and that entered the royal archive. Today, these petitions can be found in AGI, Patronato, legajos 70–75.

[28] Advertencies of Viceroy Enríquez to Conde of La Coruña, Sept 25, 1580, in Hanke, *Los virreyes*, 1: 211–12; Mariano Cuevas and Genaro García, eds. *Documentos inéditos del siglo XVI para la historia de México* (Mexico City: Talleres del Museo Nacional de Arqueología, Historia y Etnología, 1914), 441.

[29] Report Marquis of Montesclaros, Aug 2, 1607, in Hanke, *Los virreyes*, 2: 280; Letter from Luis de Velasco II to King Philip II, May 24, 1592, in Cuevas and García, *Documentos inéditos*, 442.

To protect their authority and that of the Crown, several proposed to make personal virtue and merit the main criteria in the distributive process.[30] As the Marquis of Montesclaros noted in 1604, to determine a person's worthiness, "one has to take into consideration the virtue of each, rather than equating conquistadores with *corregidores* (judicial officials). For doing so will animate them to earn by means of their personal talents what at the moment they believe to be theirs by birthright."[31]

In his observations regarding the descendants of the conquistadores, Sánchez de Múñon squarely addressed this conflict about the place of the descendants of the conquistadores in the hierarchy of the meritorious in his own way. On the one hand, he sympathetically acknowledged the lack of opportunities New Spain had to offer. On the other hand, by presenting these descendants as the ideal participants in the conquest of Asia, he called them out to live up to their claimed status. Calling for the Crown to do the same, he listed some of the benefits that could be expected from pressuring these men to travel to the Philippines: It would be cost efficient, as many of them had already adopted a martial lifestyle; they were already accustomed to the foods and climate of the Indies, making them less susceptible to the region's diseases of the Indies and enhancing their physical ability to carry out their mission; and, perhaps most importantly for his audience, New Spain would be freed of potential troublemakers

---

[30] Compare for instance: Memorial of Marquis of Villamanrique, 1592, in Hanke, *Los virreyes*, 1: 285, and Report Marquis of Montesclaros, in: Hanke, *Los virreyes*, 2: 280. Alejandro Cañeque has pointed out that this proposal partly originated out of self-interest. As viceroys owed much of their authority to their ability to grant rewards to their retainers, they had little to gain from rewarding petitioners based on birthright, as such recipients would not be bound to them by any debt of gratitude or submission. Cañeque, *The King's Living Image*, 144. Complaints about the viceroys granting positions and favors to family members and loyal cronies in their retinue were common. Brading, *The First America*, 296; María Alba Pastor, *Crisis y recomposición social*, 132–33.

[31] Letter from Count of Monterrey, Apr 31, 1604, in Hanke, *Los virreyes*, 2: 282. It is important to acknowledge that this position was not absolute. Rather, it had a specific function within the distributive struggles involving the descendants of the conquistadores. As Christoph Rosenmüller has pointed out, it was generally believed, both in Spain and New Spain, that "combination of the proper social origins, the aptitude for a position, and the services to the king and the political community enabled virtuous service." Petitioners not descended from established Christian bloodlines were often seen as innately corrupt and, therefore, unfit for any authoritative position. Rosenmüller, *Corruption and Justice in Colonial Mexico*, 71–73.

who could conspire with *mulatos*, mestizos, free blacks, and slaves against the royal authority.[32]

Discussions about how to incentivize reluctant descendants of the conquistadores to serve the Crown and move into uncharted territory played into a negative discourse emerging around this time about the qualities of the descendants of the conquistadores and American-born creoles (more on the latter in Chapter 4). Critiques like those of the viceroys and Sánchez de Múñon contributed to devaluing the status of a son or grandson of a conquistador and helped open the category of *benemérito* for others to claim royal favor. In this process, lack of mobility was not always a disqualifying factor, though. Someone who succeeded in finding a way to make his family's rootedness and mobility work together for him was Miguel López de Legazpi's oldest son, Melchor López de Legazpi Garcés. By invoking both dimensions in his self-fashioning accounts, he managed to carve out a place for his family among Mexico's elite.

FASHIONING THE LEGAZPIS

Melchor López de Legazpi was born in Mexico in 1535. Unlike his nephews, Felipe and Juan de Salcedo, he did not join his father's expedition to the Philippines but, rather, stayed behind to assume the care of his mother and younger sisters. His role in the family-positioning endeavor commenced at the end of 1565 when he, a man of letters, traveled in the company of Felipe de Salcedo and Andrés de Urdaneta to the Spanish court to present the petitions coming from the Philippines.[33] Legazpi, Salcedo, and Urdaneta's arrival at the Spanish court incited discussions about the legitimacy of the conquest of the Philippines.[34] While the legal

---

[32] AGI, México, 105.

[33] Melchor received permission from the viceroy to travel to the Court and leave his office for a period of two years. *Actas*, VI, Bk. 7, 263. Petitions of Legazpi and his son Melchor, AGI, Patronato, 23, R.26, f. 1.

[34] Regarding discussions on the question of whether the Spanish Crown had a justified claim to the Philippine Islands, see David C. Goodman, *Power and Penury: Government, Technology and Science in Philip II's Spain* (Cambridge: Cambridge University Press, 1988), 56–57; José Antonio Cervera Jiménez, "Andrés de Urdaneta y su trabajo como científico: el problema de la demarcación de Filipinas," in *Urdaneta novohispano: la inserción del mundo hispano en Asia*, ed. María Cristina E. Barrón Soto (Mexico City: Universidad Iberoamericana, 2012), 67–90; Guillaume Gaudin, "Parecer sobre las dudas que hay cerca de la demarcación del tratado de Zaragoza en Filipinas (1568), e Instrucción del virrey de Nueva España, don Martín Enríquez al capitán Juan de la Isla

and cosmographical experts were still coming to grips with this problem, petitions for favor were not officially taken into consideration. Consequently, Melchor had to wait two and a half years at the court – a stay that put a heavy financial burden on a family that, as he himself explained in a letter to the Council, had already sacrificed so much because his father had "sold everything, leaving his children and house to the Crown's protection."[35]

As he waited for the situation to change, Melchor did his best to make sure his family was not forgotten. He submitted a petition repeating his father's requests and another asking the monarch to remunerate his expenses for staying in Castile by appointing him to the position of *contador* (royal accountant) of Mexico City.[36] In 1568, he also convinced the Council of the Indies to send a request to Mexico's audiencia to investigate Miguel López de Legazpi's "merits, quality, sufficiency, and services."[37] Dr. Jerónimo de Orozco, the *oidor* in charge of the investigation, started hearing witnesses in the viceregal capital on October 7, 1568. The questionary used for this purpose focused on four aspects of Legazpi's public persona, asking witnesses whether they recognized Legazpi's qualities as a hijodalgo and caballero; believed Legazpi to possess the qualities and talents required to lead the expedition to the Philippines; knew that Legazpi had invested his entire fortune in the expedition and resigned as treasurer of the *Casa de la Moneda* (royal mint), leaving him poor and in need; and had heard anything contradicting the idea that Legazpi had not yet been rewarded. The four witnesses all testified positively to Legazpi's qualities and merits and confirmed that it was well known that he had not been repaid in any form for his and his family's expenses. In accordance with these testimonies, Orozco issued a recommendation for the Crown to heed Legazpi's requests.

Around the same time, Melchor himself interviewed six witnesses who had arrived at the Spanish court from the Philippines and New Spain. The portrait of Legazpi produced via his questionary differs in several ways from the one delineated in Mexico City. With respect to Legazpi's qualities, Melchor asked for instance whether the witnesses knew his father to

---

sobre lo que debe hacer para ir al descubrimiento de la China," *Relaciones Estudios de Historia y Sociedad* 40, no. 160 (2020): 102–22.

[35] AGI, Patronato, 23, R.26, f. 7r.   [36] Ibid., f. 12r.

[37] Información de méritos y servicios of Miguel López de Legazpi, Oct 7, 1568, AGI, Patronato, 52, R.1.

be "one of Mexico's oldest *"antiguos pobladores"* (first settlers), who had lived there for forty years and is one of its principal residents."[38] To people in New Spain, this fact may have seemed irrelevant to determining whether merit had been earned in the Philippines. Perhaps they also did not recognize Legazpi's status as first settler, as he had only arrived in 1528. Melchor, in turn, may have reasoned that, according to the New Laws, the status of settler equaled that of a conquistador.[39] Stressing his father's status as a *benemérito* in New Spain could help his own petition for the position of Mexico's treasurer, with which he hoped to make up for the fifteen thousand pesos he had spent while at the court and which he needed "to support his father's social rank or that of his siblings."[40] After all, as a son of a first settler, he was linked to the land and could claim a reward for his father's services.

These testimonies and the portrait they painted of the Legazpi family eventually became relevant when, at the end of 1569, the Council of the Indies finally had a chance to discuss pending matters related to the Islas del Poniente with the king.[41] During a meeting on December 21, Philip II agreed to appoint Miguel López de Legazpi as governor and captain general of the Philippines for life, granting him an annual salary of 2,000 ducats. In addition, he gave permission for the conquest and settlement of two of the Ladrones Islands (today's Mariana Islands), bestowing on Legazpi the title of *adelantado* (provincial governor) of the Ladrones Islands in return.[42] Salcedo received permission to present himself to the Council of Orders for a habit of the Order of Santiago, and the king approved Melchor's request for the position of *contador*.[43] Not entirely satisfied by this outcome, Melchor asked the Crown to extend his father's authority and grant him permission to conquer New Guinea.[44] This petition was unsuccessful, although it may have helped in securing a

---

[38] AGI, Patronato, 23, R.26, f. 15r.   [39] Icazbalceta, *Nueva colección*, 2: 221
[40] Ibid., f. 16r.
[41] On November 16, 1568, the king had already written Miguel López de Legazpi to praise his work and provide new instructions. Reply to Miguel de Legazpi, in Blair and Robertson, *Philippine Islands*, 2: 235–38.
[42] Consultation by the Council of the Indies, Dec 21, 1568, AGI, Indiferente General, 738, N.92. For the precise terms of this *merced*, see also the official appointment of Miguel López de Legazpi as governor, captain general, and adelantado: AGI, Filipinas, 339, L.1, ff. 28r–33r.
[43] This request can also be found in AGI, Patronato, 23, N.26, f. 12r. Melchor's official appointment as *contador* took place on August 3, 1569. AGI, Contratación, L.1, ff. 49v.– 50.
[44] AGI, Patronato, 23, R.26, ff. 28–29.

one-time payment of 2,000 ducats.[45] Having exhausted all his possibilities, Melchor traveled home in the spring of 1570.[46]

Back in Mexico, Melchor's status gradually improved. He took up his position as treasurer of the Casa de la Moneda and, in 1572, he married Luisa de Albornoz y Acuña, granddaughter of Rodrigo de Albornoz, a conquistador and one of the first Spaniards to govern Mexico in the absence of Hernán Cortés, and daughter of García de Albornoz, who had been sent into exile for being too much on the side of the alleged conspirators in 1566.[47] One year later, news about Miguel López de Legazpi's death arrived from the Philippines, due to which Melchor inherited his father's possessions, two encomiendas, and the title of *adelantado*.

One of Melchor's biggest worries following this news was that, in order to benefit from his inheritance, he would have to leave New Spain and move to the Philippines. He was planning to return to Spain to ask the Crown to exempt him from doing so, but Viceroy Enríquez encouraged him to stay. Instead, the viceroy wrote the king on his behalf, asking him to reward Melchor the privilege of enjoying these benefits within the viceroyalty for the sole reason of him then being able to take care of his siblings, who lived there in poverty.[48] The same viceroy who two years later would complain about how little American-born Spaniards were inclined toward traveling to the Philippines apparently had little problem with Melchor staying behind. In 1575, he clearly did not have the members of the elite in mind. Seen in this light, the poverty to which Legazpi and the viceroy referred was relative as well, measured, as so often, in terms of his status and ideas about what a person of that status deserved rather than actual financial means.[49]

Melchor's gradual integration into Mexico's elite provoked both criticism and praise. In his *Tratado del descubrimiento de las Indias* (Treatise on the Discovery of the Indies, 1578), Juan Suárez de Peralta mentioned Melchor in a story that accused Miguel López de Legazpi of greed for accepting leadership of the expedition to the Philippines. As the position

---

[45] AGI, Filipinas, 339, L.1, ff. 35v.–36r.

[46] Concession to travel for Melchor de Legazpi's slave, Mar 11, 1570, AGI, Indiferente General, 2052, N.62.

[47] Dorantes Carranza, *Sumaria relación*, 259; process against García de Albornoz, 1568, AGI, Patronato, 220, R.4.

[48] Letter from Viceroy Enríquez to King Philip II, Oct 23, 1573, AGI, México, 19, N.142; Letter Viceroy Enríquez to King Philip II, Dec 5, 1573, in *Cartas de Indias*, no. LIV, 295.

[49] Huber, *Beute*, 349–50.

of treasurer of the Casa de la Moneda had already provided the Legazpi family with "food in Mexico," Suárez de Peralta wrote, the father's decision to lead the expedition had deprived someone else of a chance to make a living.[50] Others had been equally amazed by Legazpi's decision to give up his position, but they wondered why someone would give up his security for such a risky enterprise.[51] In Suárez de Peralta's case, it is hard not to relate his observation concerning Miguel to another he made about Melchor holding the title of Adelantado de las Islas de los Ladrones while still residing and occupying an office in Mexico. Even if Suárez de Peralta's explicit critique only targeted the elder Legazpi, Melchor might still have felt the sting of himself being accused of similar vices as well.

Nevertheless, more positive images emerged by the beginning of the seventeenth century. In 1603, Viceroy Juan de Mendoza y Luna (1603–7), the Marquis of Montesclaros, referred to Melchor as *"merced,"* an honorary title that came with his dignity as *adelantado*, in a report for the Crown in which he discussed the loose ways in which titles were used and misused in the viceroyalty.[52] Around the same time, Baltasar Dorantes de Carranza confirmed the family's status as a member of New Spain's "nobility of conquistadores and pobladores" in a text known today as the *Sumaria relación de las cosas de la Nueva España* (Summary Account of the Things of New Spain).[53] Dorantes de Carranza wrote this text to instruct Montesclaros about New Spain, its history, and the qualities of its residents. In addition, he provided detailed information on the lineages of 195 conquistadores and 77 *pobladores*, plus their scions, whom he deemed to be the true *beneméritos* of New Spain.

These lists were meant to help the viceroy to end the injustices being done in New Spain. According to Dorantes de Carranza, too often the viceregal authorities neglected the New Laws or were tricked into believing people pretending to be descendants of either a first conquistador or *poblador*. Although the former ranked higher than the latter in the hierarchy of merit, Dorantes's objective in the *Sumaria relación* was to convince the new viceroy that 77 settler families – including his

[50] Juan Suárez de Peralta, *Tratado del descubrimiento de las Indias*, ed. Teresa Silva Tena (Mexico City: Consejo Nacional para la Cultura y las Artes, 1990), 171–72.

[51] Miguel Luque Talaván, "'Al Rey la hacienda y la vida se ha de dar:' Las reclamaciones económicas de los Legazpi a la Corona," in *España y el Pacífico: Legazpi*, ed. Leoncio Cabrero (Madrid: Sociedad estatal de conmemoraciones culturales, 2004), 1: 394–95.

[52] Report Marquis of Montesclaros, Nov 20, 1603, in Hanke, *Los virreyes*, 2: 275.

[53] Dorantes de Carranza, *Sumaria relación*, 259–60.

own – deserved an equal or even higher spot. Blaming the conquistadores for their atrocities against the Native populations, he argued that this group of settlers had been involved in peaceful settlement of the territory and were extremely dedicated to rendering services to the Crown.[54] The Legazpis perfectly embodied Dorantes's argument. As a settler family – according to the *Sumaria relación*, López de Legazpi arrived in Mexico in 1535 – they had successfully become part of the viceregal elite, preserving its ties to the land on the one hand and rendering services in other parts of the empire on the other. Yes, Melchor had earned the title of *adelantado* and his office in the royal treasury due to his father's services, but by serving as *alcalde mayor* in Puebla de los Angeles, he further added merit to the lineage himself. According to Dorantes, Melchor's oldest son, García de Leagzpi y Albornoz, would continue doing so.

Dorantes de Carranza was right about future Legazpis serving the king. Still, much more valuable than any of their own individual feats, was the image of a deserving subject that Melchor had produced and got inserted into the royal archives. After his death, Melchor's widow and children fashioned themselves in a series of petitions in largely the same way as their husband and father had done during the previous decades. In the context of the investigation initiated by Mexico's audiencia in 1606, doña Luisa de Albornoz underlined the qualities of both lineages out of which her children were born. Her case evolved around the title of *adelantado*, the moment that both families had arrived in the Indies, the many services their members had rendered, and their (relative) poverty. As proof of her claims, she included the questionary that Melchor had

---

[54] Ibid., 225. Scholars have generally interpreted this text as a passionate defense of the creole elite. For instance, Ernesto de la Torre found in the work traces of the insolence, vanity, and dissatisfaction of the descendants of the conquistadores and settlers, resulting in a text that represents "with perfection the spirit of New Spanish creoles." Dorantes de Carranza, *Sumaria*, ix. Compare also Pagden, "Identity Formation," 56; Aurora Diéz-Canedo, *Los desventurados barrocos: sentimiento y reflexión entre los descendientes de los conquistadores: Baltasar Dorantes de Carranza, Juan Suárez Peralta y Gonzalo Gómez de Cervantes* (Mexico City: Universidad Pedagógica Nacional, 1990); David M. Solodkow, "La aristocracia de los desposeídos: Baltasar Dorantes de Carranza y la primera generación de criollos novohispanos," in *Poéticas de lo criollo*, eds. Vitulli and Solodkow, 106–7. I have examined Dorantes de Carranza's efforts to increase the estimation of the *pobladores* as *beneméritos* elsewhere: Nino Vallen, "The Self and the World in Baltasar Dorantes de Carranza's Sumaria relación de las cosas de la Nueva España," in *Distributive Struggle and the Self in the Early Modern Iberian World*, eds. Böttcher, Rinke, and Vallen (Stuttgart: Verlag Hans-Dieter Heinz, Akademischer Verlag, 2019), 156–61.

elicited during his time in Madrid and the responses to it.[55] In 1612 and 1630, don García de Albornoz Acuña y Legazpi repeated this process. He asked for an encomienda with a rent of 4,000 ducats in New Spain or, if there was no other possibility, one with a rent of 6,000 ducats in the Philippines with the privilege of, for family-related reasons, not having to live there.[56] He also petitioned for a habit of one of the three military orders, a request that was conceded by allowing him to present himself to the Order of Santiago.[57] Finally, his younger brothers, Antonio and Miguel, used the successful family strategy to acquire a royal grant worth 1,000 ducats of annual income from an encomienda in the Philippines, which they too hoped to enjoy in New Spain.[58] Although these documents mention some administrative functions, their main focus remained on what their "grandfather did in Your Majesty's service" and their need to stay in the viceroyalty.[59]

Over the course of almost seven decades, the Legazpi y Albornoz family fashioned a powerful image of itself. As the temporal distance to the events on which they based their status of *personas beneméritas* increased, some details of their story were changed. The role of the Salcedos was sometimes reduced, whereas on other occasions their title was conveniently altered into the more appealing "Adelantado de las islas Filipinas."[60] Still, the basis of their tried and tested formula for success remained the same, combining their rootedness in New Spain with the merits of the family founder's actions in the Philippines into a story that stressed their need to receive their rewards in the viceroyalty. Instead of actually serving on the empire's frontiers, as their title suggested, the heads of the family managed to strengthen the family's position right in the center of the viceroyalty, eventually becoming part of New Spain's titled nobility.[61] The case of the Legazpi thus illustrates the reluctance of

---

[55] Petition from Doña Luisa de Albornoz, widow of Melchor de Legazpi, Mar 3, 1605, AGI, Patronato, 53, R.13.

[56] Consultation about favors for García de Albornoz, Sept 20, 1613, AGI, Filipinas, 1, N.147.

[57] García de Albornoz y Acuña y Legazpi, 1614, AHN, OM-Expedientillos, N.369; García de Albornoz y Acuña y Legazpi, 1615, AHN, OM-Caballeros_Santiago, Exp.228.

[58] Petition from Legazpi's grandsons for an encomienda without residence, Jun 22, 1616, AGI, Filipinas, 37, N.29.

[59] Inventario de bienes: García de Albornoz Legazpi Acuña, Apr 19, 1622, AGI, México, 262, N.4.

[60] Memorial of García de Albornoz y Legazpi, ca. 1627, AGI, Filipinas, 5, N.339.

[61] Luisa de Albornoz Legazpi y Acuña, who was the oldest daughter of García de Legazpi y Albornoz and doña María Ortíz Oráa, married Juan de Altamirano y Velasco, who obtained the title of Count of Santiago de Calimaya in 1625. José Ignacio Rubio Mañé,

inhabitants of New Spain to move to the Philippines, while at the same time revealing how these islands came to play a role in the public identity that allowed this creole family to rally sufficient support to rise to the highest ranks.

The success of the Legazpi family was exceptional – as had been Miguel López de Legazpi's military feats. Still, there were certainly others who found opportunities in this terraqueous space to demonstrate their readiness to serve the king and acquire the political capital needed to negotiate royal favor. Some were themselves veterans of the Legazpi expedition, who had received rewards in the Philippines but also hoped to enjoy them in New Spain.[62] Their number remained small, however, and the fact that their claims were even considered appears to have been related to injuries they had suffered during their service for the Crown. But colonization of the Philippines was not the only potentially enriching phenomenon attracting people to the Pacific. Another incentive came from the English pirates who wreaked havoc along the west coasts of South and Central America in 1578 and, again, in 1587. The documentation surrounding these events provides some revealing insights into the ways responsibilities were distributed and how these processes were influenced by the self-fashioning of some of the main protagonists of these minimally successful chasings.

PRIVATEERS AND THE MERITORIOUS

In 1578, reports of the English privateer Francis Drake heading north along the Pacific coast prompted fear across the viceroyalty, even among residents of Mexico City.[63] With memories of Drake's earlier raids on the Spanish Main in 1572 still fresh, news of his pillaging along the Pacific coast got better-off New Spanish residents worried about their safety and possessions. Yet, this fear of attack was also blended with a certain sense

---

El virreinato: expansión y defensa, primera parte (Mexico City: Instituto de Investigaciones Históricas, UNAM, 1959), 2: 120n.

[62] AGI, Patronato, 53, R.4; AGI, Patronato, 53, R.6.

[63] Zelia Nuttall, ed. *New Light on Drake: A Collection of Documents relating to His Voyage of Circumnavigation* (London: Hakluyt Society, 1914), 226. On Drake's journey along the American west coast, see: Peter Gerhard, *Pirates of the Pacific, 1575–1742* (Lincoln: University of Nebraska Press, 1990 [1960]), 57–101; Harry Kelsey, *Sir Francis Drake: The Queen's Pirate* (New Haven, CT: Yale University Press, 2000), 137–92; Samuel Bawlf, *The Secret Voyage of Sir Francis Drake, 1577–1580* (Vancouver: Douglas & McIntyre, 2003), 321–66.

of excitement, as some realized that Drake's arrival created a unique opportunity to render service to the Crown. Reports recount how, in a matter of days, 800 men were mobilized for the defense of the viceroyalty's east and west coasts;[64] 200 of them were sent to San Juan de Ulloa on the Atlantic coast, while the other 600 headed for the Pacific coast. A total of 200 went to Guatemala under the command of Juan Cortés, another 200 to Huatulco with captain Pedro de Robles, and 200 more were supposed to chase the pirates. A conflict developed, however, over who would lead this pursuit. Foremost candidates for this task were don Carlos de Luna y Arellano, the mariscal de Castilla and a man with close links to the first conquistadores; his kinsman don Luis de Velasco, son of the former viceroy; and don Hernando de Robles, a recent arrival who served as *alcalde del crimen* (criminal judge) of Mexico's audiencia. It was the latter whom Viceroy Enríquez decided to put in charge of the hunt for the dreaded pirates.

The appointment pleased Robles and, in a letter from September 4, 1579, he gloated of his feats. In only twenty-nine days, he wrote, he had rallied 200 men and brought them to Acapulco, where he handed them over to his son, don Felix de Robles.[65] Having received new instructions ordering him to return to Mexico, his role in the pursuit of Drake's *Golden Hind* thus remained limited. Such a minimal contribution did not stop Robles, however, from writing the king that "I consider having been very well employed, as that what I have done and borne has been in Your Majesty's service."[66] Not everyone agreed, though. Two weeks later, Luis de Velasco informed the king that the entire enterprise had been a farce. Frustrated about the fact that Enríquez had refused his offer to lead the company for which he and Luna y Arellano had recruited most of the men, he blamed Robles for arriving at Acapulco after Drake was already long gone.[67] But that was not all. Robles had not actually handed over responsibility for the pursuit to his son but, rather, to the local *proveedor* (purveyor of the garrison), don Juan de Guzmán. With a two-month head start it would be impossible for Guzmán to catch Drake, except in the unlikely event that the privateer was repairing his ship somewhere along the coast. Rather than pursuing the English privateers,

---

[64] Nuttall, *New Light on Drake*, 226–27.
[65] Letter from Dr. Fernando Robles, Sept 4, 1579, in Ibid., 227–29. See also Miles Philips' statement: Ibid., 226–27.
[66] Ibid., 229.
[67] Letter from Luis de Velasco to King Philip II, Sept 17, 1579, AGI, Patronato, 266, R.31.

concluded Velasco, word ought to be sent to the Philippines warning the authorities of Drake's likely arrival, barring the possibility of him having found a northern strait to the Atlantic.

The futility of the pursuit notwithstanding, Robles did not give up in his attempts to turn it into an event during which merit had been earned. In the autumn of 1582, by now in the function of *oidor* on Mexico's audiencia, he received the *información de merítos y servicios* of his own son.[68] In his list of qualities and merits, Felix de Robles mentions his role as deputy captain general and *alférez general* (staff officer), along with his expenses for maintaining the soldiers. Neither his personal statement nor the witnesses to it mention the actual pursuit. While the latter confirm the self-image that Felix de Robles sketched of himself as a capable man of virtue, fit for either a military or an administrative office, they knew little more than that he had held the said offices. Several years later the elder Robles also oversaw the assessment of Carlos de Luna y Arellano. Sharing the supposed merit this time, Luna y Arellano recorded his role in assembling the 200 men that Robles had taken to Acapulco, an act through which he had fulfilled his responsibilities as a "great caballero."[69] Except for these few cases, the archive remains silent about others having served the Crown during these events. Despite the hopes that Drake's arrival had elicited among New Spain's elite, in the end only minor merits were earned by a few for their alleged roles in his pursuit.

Things were even worse in 1587, when the English privateer Thomas Cavendish appeared near New Spain's western coast. On this occasion, the self-fashioning of one of the protagonists prior to the events themselves directly impacted the dramatic outcome of the latter. Like his predecessor, Viceroy Villamanrique decided to put a *letrado* (literally man of letters; usually a lawyer or judge) in charge of this pursuit.[70] His choice fell on Diego García de Palacio, whose career had taken a high arc since the time he had proposed his plan to conquer China. To reward him for his many years of service, the king appointed him to the position of criminal prosecutor in Mexico City in May 1578.[71] Even before he departed from Guatemala to take up his new office, he had already been

---

[68] Información de los méritos y servicios of Félix Robles, Oct 20, 1582, AGI, Patronato, 77, N.1, R.15.

[69] Información de calidad, méritos y servicios of the mariscal Carlos de Luna y Arellano, Mar 10, 1585, AGI, Patronato, 78b, N.2, R.4.

[70] Instructions for Diego García de Palacio, Sept 10, 1587, AGI, Patronato, 265, R.49.

[71] Consultation Council of the Indies, Apr 11, 1578, AGI, Indiferente General, 739, N.63.

promoted to *oidor*.[72] After his arrival in the capital in 1580, he acquired a doctorate from the Real Universidad de México and, shortly thereafter, was elected its rector. His rapid social ascent in New Spain made Palacio some enemies, however, and during a 1586 *visita* (extraordinary performance review) accusations of corruption and abuse of powers were brought against him, costing him his position on the audiencia.[73]

Attempting to put his derailed career back on track, García de Palacio sought to obtain a position as captain general of the galleons heading for the Philippines. To convince others that he possessed the qualifications for such a job, he published a nautical manual, entitled *Instrucción nauthica* (Nautical Instruction), in Mexico in 1587. Providing an introduction to nautical astronomy, navigation, shipbuilding, rigging, crew composition, and naval tactics, this treatise played a similar role in García de Palacio's self-fashioning as the *Suma de geographia* had for Martín Fernández de Enciso, each using his text to present himself as an expert in navigation. This was not the first time that García de Palacio had used his learning to present himself as someone fit for specific responsibilities. When he had presented his plan for the conquest of China, he also sought to dissipate any doubts regarding his knowledge of military activities by sending the king a military manual. With this work he had hoped to show that "natural inclinations" had forced him to familiarize himself with the art of war and that he possessed the "required qualities for such an office."[74] Printed in Mexico in 1583, the *Diálogos militares* (Military Dialogues) also presented García de Palacio's stance in the ongoing controversies about the value of blood and service in the distribution of royal favor, as he concurred with New Spain's viceroys that an individual's personal virtue was what substantiated the noble qualities of his ancestors.[75] Experienced in pleasing his audience at the viceregal court, the *Instrucción* helped him to publicly present his skills and knowledge. In fact, Villamanrique was so impressed that he felt justified in replacing don Cristóbal de Cárdenas y Mendoza, whom the governor of Panama had put in charge of the pursuit of Cavendish, with García de Palacio,

---

[72] Informaciones de oficio y parte: Diego García de Palacios, Dec 22, 1580, AGI, México, 215, N.24, f. 2v; Othón Arróniz, *El despertar científico en América: la vida de Diego García de Palacio* (Mexico City: Universidad Autónoma Metropolitana, 1980), 89–92.

[73] Edmundo O'Gorman, "Nuevos datos sobre el Dr. Diego García de Palacio," *Boletín del Archivo General de la Nación* XVII, no. 1 (1946): 3–31.

[74] AGI, Patronato, 24, R. 47, doc. 3.

[75] Diego Garcia de Palacio, *Diálogos militares* (Madrid: Ediciones Cultura Hispanica, 1944 [1583]), f. 37v.

characterizing him as "very eloquent and intelligent in matters related to war on sea and on land."[76]

This decision could not have turned out any worse. After Cavendish had terrorized South American coasts for several months, Spanish authorities in New Spain had had more than enough time to prepare a fleet to chase the English privateers. But the squabbles over appointments resulted in costly delays that allowed them to hide out on an island north of Mazatlán, waiting undisturbed for an unsuspecting galleon to arrive from the Philippines. When Cavendish's men spotted the *Santa Ana* on November 4, 1587, the heavily loaded and unprotected vessel was a sitting duck.[77] To the horror of Mexico's merchant elite, Cavendish escaped with an impressive treasure, comprising Asian silks and merchandise as well as 122,000 pesos in gold. Meanwhile, García de Palacio barely made it thirty leagues out of port. Whereas Villamanrique blamed this debacle on particularly strong western winds, others criticized him for appointing García de Palacio.[78] Although personal animosity and political posturing likely played a role in their accusations, it was not the first time something like this had occurred to the lettered captain. In 1579, the president of Guatemala's audiencia, don Diego García de Valverde, reported to the king how he had put García de Palacio in charge of the pursuit of Drake. However, no sooner had García de Palacio received orders to begin the chase than he claimed to have fallen ill. Considering the illness but a mere excuse, García de Valverde ridiculed García de Palacio's book about the art of warfare at sea and on land, noting cynically that "in serving Your Majesty to say and to do are not the same thing."[79]

Valverde's criticism and Diego de García's failure, twice, to give serious chase to the English pirates, provide a constructive counterweight to critiques blaming the descendants of the conquistadores and first settlers for making absurd claims of entitlement. Newcomers, too, relied on excessive self-fashioning when they sought to prove their worthiness for

[76] Letter from Viceroy Villamanrique to the King, Oct 28, 1587, in Arróniz, *El despertar científico en América*, 179.

[77] Report from Thomas de Alzola, captain of the Santa Ana, about the ship being captured by English pirates, AGI, Patronato, 265, R.51; Lytle Schurz, *The Manila Galleon*, 47; Gerhard, *Pirates of the Pacific*, 89–94.

[78] Letter from Viceroy Villamanrique, Jan 15, 1588, AGI, México, 21, N.35. Notes contesting the memorial of the Marquis of Villamanrique, 1592," in Hanke, *Los virreyes*, 1: 313.

[79] Manuel Rubio Sánchez, *Historia del Puerto de la Santísima Trinidad de Sonsonate o Acajulta* (San Salvador: Editorial Universitaria, 1977), 33–34.

an office in the places where they had arrived. The Robles did so through the common practice of exalting journeys and services that were of little actual value, whereas Garcia de Palacio's book publishing had helped him to gain public recognition for certain skills he had, even if he was not much on putting them into practice. Such acts of self-fashioning helped them to influence assessments and improve their position in the changing hierarchy of the meritorious. Although the pursuit of pirates during the 1570s and 1580s turned out to be of little use, the possibilities for earning merit in the Pacific did actually improve after the capture of the *Santa Ana*. Not only did some benefit from the opportunities brought by new colonizing projects but also, increasingly, from the Court's new practice of rewarding people with more desirable offices for services rendered somewhere else in the empire.

MEN OF MERIT IN THE SOUTH SEA

The loss of the *Santa Ana* taught viceregal authorities an important lesson. In order to prevent other ships from suffering a similar fate, Spaniards had to become more active in the regions that they had abandoned since the 1540s. A first step toward this goal was taken in 1582, when Viceroy Lorenzo Suárez de Mendoza (1580–84) ordered Francisco Gali to find a better return route from the Philippines, map the California coast, and search for the Strait of Anian – a presumed passageway in the Pacific Northwest that had become the subject of much speculation in the wake of Drake's Pacific voyage.[80] Plagued by misfortune, the expedition yielded few results. A second attempt followed in 1596, when Viceroy Velasco instructed the Portuguese pilot Sebastián Rodríguez Cermeño to continue mapping the coasts of today's California and find a maritime route that could speed up interactions between New Spain and the new colonies in New Mexico.[81] In the following years, interest in the

---

[80] The history of ideas about this strait is covered in: Martín Fernández de Navarrete, Relación de Lorenzo Maldonado sobre el descubrimiento del Estrecho de Anian, 1800, RAH, 11-3-1-8234, doc. 25; Godfrey Sykes, "The Mythical Straits of Anian," *Bulletin of the American Geographical Society* 47, no. 3 (1915): 161–72; Brenden Rensink, "'If a Passage Could Be Found': The Power of Myth (and Money) in North American Exploration," *We Proceed On* 36, no. 2 (2010): 8–17; Barry M. Gough, *Juan de Fuca's Strait: Voyages in the Waterway of Forgotten Dreams* (Madeira Park: Harbour Publishing, 2012).

[81] Dora Polk, *The Island of California: A History of the Myth* (Lincoln: University of Nebraska Press, 1995), 243.

northwestern Pacific grew further, mainly as a result of the discovery of pearl oyster beds off the California coast and a long-running debate about the creation of new settlements along the route between Manila and Acapulco.[82]

In their efforts to resolve the geostrategic questions raised by transpacific trade, New Spain's viceroys collaborated with pilots, clergymen, and a series of entrepreneurs interested in exploiting the pearl beds. Most of these men were newcomers to the Indies, who hoped to benefit from the widespread lack of interest in the region among New Spain's population, were few appeared to have been willing to risk the personal costs involved in colonizing regions that had once turned out to be useless. In their negotiations with royal authorities and the Crown over *capitulaciones*, these new men deployed familiar strategies. Via letters, maps, and bureaucratic procedures, they showed their skills, knowledge of the region, and earlier services to demonstrate that they were worthy of the responsibilities that came with colonization of the region.[83] But their self-fashioning was not only meant to get royal approval for developing activities in the Pacific, as some tried to gain a foothold in the center of New Spain as well.

Few of them were as successful in doing so as Sebastían Vizcaíno. A native of Extremadura and self-proclaimed nobleman, Vizcaíno had been a crew member of the *Santa Ana* when Cavendish seized the vessel.[84] This harrowing experience did not, however, deter him from staying active in the waters of the Pacific during the following three decades. Enjoying the confidence of Viceroy Velasco and his successor, the Count of Monterrey, Vizcaíno would quickly become one of the most active Spaniards in the Pacific – a fact he never forgot to mention when

---

[82] Spate, *The Spanish Lake*, 111–15; W. Michael Mathes, *Vizcaino and Spanish Expansion in the Pacific Ocean, 1580–1630* (San Francisco: California Historical Society, 1968); León-Portilla, *Cartografía*, 79–102.

[83] An example of the knowledge about the Pacific produced during these negotiations can be found in Nicolás de Cardona, *Descripciones geográficas e hidrográficas de muchas tierras y mares del norte y sur, en las Indias, en especial del descubrimiento del Reino de California*, ed. Pilar Hernández Aparicio (Madrid: Turner, 1989 [1632]).

[84] In his 1603 petition, Vizcaíno described himself somewhat bewilderingly as "a *caballero de cuantía* (non-noble mounted warrior), hijodalgo and [man of] notorious calidad." Información de oficio: Sebastían de Vizcaíno, Oct 1, 1603, AGI, Patronato, 30, R.1, image 11. We do not know with certainty whether any of these claims were true. However, several years prior, in 1597, when the family tried to prove his son's nobility to keep him out of jail, they presented documentary proof confirming the noble status of his wife. Letter of confirmation of nobility, 1597, Library of Congress, HT653.M6 V5 1600.

communicating with the Crown. In an *información de parte y oficio* presented to Mexico's audiencia in 1603, for example, he listed his various feats in support of his request for encomiendas, judicial or military offices, and habits of the military orders for himself and his sons.[85] The services rendered to that moment included his leading role in the colonization of Baja California in 1593, his pursuit of the three English ships sighted by Indian fishermen in Mazatlán in 1597, and the explorative voyage along the American west coast in 1602.[86]

Although the audiencia considered it appropriate to reward these services with a naval or military office, Vizcaíno would have to wait several years before he could enjoy the fruits of his work. The cause of this delay was the appointment of the Marquis of Montesclaros as viceroy of New Spain. Although his predecessor promised Vizcaíno the position as captain general of the Manila galleons, Montesclaros preferred to pick his own candidate. Frustrated in his ambitions by the viceroy's favoring of his own clients, Vizacaíno returned to Spain to force a royal intervention. During this stay, he reiterated his various services, emphasizing this time his role in the discovery of the bay of Monterrey in 1602. This strategic decision to present himself as a discoverer paid off, because he was rewarded the encomienda of the province of Ávalos (current-day state of Jalisco) in 1607.[87] By acquiring an encomienda grant, he achieved a feat of which many descendants of the conquistadores and first settlers had been dreaming. But that was not all. The Crown also decided that, because of his experience, Vizcaíno should be put in charge of the search for the Islas Rica de Oro y Rica de Plata, which were supposed to be located somewhere between Japan and the California coast. This commission was the first of several that would bring Vizcaíno to the Philippines, Japan, and Salagua, where he fought the Dutch corsair Joris van Spilbergen in 1615.

Due to his long career in the Pacific, Sebastian Vizcaíno was able to establish himself in New Spanish society. Although his actual achievements were relatively small, he demonstrated how showcasing one's mobility in this region could be useful to one's social ascent. The number of newcomers hoping to achieve a similar result grew considerably during these three decades. Most of these men spent less time in the Pacific Basin than Vizcaíno had but, like him, benefited from the Crown's practice of promoting officials and officers serving along the empire's frontiers. Some

---

[85] AGI, Patronato, 30, R.1, image 11.   [86] Gerhard, *Pirates of the Pacific*, 96.
[87] Vizcaíno to King, Dec 3, 1607, AGI, México, 27, N.18, images 43–46.

of them continued their careers in New Spain, as with Pedro de Rojas, Antonio de Morga, and Hernando de Mújica, while others, like Luis Fernández de Córdoba y Arce and Sebastían Hurtado de Corcuera, did so in Peru, Chile, Panama, or the Canary Islands.[88] They were men who traveled to the "end of the world," as one governor of the Philippines put it in 1621, with the hope that "after three years they could enter honorable or profitable offices."[89] This route to social ascendence was not an easy one, however. In addition to the long and dangerous journeys and the inhospitable environments these men encountered in Asia, the actual rewards for these hardships were not always as good as expected. Distance and danger could not always make up for the petitioners' lack of social status or connections.

Illustrative of these difficulties are the experiences of Rodrigo de Vivero y Aberruza, one of the few members of New Spain's *encomendero* elite who accepted a position in the Philippines. Vivero was born in Tecamachalco, Puebla, in 1564, the son of don Rodrigo de Vivero y Aberruza, a cousin of New Spain's second viceroy, Luis de Velasco, and doña Melchora de Aberruza, widow of the late conquistador and *encomendero* Alonso Valiente.[90] In his early teens, Vivero traveled to the Spanish court, where he served as a page and servant to Queen Ana.[91]

---

[88] Royal provision granting to Pedro de Rojas the office of alcalde del crimen of the Audiencia of Mexico, Apr 6, 1593, AGI, México, 1092, L.14, ff. 114r–115v; Petition by Antonio de Morga for a position on the Audiencia of Mexico or Peru, Jul 1, 1598, AGI, Filipinas, 18B, R.8, N.98; Consultation about a *merced* for Antonio de Morga, Jun 20, 1602, AGI, Filipinas, 1, N.43; Petition by Hernando de Mújica for an office in Guadalajara, Oct 3, 1615, Filipinas, 37, N.15; Royal provision giving title of royal accountant in Guadalajara, Apr 23, 1616, AGI, Indiferente, 450, L.A4, ff. 132–133v. On the career of the infamous Sebastián Hurtado de Corcuera, who was convicted on 45 of 49 charges during his residencia but, after having been acquitted by the Council of the Indies, nevertheless received the governorship of the Canary Islands, see: Nuria González Alonso, "Sebastián Hurtado de Corcuera: Gobernador de Panamá y de Filipinas," *Anales del Museo de América* 20 (2012): 199–218; William J. McCarthy, "Cashiering the Last Conquistador: The Juicio de Residencia of Don Sebastián Hurtado de Corcuera, 1635-1644," *Colonial Latin American Historical Review* 18, no. 1 (2013): 35–61.

[89] Letter from Fajardo de Tenza, Dec 10, 1621, AGI, Filipinas, 7, R.5, N.65, f. 9.

[90] For a more detailed discussion of Vivero's family, see: Juan Gil, "Don Rodrigo de Vivero. Un criollo en Filipinas y Japon," in *El Mar del Sur en la historia: ciencia, expansión, representación y poder en el Pacífico*, eds. Rafael Sagredo Baeza and Rodrigo Moreno Jeria (Santiago de Chile: Universidad Adolfo Ibáñez, 2014), 65–70.

[91] Vivero started referring to this service only in 1598, after having omitted it in earlier petitions brought before the viceregal authorities. Witnesses asked to verify his claims could not confirm the exact duration of his stay at the court, though. *Información de méritos y servicios*, AGI, México, 218, N.25, images 20–68.

Once he returned to New Spain in 1581, he joined his uncle, Luis de Velasco, son of the former viceroy, to fight against the Chichimecas. When preparations for the pursuit of Cavendish began, he also traveled to Acapulco.[92] Shortly thereafter, he married doña Leonor de Ircio y Mendoza, granddaughter of the notorious conquistador Martín de Ircio, which helped him to establish another indirect bond with the conquistadores.[93]

His social status and readiness to serve the Crown notwithstanding, Vivero had a hard time convincing viceregal authorities to make use of his services. In fact, in 1588 Mexico's audiencia was unwilling to give a positive recommendation to the Crown after having heard witnesses on a petition he submitted.[94] Vivero's luck changed, however, when his uncle was appointed viceroy of New Spain in 1589. Two years later, Velasco bestowed on his nephew the position of *alcalde mayor* in Michoacán and castellan of San Juan de Ulua in 1595. In this position, Vivero attracted the attention of the Council of the Indies, which considered him a possible candidate for the position of governor of Cuba in 1597. The king decided otherwise, though, appointing him first as *alcalde mayor* of the mines of Taxco and, later, as governor of New Biscay.[95]

After having resigned from the latter position in 1602, Vivero's career stagnated. A 1604 petition to Mexico's audiencia was successful but the Crown did not follow up on the *oidores'* recommendation for "any kind of legal or military offer that becomes available in these parts" and an encomienda with an annual tribute of 4,000–5,000 pesos.[96] Once again it was Velasco, having returned as viceroy in 1607, who had to come to Vivero's help. When his first candidate for the position of interim governor of the Philippines declined, Velasco turned to his nephew. Vivero grasped the chance offered to him eagerly and served a nine-month stint in Manila. On September 30, 1609, shortly after having initiated his return voyage, Vivero became shipwrecked on the Japanese coast.

---

[92] José Ignacio Conde y Díaz-Rubín and Javier Sanchiz Ruiz, *Historia genealógica de los títulos y dignidades nobiliarias en Nueva España y México: Casa de Austria (siglos XVI-XVII)* (Mexico City: Universidad Nacional Autónoma de México, Instituto de Investigaciones Históricas, 2012), 2: 26.

[93] It is because of this marriage that Dorantes de Carranza mentions Rodrigo de Vivero as one of the grandsons of the conquistador Martín de Ircio, whose family, in his opinion, deserved the most important positions in the viceroyalty. Dorantes Carranza, *Sumaria relación*, 187–88.

[94] AGI, Mexico, 219, N.5, images 1–21.

[95] Conde y Díaz-Rubín and Sanchiz Ruiz, *Historia genealógica*, 26–27.

[96] AGI, Mexico, 218, N.25, Image 75.

Many lives and fortunes were lost in the disaster, but once Vivero and his men had been brought before the Japanese authorities, he saw a possibility to turn his bad luck into something positive.[97]

Thrown on the coast of present-day Chiba, Vivero and the other survivors were brought to Iwawada, from which notice of their arrival was sent to the lord of Otaki.[98] In the latter's company, Vivero traveled to Edo, where he stayed in a Franciscan convent and had an audience with "the prince," the second shogun, Tokugawa Hidetada. After his meeting with Hidetada, he traveled to Sunpu to meet the "emperor," the retired shogun, Tokugawa Ieyasu. According to Vivero's own accounts, both rulers received him well, and he used their benevolence to discuss proposals for collaboration.[99] He asked the two rulers to grant the Spanish Mendicant Orders the right to preach in their realm, establish friendly relationships with the Spanish monarch, and expel the Dutch. The historian Juan Gil has argued that these requests betray the influence of the Franciscan friars who accompanied Vivero during part of his journey and who had been seeking ways to increase their influence for some time.[100] These talks gave occasion to the short-lived rapprochement between Japan and the viceroyalty.[101]

Four years later, Vivero used the arrival of the Japanese embassy to Mexico, led by Hasekura Rokuemon Tsunenaga, as a pretext to petition viceregal authorities to extend the grant for the encomienda of Tecamachalco in perpetuity or else for at least four lifetimes – a request that the viceregal authorities came to support.[102] In his petition, he

---

[97] In all, fifty-six people drowned in the disaster, while two million pesos worth of goods was lost, including a "large bed ... and some diamonds and rubies, with a total value of hundred thousand ducats" that were Vivero's. "Segunda relación," in Juan Gil, *Hidalgos y samuráis: España y Japón en los siglos XVI y XVII* (Madrid: Alianza editorial, 1991), 194.

[98] Gil Fernández explores Vivero's stay in Japan and his plans to establish connections with New Spain in, *Hidalgos y samuráis*, chapter 2. See also, Lothar Knauth, *Confrontación transpacífica: el Japón y el Nuevo Mundo hispánico, 1542–1639* (Mexico City: UNAM, Instituto de Investigaciones Históricas, 1972), 190–97; Mathes, *Vizcaíno*, 121–34.

[99] "Primera relación," in Gil, *Hidalgos y samuráis*, 171–77.

[100] Gil, "Don Rodrigo de Vivero," 97–102.

[101] For a more detailed study of these negotiations and the history of Japanese–Philippine relationships at the turn of the sixteenth century, see Ubaldo Iaccarino, *Comercio y diplomacia entre Japón y Filipinas en la era Keichō (1596–1615)* (Wiesbaden: Harrassowitz Verlag, 2017), 189–203.

[102] Letter from Marquis of Guadalcázar with petition by Rodrigo de Vivero, May 22, 1614, AGI, México, 28, N.18. Conde y Díaz-Rubín and Sanchiz Ruiz, *Historia genealógica*, 29. On the reception of Tsunenaga's embassy in Mexico, see Miguel León-Portilla, "La embajada de los japoneses en México, 1614. El testimonio en Náhuatl del cronista Chimalpahin," Estudios de asia y África XVI, no. 2 (1981): 215–41.

fashioned an image of himself as the perfect *benemérito*, worthy of, in the words of Viceroy Diego Fernández de Córdoba (1612–21), Marquis of Guadalcázar, "a presidency or government of importance." Most attention was paid to his social status and family relations, as well as the services that had been documented in an earlier *información de parte y oficio*.[103] The brief summary of these services highlighted his role in the wars against the *Chichimecas*, especially in the crushing of the rebellion of the *Acaxes*.[104] His activities in Asia, in turn, appeared more as a side note. The viceroy's recommendation and Vivero's summary of his services both mentioned him serving as interim governor of the Philippines, and Vivero briefly referred to his role in a trading deal with the Japanese. It is surprising that not more effort was made to use the arrival of the Japanese to highlight his services in Japan.

The petition reveals that the value ascribed to the journey across the Pacific, the suffering that this had caused Vivero, and the services he had tried to render in Japan was relatively limited at this time. Two circumstances could have played a role here. On the one hand, as captain general of the galleon fleet, Vivero was partly responsible for the disastrous voyage – and with so little time having passed, there was no need to remind others of the loss of life and wealth – though some years later Vivero would be able to exploit his suffering in the shipwreck.[105] On the other hand, it was not so clear whether his efforts to negotiate direct relations between New Spain and Japan would actually have been considered a service to the Crown. Not only did the Jesuits in Japan fiercely oppose such a plan, so did the authorities in Manila, the Portuguese, and even some Spanish captains.[106] In the context of this polemic, the question arose of whether Vivero had not actually overstepped his authority. Finally, it did not help that the Japanese embassy inspired a great deal of antagonism. The journey certainly did not lead to an automatic promotion; for that Vivero had to wait almost another decade, many of which were spent at the court.

Each of the men we have come across here experienced the Pacific world differently, and the ways in which they used these experiences to

---

[103] Información de parte y oficio of Rodrigo de Vivero, Jan 22, 1587, AGI, México, 218, N.25.

[104] AGI, México, 28, N.18, Image 4–5.

[105] Letter Vivero, Panama, Jun 30, 1624, AGI, Panamá, 17, R.8, N.144.

[106] For an extensive discussion of the opposition against the project of establishing direct trading connections between Japan and New Spain, see Gil, *Hidalgos y samurais*, 226–51; Iaccarino, *Comercio y diplomacia*, 255–83.

fashion a deserving self varied accordingly. Still, it is possible to distinguish some patterns in the ways they presented themselves: facing the challenge of making up for lack of social status, connections, or ties to the land, they traveled into the Pacific to gain symbolic capital to renegotiate their rank in the hierarchy of the meritorious. Some benefited from this improved position by landing positions or rewards in New Spain, whereas others continued their quests, always looking for something better.

A PLEA AGAINST MOBILITY

Historians have long recognized the impact of newcomers from the Peninsula on existing struggles over the distribution of benefits in New Spain.[107] Indeed, struggles between newcomers and the descendants of the conquistadores and settlers played an important role in shaping narratives about the emergence of a creole subjectivity. Ideas often seen as evocations of such an identity betray the latter's efforts to defend their position in the hierarchy of the meritorious in an increasingly mobile world. The most common motif, of course, was the claim that people born in a specific kingdom should enjoy its benefits, especially when their ancestors had conquered and settled it. But equally important were views about undesired newcomers taking places that ought to have been reserved for locals.[108] In this vein, scholars have often cited Baltasar Dorantes de Carranza's rants against the *advenedizos*, as newcomers were known, as well as their excessive self-fashioning and role in corrupting government.[109]

Undoubtedly, these distributive struggles produced a clear sense of a deserving self and an undeserving other – an American-born creole deserved New Spain's benefits more than a mobile newcomer. Problems arise, however, when we turn this strategically produced dichotomy into

---

[107] Brading, *The First America*, 305, 316–17; Bacigalupo, *A Changing Perspective*, 128–29.

[108] See, for instance, the late sixteenth–century epic poem *Nuevo Mundo y conquista* in which Francisco de Terrazas, son of a conquistador going by the same name, lamented that when it came to rewarding the descendants of the conquistadores the laws were not observed. Francisco de Terrazas, *Poesías*, ed. Antonio Castro (Mexico City: Porrúa, 1941), 84–85. An explicit discussion about the New Laws and the promises they made to the descendants of the conquistadores and *pobladores* can also be found in Dorantes de Carranza, *Sumaria relación*, 222–24.

[109] Dorantes de Carranza underscores the points he seeks to make with fragments from the work of the satirical poet Rosas de Oquendo. Dorantes de Carranza, *Sumaria relación*, 135–38.

something absolute, which obscures the fact that the hierarchy of merit was defined by multiple factors, often addressed separately by individuals as they sought to prove why they more than others were worthy of royal favors. It also shrouds how, in so doing, both creoles and Peninsulars constantly sought to find a balance between rootedness and mobility in ways that benefited their claims in specific circumstances. In order to get a better understanding of these dynamics, let us return to Rodrigo de Vivero and a text he wrote toward the end of his life, known today as *Abisos y proyectos para el buen gobierno de la monarchía Española* (Notices and Projects for the Good Government of the Spanish Monarchy).

Vivero probably wrote his text between 1629 and 1636, after he had served for almost eight years as governor of Panama. His Panamanian years had been hard on him. As he wrote to readers, "with so many merits gained and so much time lost in Spain, in the Mexican Indies (*Indias mexicanas*), in China, in Japan," in Panama "I saw myself buried and all my hopes lost."[110] This time his suffering was not entirely in vain, however. Having badgered the Crown for five years, in 1627 he received the titles of Viscount of San Miguel and Count of the Valley of Orizaba.[111] Vivero was ecstatic about his promotion and soon thereafter returned to New Spain. But upon his arrival he faced a challenge of a different nature, as the Marquis of Cerralbo reported. Life in the viceregal capital was expensive, and Vivero lacked the means to sustain a lifestyle suitable for a man of his standing. As a result, Vivero was forced to retire to his home in Tecamachalco.[112]

Impoverished and once more removed from the center of power, Vivero, at the age of 65, did not yet think of retirement from the royal service. On the contrary, as Viceroy Cerralbo explained to the king, the count could be an important asset to himself and the Crown, because of his many years of experience. Not only did he lament the fact that Vivero had left the capital and could not serve his as advisor; he also suggested employing him as president of the audiencia of Guadalajara when this

---

[110] Monbeig, *Du Japon et du bon gouvernement*, 51.

[111] For these petitions, see: AGI, Panama,17, R.6, N.94; AGI, Panama, 17, R.7, N.13; AGI, Panama, 31, N.1; AGI, Panamá, 17, R.8, N.144 AGI, Panamá, R.1, N.9. Royal provision granting the title of Viscount of San Miguel to don Rodrigo de Vivero, Feb 14, 1627, AGI, Indiferente, 451, L.A10, ff. 68–69v; Royal provision granting the title of Count of the Valley of Orizaba to don Rodrigo de Vivero, Feb 14, 1627, AGI, Indiferente, 451, L.A10, ff. 97v–98.

[112] Gil, "Don Rodrigo de Vivero," 123.

position became vacant.[113] Such ideas may have inspired Vivero to start writing again. He had done so before, trying twice to write about his experiences in Japan.[114] But this time, he decided not to recount his own journeys but to use his experiences to reflect upon mobility instead. Finding inspiration in the works of Spanish *arbitristas* (writers proposing policy solutions for social and economic problems), such as Pedro Fernández de Navarrete and Manuel Gaytan de Torres, he presented himself, as the historian Serge Gruzinski has argued, as an imperial expert who, due to his mobility, had the capacity to think about the world and the Spanish empire as a larger union of interdependent zones and, consequently, propose a wide range of solutions to reshape these connections and manage the empire in the most efficient way.[115]

Several of these proposals were concerned with the mobility of officials and soldiers in the Spanish empire in general and the Pacific in particular. The first issue he addressed in the *Abisos* was the practice of rewarding services with offices.[116] The Crown should stop using offices as rewards, Vivero contended, because too often people were given positions for which they were either unfit or that brought them to places of which they had no knowledge. He also noted that a system that required people to petition for offices was inherently flawed and typically led to excesses. Petitioners who traveled to the court contributed nothing and impoverished themselves as they waited for their petitions to be processed. Furthermore, the difficulty in honoring all claims equitably resulted in protests against the viceroys, which damaged their and the king's reputations. Vivero's proposal for changing this practice was twofold. He suggested that, instead of offices, the Crown should grant pensions and

---

[113] Ibid. Cerralbo still consulted Vivero, even when he was in Orizaba. In 1631, for example, he gave a statement in the context of the hearings about the desirability of the exploration and subsequent colonization of California. Although Vivero had never been there, information he received from other sources regarding the region was nonetheless valued. AGI, Patronato, 30, R.2. This document has been translated in W. Michael Mathes, *Spanish Approaches to the Island of California, 1628–1632* (San Francisco: The Book Club of California, 1975), 45–49.

[114] The "Primera relación," and "Segunda relación" have both been printed in Gil, *Hidalgos y samurais*, 171–77, 192–207.

[115] Gruzinski, *Las cuatro partes del mundo*, 264–65, 289–98. *Arbitrista* writing took different forms but had as a common threat the authors' concern with the decline of Spain's economy and the solutions to reverse such a trend. On the impact of *arbitrista* thinking on the *Abisos*, see Monbeig, *Du Japon et du bon gouvernement*, 34–35, 42–43.

[116] RAH, Colección Muñoz, V.10 (9-4789), f. 58. Vivero, "Abisos y proyectos," 78. A similar argument was made by other descendants of conquistadores. Compare, for example, Dorantes de Carranza, *Sumaria relación*, 105.

memberships to the military orders. At the same time, the monarch should gather knowledge about his worthy subjects in every corner of the empire so that he would then possess a list for each kingdom and province, from which he could pick the most suitable candidates.

To demonstrate the usefulness of his proposed method, Vivero drew on his experiences in Asia. Both the Chinese and the Japanese, the reader learns, applied a similar approach with excellent results, as is shown with the help of an explanation about their procedures for selection of royal officials.[117] Vivero explained how two secretaries selected several appropriate candidates for an office, whom they presented to the king. He then decided who was the best candidate, ordering this person to read the laws and accept the salary earned by their predecessor. Once in office, all royal officials were subjected to secret visits. The punishment for violation of the Crown's orders was death. Impressed by the apparent efficiency of this system and the complete absence of corruption in these lands, Vivero concluded that "[it] may appear confusing to us that people without God [can] demonstrate to us how to keep such precepts."[118]

Although Vivero's use of the Chinese and Japanese as mirrors for reform was unique, his critiques were rather commonplace, as they reflected a well-established discourse that had taken shape since the ascent of the Count-Duke of Olivares to the position of chief minister in 1621.[119] Yet, he deviated from this discourse by introducing his own proposals for the reduction of mobility in New Spain, one of which was concerned with connections between the viceroyalty and the Philippines. Vivero observed that Spanish expansion in Asia had reached its limits, as both China and Japan had turned out to be too powerful to subject. In this light, the decision to maintain the Philippines was, in his eyes, one that had grave consequences for the strength of the empire. During the preceding fifty years, he noted, 50,000 men had died on the islands, while great amounts of silver had been lost to foreign enemies.[120]

---

[117] RAH, Colección Muñoz, V.10 (9–4789), f. 58v; Vivero, "Abisos y proyectos," 79.

[118] Rodrigo de Vivero, "Abisos y proyectos," 80. In the Real Academia manuscript, only "*Nuestra confusion!*" (Our confusion!) is written, without making any reference to the people without God.

[119] The Count-Duque of Olivares himself contributed to the discussion about royal patronage and the necessity to moderate the granting of *mercedes* in his *Memorial de las mercedes* (1621). John H. Elliott, José F. de la Peña, and Fernando Negredo *Memoriales y cartas del Conde Duque de Olivares* (Madrid: Edición Alfaguara, 1978), I: 3–11.

[120] RAH, Colección Muñoz, V.10 (9–4789), f. 73r.; Vivero, "Abisos y proyectos," 104.

To convince the Crown to stop wasting lives and resources on a province that could not maintain itself, he related the story of the Japanese "Emperor Taycosama" – an erroneous reference to Toyotomi Hideyoshi, who was the de facto ruler of Japan but not its actual emperor. Taycosama had been persuaded by some of his captains to assemble a force of 80,000 soldiers to conquer the kingdom of Korea. When, after one year of occupation, it turned out that the land was of no use, he decided to leave. According to Vivero, King Philip IV should do the same with the Philippines. If that was not an option, he should at least consider closing the port of Acapulco because, of the soldiers who passed through New Spain, "half die due to the variety of bad climes, while the other half run away," which served no purpose whatsoever.[121]

Such a trenchant call for the severing of New Spain's connections with the Asian-Pacific region typifies Vivero's vision about the viceroyalty's place in the world. In Chapter 5, this view is discussed in more detail in relation to the question of trade. Here it suffices to note that, rather than celebrating New Spain's role as a pivot in a globalizing world, Vivero urged the Crown to turn New Spain once more into an imperial frontier. Such a position seems remarkable for someone who only two decades earlier had advocated so passionately for the establishment of direct interaction between the viceroyalty and Japan.[122] But in a way this change of mind mirrored the shift in Vivero's attitude toward mobility, as displayed in the *Abisos*.

Having personally traveled in the service of the Crown for a large part of his life and having used these services to negotiate a better position for himself, he now opposed this practice. In fact, he even adopted a defense of the rights of the natives to govern the land in which they had been born. Contrary to earlier creole writers, such as Baltasar Dorantes de Carranza, he even referred to the "criollos of the Indies." "Who," he entreated, "had introduced [this name] with such a poor reputation?" – a reputation that contradicted their well-established role in the conquest of Chile and the Philippines.[123] Creoles differed in no way from the natives of Seville, Cordoba, and Madrid, whose fathers and grandfathers had once come from France or Holland, arriving to their new patria without risking their lives in the service of the king. The creoles of New Spain, on

---

[121] Ibid., 105.

[122] Copy of letter from Rodrigo de Vivero to King, May 3, 1610, AGI, Filipinas, 193, N.3, images 21–29.

[123] RAH, Colección Muñoz, V.10 (9–4789), f. 97; Vivero, "Abisos y proyectos," 121–22.

the contrary, were the sons, grandsons, and descendants of the 500 men who had defeated 800,000 Indians. Among them there were persons of great blood and quality, who deserve grants of land, labor, and haciendas for the services they had rendered in the Indies.

Vivero's observations affirm the growing importance of the category criollo for distributive struggles in New Spain. But they also shed light on his own balancing act of arguing against the mobility of some without discarding the value of his own movements as a source of merit. The latter was, in fact, crucial to the self-image that he had fashioned for his bid for the office of president of an audiencia or possibly even that of viceroy. As he observed in his discussion about such appointments, those in charge of the government should have much experience governing in other places.[124] Mobility, at this level then, remained a qualifier that Vivero consciously used to distinguish himself. After all, few people in New Spain had a similar track record – documented and recognized by the Crown – as he did. On the other hand, by making an argument for the positive effects of putting American creoles in charge of the land in which they had been born, he obviously argued against those persons coming from Europe who lacked experience in the Indies. Rootedness and mobility were both important to his image of a deserving self, each fulfilling a role in explaining why Vivero, from among a certain group of potential candidates, deserved the king's favor the most.

We do not know whether Vivero ever presented this intervention into the contemporary discussions about the connections between mobility, rootedness, and merit. He probably did not, seeing that it was his grandson who brought his papers to Spain, long after Vivero's death in 1636. Still, the *Abisos* provide revealing insights into the importance of these debates and the impact they had on people's perceptions of themselves and the world. Although he embraced being a creole, Vivero saw little reason for celebrating New Spain's integration into a globalizing world. Too many, he believed, were the problems caused by the mobility of royal officials and soldiers. If it were up to Vivero, the Pacific would become the empire's outermost frontier again, while the Spaniards focused their attention on the Atlantic region. Vivero's views were certainly not shared by all inhabitants of New Spain. But among the traditional elite of *encomenderos* and ambitious creoles, with or without direct links to the conquistadores, it was not an exceptional view either. Rather than being a

---

[124] RAH, Colección Muñoz, V.10 (9–4789), f. 58v.; Vivero, "Abisos y proyectos," 78.

space of opportunities, they saw the Pacific as a region where little was to be gained for themselves, while giving others the chance to challenge their privileged positions. The two chapters that follow will examine how the mobilities associated with clergymen and trade added to such sentiments.

What this chapter also has shown is the importance of categories or collective identifiers in distributive struggles. Mobilized in discussions about the distributive process or the social order in general, these markers became the subject of diverging assessments of the worthiness or unworthiness of those identified through them. Descendants of the con-quistadores earned a reputation as unwilling to serve the Crown or criollos being seen as innately unqualified. The significance of these stereotypes increased as they were instrumentalized, forcing those belonging to these groups to address them as they sought to demonstrate their own worthiness. Chapter 4 explores this development in more detail by examining how the category criollo came to be discussed as New Spain developed into a way station on the missionary routes connecting Europe to Asia. The arrival of clergymen traveling to the Philippines fueled the conflict over rootedness and mobility, prompting new demands for regulation of the friars' movements as well as new notions of a deserving self.

4

The Creole

Distributing Royal Patronage on the Westward Religious Itinerary to Asia

Between 1605 and 1617, the Discalced Augustinian friar Rodrigo Aganduru Moriz traveled between Spain and the Philippines on three different occasions. A decade later, writing about his experiences, he recalled that in Mexico City the sun was shining every day of the year, even during the rainy season, when it poured tempestuously but only after vespers. Awed by the land's "unique qualities," he noted that "the heavens appear to have established a pact with the Mexican terrain, so as not to impede itinerants their day's journeys."[1] While Aganduru Moriz created an impression of divine intervention facilitating crossing through the viceroyalty, other travelers reported quite different experiences. Some friars and nuns wrote about the hardships they encountered as they journeyed from Mexico City to Acapulco, a route that took them across steep mountain passes, over rivers, and into mosquito-infested, unbearably hot territory.[2] Others bemoaned being harassed by locals who tried

---

[1] *Crónica que versa sobre la historia geográfica de diversas islas orientales y occidentales, mencionando en sus apartados las Islas Canarias, algunas islas de América, la Nueva España, América del Norte, Sudamérica y Japón.* Undated, BP, R480/004, f. 102r. Aganduru never published this text, though pieces of it made it into Luis de Jesús's *Historia general de los religiosos descalzos del orden de los hermitaños del gran Padre y Doctor de la iglesia de S. Augustin de la Congregación de España y de las Indias* (Madrid, 1681), 2: 78.

[2] See, for example, the experiences described by Sor Ana de Cristo, a Franciscan nun who traveled the China Road between Mexico City and Acapulco in the spring of 1621. Sarah E. Owens, *Nuns Navigating the Spanish Empire* (Albuquerque: University of New Mexico Press, 2017), 64–67. Also worth considering are the writings of the Dominican Domingo Fernández de Navarrete, who had to wait two years in New Spain before he could continue his journey to Manila. Domigo Fernández de Navarrete, *Tratados históricos,*

to prevent any of them, even the sick, from staying in the viceroyalty.[3] The crossing of New Spain clearly was not as pleasant as Aganduru Moriz made it seem. Meanwhile, the opposition travelers encountered suggests that, as the viceroyalty became a way station on the journey from the Iberian Peninsula to Asia, mobility once again became a point of contention.

This chapter examines what affects movement of the clergy along this Asia-bound religious itinerary had on disputes over royal patronage in New Spain. Although they may have had heavenly bliss on their minds, the arrival of friars, secular clergymen, and nuns from the Peninsula more than once fueled existing conflicts and created others. New or more austere branches of the Mendicant Orders suddenly became active in the viceroyalty, which impacted the relationships among the local clergy. The balance of power also shifted within individual monasteries in New Spain, as Peninsular friars who deserted their missions along the way found a new home in them. On the other hand, among those who did make it to Asia there were friars who distinguished themselves in such ways that their feats were deemed worthy of being celebrated by others.[4] All of these developments affected struggles over tribute, novices, and souls, as well as the ways in which individuals negotiated patronage for their projects or personal advancement.

Those involved in these disputes spoke increasingly frequently about the criollo, a social category that became the subject of heated controversies over whether American-born clerics possessed the qualities or not to fulfill sacerdotal duties or administrative positions.[5] Scholars have interpreted the meaning of these debates in varying ways.[6] One influential

---

políticos, éticos y religiosos de la monarchia de China (Madrid: Imprenta Real, por Juan García de Infançon, 1676), 299–301.

[3] Report from Diego Aduarte, Jan 20, 1606, AGI, Filipinas, 79, N.75.

[4] For example, in his history of the Franciscan Provinces of San Pedro and San Pablo of Michoacán, the Franciscan friar Alonso de la Rea praised the Japanese convert Luis de San Francisco, who took the habit in Valladolid (modern-day Morelia) and was martyred in Ōmura, Japan, in 1624. Alonso de la Rea, *Crónica de la orden de N. Seráfico P.S. Francisco, Provincia de S. Pedro y S. Pablo de Mechoacan en la Nueva España*, ed. Patricia Escandón (Zamora: El Colegio de Michoacán, 1996), 213–15.

[5] Scholars believe that etymologically the term *criollo* stems from the Latin word *creare* (to make, to create). It was probably in Brazil were the term *crioulo* was used for the first time to distinguish black slaves born in the Americas from those brought from Africa. Bauer and Mazzotti, "Introduction," 3.

[6] Bacigalupo, *A Changing Perspective*, 69–94; Lavallé, *Las promesas ambiguas*, 63–77; María Alba Pastor, "Criollismo y contrarreforma. Nueva España entre 1570 y 1630," *Ibero-amerikanisches Archiv* 22, no. 3/4 (1996): 247–66; Mark A. Burkholder, *Spaniards*

body of scholarship traces back to these discussions the roots of a "creole patriotism" or "creole epistemology" out of which developed the autonomy movements of the nineteenth century.[7] More recent studies, however, question such readings. Not only have they refuted the idea of the emergence of the identifier criollo being linked to a diminishing loyalty to the Crown but also revealed that criollos often pursued competing theological and political programs.[8] This changing understanding of the creoles' relationship with the Crown and among themselves has led historians to reconsider and downplay the importance contemporaries ascribed to this collective identity as a factor in explaining their actions and solidarities. Still, I contend, the marker criollo did have concrete uses.

While analyzing interactions along the religious itinerary between Spain and Southeast Asia, this chapter considers the criollo as a meaningful category for the distributive struggles taking place in New Spain from the 1570s. I argue that it acquired such a function due to two factors: First, its role in the establishment of hierarchies of worthiness that were based on the belief that place (of origin) was a key factor that engendered certain qualities and talents in people.[9] Second, new laws and practices positively valuing the status of being native or *natural* in Spanish. By examining how friars, secular clergymen, and royal officials encountered and responded to assessments of the Spanish natives of the Indies in connection with movement along the religious itinerary, the chapter draws a new picture of the relationship between the creoles' and the viceroyalty's place in a world of global missions.

ESTABLISHING THE RELIGIOUS ITINERARYS

Until 1565, European clergymen, mostly Jesuits, had traveled to the Far East via the route that Portuguese ships took along the Cape of Good Hope and through the Indian Ocean. Individual clergymen coming from

---

in the Colonial Empire: Creoles vs. Peninsulars? (Malden, MA: Wiley-Blackwell, 2013), 28–58.

[7] Brading, *First America*, 297–300; Alberro, *El águila y la cruz*; Jorge Cañizares-Esguerra, "Racial, Religious, and Civic Creole Identity in Colonial Spanish America," *American Literary History* 17, no. 3 (2005): 420–37.

[8] Conover, *Pious Imperialism*, 83; Alicia Mayer González, "Religious Thought in Carlos de Sigüenza y Góngora (1645–1700): A Mirror of 'criollo' Spirituality in New Spain," *Jahrbuch für Geschichte Lateinamerikas*, no. 43 (2006): 91–118.

[9] On the common belief that individuals and political communities owed their physiologies, characters, customs, and manners to their specific location in the world, see also Wey Gómez, *The Tropics of Empire*, 59–106.

the territories of the Spanish kings traveled this way to Goa, Macao, and beyond. But larger Spanish missions did not take this route.[10] To do so would have required the permission of the Spanish Crown, which had agreed to only exercise its right of patronage (*patronato real*) in the lands west of the demarcation line defined in the Treaty of Tordesillas.[11] This situation changed with the discovery of the route from Asia to the Americas. Transpacific travel allowed the Spanish kings to establish their own churches and monasteries in Asia and facilitate the movement of clerics to the region without violating the agreement with the Portuguese. The first to benefit from these new opportunities were the five Augustinians who came with Miguel López de Legazpi to the Philippines. Having initiated the evangelization of the natives of Cebu, Luzon, and Panay, they established the Province of the Most Holy Name of Jesus of the Philippines and set in motion new forms of mobility between the islands and the court.

Fray Andrés de Urdaneta and Fray Andrés de Aguirre initiated this movement in 1565, when they sailed with Felipe de Salcedo from Cebu to complete the eastern-bound journey across the Pacific.[12] After a brief layover in Mexico, the two friars continued their voyage to present to the king the first results of Legazpi's expedition and request royal support for their mission.[13] In 1572, Fray Diego de Herrera, another of the founders of the Philippine Province, followed their example to ask the king to financially support expansion of the Augustinian mission in East and Southeast Asia, especially in the great kingdom of China.[14] Not only were the three Augustinians the first of their order to complete the long journey between

---

[10] The most famous friar to travel this way was the Navarrese Jesuit Francis Xavier. Between 1541 and 1552, he traveled from Lisbon to Goa, Malacca, the Moluccas, Canton (China), and Kagoshima (Japan), laying the basis for the Jesuit missions in Asia under the Portuguese *Padroado* (royal patronage).

[11] On the *patronato real* or royal authority in ecclesiastical affairs, see John F. Schwaller, *The History of the Catholic Church in Latin America: From Conquest to Revolution and Beyond* (New York: New York University Press, 2011), 35–48.

[12] Gaspar de San Agustín, O.S.A., *Conquistas de las Islas Filipinas (1565–1615)*, ed. Manuel Merino, O.S.A. (Madrid: Consejo Superio de Investigaciones Científicas, 1975), 203–9.

[13] Historians have mainly studied Urdaneta's voyage because of his role in the discussions about the geographical location of the Philippines and the question of whether the Spanish Crown had a legal claim over the islands according to the terms of the existing agreements with the Portuguese. Goodman, *Power and Penury*, 58–65; José Antonio Cervera Jiménez, *Tras el sueño de China: agustinos y dominicos en Asia Oriental a finales del siglo XVI* (Madrid: Plaza y Valdés Editores, 2013), 105–36.

[14] Ollé, *La empresa de China*, 84–86.

the two extremes of the Spanish empire; they also played an important role in the mobilization of others. During their time in New Spain and Spain, they recruited their own brethren and inspired members of other religious orders to become involved in the evangelizing endeavor in Asia. Herrera's stay at the court led, for instance, to the Discalced Franciscans organizing their first mission to the Philippines.[15] Headed by Fray Pedro de Alfaro, this group of fifteen Discalced Franciscans arrived on the islands in the summer of 1576, to lay the foundations for what would become the Franciscan Province of Saint Gregory of the Philippines, in 1586.[16]

The number of clergymen traveling between Spain and the Philippines further increased in the following years. In 1578, two more Augustinian friars traveled back to the court. Fray Fransciso de Ortega went to recruit new friars and petition the Crown for financial assistance, while Jerónimo Marín, son of the conquistador Luis Marín, returned to the Peninsula to report on his and Fray Martin de Rada's journey to China.[17] In 1580, two larger groups made the journey in the opposite direction. The first was made up of eighteen Dominicans led by Fray Domingo de Salazar, whom Pope Gregory XIII had appointed as the first bishop of Manila in 1579 and who now went to establish a new province in the Philippines. A plague outbreak during the Atlantic crossing abruptly ended this project. When Salazar continued his journey at the end of March 1581, he did so in the company of but one other Dominican, as well as 3 Jesuits, 18 Discalced Augustinians, 6 Discalced Franciscans, and 7 clerics.[18] The second group that left Spain in 1580 was made up of 34 Discalced Franciscans, traveling under the guidance of the custodian Miguel de Talavera.[19] Although

---

[15] Letter from Pedro de Alfaro, Jun 3, 1577, AGI, Filipinas, 84, N.7.

[16] Ubaldo Iaccarino, "Early Spanish Intruders in China: The 1579 Mission of Pedro de Alfaro, O.F.M., Reconsidered," *Journal of Jesuit Studies* 9 (2022): 253; Marcelo de Ribadeneira, *Historia de las islas del archipiélago filipino y reinos de la Gran China, Tartaria, Cochinchina, Malaca, Siam, Cambodge y Japón*, ed. Juan R. de Legísima, O.F.M. (Madrid: La editorial católica, 1947), 40–41.

[17] Gaspar de San Agustín noted that Jerónimo Marín was born in Mexico City "to noble parents and conquistadores of these realms." According to Luis Marín's entry in Mendoza's register of *beneméritos*, the conquistador had eleven children, with three of his sons joining the Augustinians. San Agustín, *Conquistas de las Islas Filipinas*, 730; Icaza, *Conquistadores y pobladores*, 1: 5–6.

[18] Lucio Gutiérrez, O.P., *Domingo de Salazar, O.P.: First Bishop of the Philippines, 1512–1594* (Manila: University of Santo Tomas, 2001), 93–96.

[19] Juan González de Mendoza, *Historia de las cosas más notables, ritos y costumbres del gran reino de la China* (Rome: Stampa de Vicentio Accolti, 1585), 343; Ribadeneira, *Historia de las islas del archipiélago filipino*, 53–54.

Talavera never actually traveled beyond New Spain, other members of this mission did make it to the Philippines and even to China.

As more and more friars began traveling along the same route to Asia, a new global imaginary gradually began to take shape. While for a long time there only had been one way to arrive to those parts of Asia that held particular promise for missionary work, now Christians were traveling along two distinct routes.[20] Visions of this new itinerary quickly emerged in reports the clergy produced about their time at sea or during the overland crossing to the Pacific. Although these accounts captured individual experiences, it soon became clear that these were embedded within a shared collective experience. Travelers conveyed an awareness that others were experiencing the same challenges and delights or would experience them once they followed in their footsteps. Indeed, by recording their personal experiences and travails, these friars helped future travelers anticipate what likely awaited them during a journey that simultaneously revealed the wonders of divine creation while also putting their faith to the test.

Few of these accounts had such an impact on the shaping of this new global imaginary as the one written by Martín Ignacio de Loyola and Juan González de Mendoza. Both men rode the wave of excitement that the Augustinian friars Martín de Rada and Jerónimo Marín had set in motion with reports of their 1575 embassy to China.[21] Reading these reports awoke in Loyola a deep desire to visit this kingdom himself.[22] González de Mendoza, in turn, benefited from the decision of the Council of the Indies to establish direct contact with the Chinese, which led to the king appointing him together with the Augustinian friars Ortega and

---

[20] An influential book describing the Portuguese route to China was Bernardino de Escalante's *Discurso de la navegación que los Portugueses hacen a los Reinos y Provincias de Oriente, y de la noticia que se tiene de las grandezas del Reino de la China* (Seville, 1577).

[21] For a discussion of Martín de Rada's journey and the reports he produced, see for example: Dolors Folch, "Biografía de Fray Martín de Rada," *Huarte de San Juan. Geografía e historia*, nr. 15 (2008): 48–61; Cervera Jiménez, *Tras el sueño de China*, 138–73.

[22] On Martín de Ignacio Loyola, see Gruzinski, *Las cuatro partes del mundo*, 283–88; José Luis Salas, O.F.M., *Fray Martín Ignacio de Loyola: "Gran Obispo de esta tierra." Eje del desarrollo humano y cristiano del Paraguay y regiones vecinas* (Asunción: Ediciones y Arte S.R.L., 2003). On the person and career of Juan González de Mendoza: Juan Manuel Pacheco S. J., "Fray Juan González de Mendoza, obispo de Popayán," *Boletín de historia y antigüedades* LIII, nr. 618–20 (1966): 301–18.

Marín as his ambassadors to the Chinese emperor.[23] However, during the early 1580s, both men also felt the effect of the Chinese distrust of the Spaniards. Loyola and his companions did so when they were arrested as spies by Chinese authorities. Meanwhile, González de Mendoza was not even allowed to travel across the Pacific after reports written by the Franciscan friar Pedro de Alfaro about his 1575 voyage to China had painted a bleak picture regarding the chances of the Chinese mission becoming a success.[24]

Loyola and González de Mendoza crossed paths in Rome in 1584, where both had come to seek papal patronage for future evangelizing. At the time, Mendoza was preparing for Pope Gregory XIII his *Historia de las cosas más notables, ritos y costumbres del gran Reyno de la China* (History of the most notable things, rites, and customs of the Great Kingdom of China, Rome, 1585), for which Loyola provided a report that would become its final part. Loyola's text, which became known as the *Itinerario*, offered a detailed description of all the lands that travelers would pass through when journeying from Spain to the Far East and back to Europe via the Cape of Good Hope.[25] By offering a description of both the journey and its final destinations, the text sought to mobilize suitable candidates by inspiring in them the religious zeal necessary to become involved in the hard but honorable work of spreading the faith. Or, as the anonymous author of the prologue to a separate edition of the *Itinerario* published in Lisbon in 1586 put it, the text could "assist those who can and have the talent to realize their objective of being sent, and ... in all those who read it, even those who cannot leave Spain, it will spark the divine love."[26]

---

[23] Diego Sola, *El cronista de China: Juan González de Mendoza, entre la misión, el imperio y la historia* (Barcelona: Universitat de Barcelona, 2018), 108–19.

[24] Letter from Juan González de Mendoza, Oct 6, 1581, AGI, Filipinas, 84, N.20.

[25] In the first printing of the *Historia de las cosas más notables* (Rome, 1585) this part was still called *Ytinerario del padre custodio fray Martín Ignacio, de la orden del bienauenturado Sant Francisco, que paso ala China en compañia de otros religiosos de la misma Orden.* González de Mendoza, *Historia*, 341–440. Later, the title was changed to *Itinerario y epítome de todas las cosas más notables que ay desde España, hasta el Reyno de la China, y de la China a España, boluiendo por la India Oriental.*

[26] Juan González de Mendoza, *Itinerario y compendio de las cosas notables que ay desde España, hasta el Reyno de la China, y de la China à España, boluiendo por la India Oriental, despues de auer dado buelta, à casi todo el Mundo: En el qual se trata de los ritos, cerimonias, y costumbres de la gente que en todo el ay, y dela riqueza, fertilidad, y fortaleza de muchos Reynos, y la descripción de todos* (Lisbon: S. Phelippe el Real, 1586), f. 4.

Wide dissemination of the *Itinerario*, both through countless reprints and translations of González de Mendoza's *Historia* and stand-alone editions, bolstered the global religious imaginary with its two increasingly standardized itineraries.[27] It became a prism through which Christians viewed the world and considered their own involvement in the spreading of God's word in the newly established religious provinces in the Far East or Far West, depending on which direction one was traveling.[28] During the following centuries, friars, nuns, and clerics would continue to travel the new route that now had been opened, producing their own descriptions of the itinerary, weaving together individual and common experiences into a recognizable story about the journey halfway around the world that each had to master to contribute toward the apostolic mission in Asia.[29]

As a region that had to be crossed between the two transoceanic voyages, New Spain came to make up an important part of this global imaginary. Like the oceanic voyages, the overland crossing of the viceroyalty came with its own challenges and opportunities created by the climes and terrain as well as the kingdom's complex political and ecclesiastical landscape. The following sections explore how the institutional development of the religious itinerary impacted relationships among the clergy in New Spain and how these interactions, in turn, shaped perceptions of the religious itinerary itself.

CLASHING INTERESTS ALONG THE ITINERARY

When European friars began crossing New Spain on their way to Asia, the New Spanish Church was passing through a phase of upheaval. After half a century during which the mendicants had been expanding their dominance in the viceroyalty's urban centers through alliances with local rulers, friars began experiencing difficulties in maintaining their control over Indigenous populations and the resources they produced. Turf wars

---

[27] The *Historia* became a true bestseller of its time. An overview of the many reprints and translations can be found in Sola, *El cronista de China*, 263–67.

[28] Padrón, *The Indies of the Setting Sun*.

[29] Some travel accounts and descriptions of the world written by missionaries in which this influence becomes visible are Sor Ana de Cristo's unpublished travelog, Rodrigo Aganduru Moriz's geographical descriptions, or the detailed description that Domingo Fernandez Navarrete included in his history of China. See Owens, *Nuns Navigating the Spanish Empire*; BP, R480/004, ff. 98r.–111r.; Fernandez Navarrete, *Tratados históricos*, 289–411.

with the secular clergy and conflicts with Native elites led to bitter and, occasionally, violent disputes.[30] The arrival of the traveling friars fueled these tensions. What caused these problems was not their mobility as such, as travel accounts testify to the warm welcome that friars and nuns coming from the Peninsula often received as they crossed New Spain.[31] Problematic, rather, was the desire of many travelers to stay, as clergy lingering in the viceroyalty shifted the relationships within individual monasteries and in the ecclesiastical landscape at large.

Traveling clergy had a variety of good reasons to want to abide in New Spain, some only temporarily but others on a more long-term basis. As they belonged to branches of the mendicant orders that had not previously been active in the viceroyalty, they wanted to establish a place where they could recover from the hardships of their transatlantic voyage while living according to their order's rules. A request that Pedro de Alfaro sent from Mexico City in December 1577 illustrates both this desire and the necessities that spurred it. The Franciscan commissary wrote the king about the harm the journey to New Spain did to the religious travelers' bodies and souls, and he believed it would be helpful to their recovery to have a house where they could receive medical treatment and find opportunities for spiritual repose.[32] Alfaro added that construction of such institutions would help the healthy to spend the time while they were waiting for the galleons' departures more usefully, as they could preach among the Natives and train novices "so that those in China can replenish themselves." In 1580, Philip II approved Alfaro's plan, issuing a royal order to Viceroy Enríquez to construct a friary near Mexico City.[33] This decision encouraged the next Discalced Franciscan commissary, Miguel de Talavera, to focus his attention on training novices in this new monastery rather than leading a mission to the Philippines as he had been ordered.[34]

---

[30] Ryan Dominic Crewe, *The Mexican Mission: Indigenous Reconstruction and Mendicant Enterprise in New Spain, 1521–1600* (Cambridge: Cambridge University Press, 2019), 199–227.

[31] Ribadeneira, *Historia de las islas del archipiélago filipino*, 41; Owens, *Nuns Navigating the Spanish Empire*, 55–56, 61.

[32] Letter from Pedro de Alfaro to King, Dec 10, 1577, in Lorenzo Pérez, "Origen de las misiones franciscanas en el Extremo Orient. Suplemento al artículo I," *Archivo Ibero-Americano* 2, no. 10 (1915): 78–79.

[33] Royal cédula for Viceroy Enríquez, Feb 15, 1580, AGI, México, 20, N.52, doc. 2.

[34] Letter from Miguel de Talavera to President Council of the Indies, Jul 20, 1581, Lorenzo Pérez, "Origen de las misiones," 92–93. Also: Ribadeneira, *Historia de las islas del archipiélago filipino*, 55–56.

Representatives of the branch of the Franciscan Order that had been active in New Spain since the conquest era did not look favorably on these developments.[35] They were quick to blame the Discalced friars for surreptitiously expanding their influence in New Spain and depriving the land of its best pastors.[36] According to the viceroy, the Count of Coruña, such complaints were the direct result of the success the Discalced friars had had in admitting "many young boys born in this land."[37] Although Franciscan priors had generally avoided allowing creoles into their ranks, they still admitted suitable creoles when they found them – a pool that had now decreased due to recruitment by the Discalced friars.[38] The viceroy warned the Crown not to allow the newcomers to build any more monasteries, as doing so would create discord between the two branches. Heeding this advice, the Crown prohibited Franciscan commissaries from improving their new friary.[39] The royal orders also obliged custodians to travel to the agreed destination, obey local prelates, and ensure that no more than four friars stayed behind in New Spain so as not to upset relations in the viceroyalty.

The effects of these regulations remained limited. As more friars, clerics, and nuns embarked on the journey, the toll that the small, crowded ships, seasickness, and the arrival in tropical regions took on their health became a matter of grave concern. Commissaries reported how members of their mission fell sick or perished during the Atlantic leg of the voyage – at times, halving their numbers.[40] Such circumstances made it difficult for the Crown to deny requests for the construction of new monasteries and convents. But the well-being of traveling clergy was not the only reason for granting such permission. Royal officials also realized that political benefits could be gained from favoring new religious orders, like the Discalced Franciscans, Mercedarians, or Carmelites. As Jessica Ramírez Méndez has demonstrated, in return for the king's patronage, these orders would come to support the authority of the monarch

---

[35] Antonio Rubial García, ed. *La Iglesia en el México colonial* (Mexico City: UNAM, 2013), 182–84.

[36] Letter from eight friars to King Philip II, Dec 15, 1580, in Pérez, "Origen de las misiones franciscanas," 84–86.

[37] Letter from Conde de Coruña, AGI, México, 20, N.52. ff. 3v–4v.

[38] Francisco Morales Valerio, "Criollización de la orden Franciscana en Nueva España, siglo XVI," *Archivo Ibero-Americano* 48 (1988): 668–71.

[39] Request for favors for Province of San Gregorio, May 23, 1584, Patronato, 25, R.17.

[40] Compare, for instance, Letter from Pedro de Alfaro to King, Jul 25, 1578, AGI, Filipinas, 84, N.11; Letter from Diego Aduarte to King, Jan 20, 1606, AGI, Filipinas, 79, N. 75, doc. 3.

and the bishops, making them a valuable ally of the secular clergy in their efforts to reduce the autonomy of the traditional mendicant orders.[41] Although the Mendicants protested this expansion process, they were unable to bring it to a complete halt.

So, the religious orders that were supposed to lead the mission in the Far East managed to become part of New Spain's ecclesiastical landscape. By 1593, Discalced Franciscans received permission to transfer their seat in Mexico City from the San Cosme hermitage to the newly built monastery of San Diego. With the transfer of their seat, the friars erected the Custodia of San Diego, which depended on the Philippine Province of San Gregorio – a dependency that lasted until 1602, when the New Spanish province became independent.[42] They also erected monasteries in Puebla, Taxco, and Acapulco, as well as new houses in Oaxaca, Taxco, Pachuco, Sultepec, Querétero, Texmelucan, and Cuauhtla. Discalced Augustinians also expanded their presence, creating friaries in Veracruz, Perote, Puebla, and Mexico City, while Dominicans established the Hospice of San Jacinto de China in Tenanitla, near Mexico City, in 1602.[43] Finally, the Carmelites received from the then viceroy, the Marquis of Villamanrique, the convent of San Sebastián Atzacoalco in 1585, which they held on to until 1607.[44]

Despite repeated royal orders, members of the missions also continued to dwell in New Spain.[45] Like soldiers and officials, they too heard discouraging stories about the transpacific crossing and life in the Philippines that were circulating in the viceroyalty and made them rethink

[41] Jessica Ramírez Méndez, "La reforma filipina del clero regular y el paso de nuevos hábitos a Indias, 1566–1585," in *Reformas y resistencias en la iglesia novohispana*, eds. María del Pilar Martínez López-Cano and Francisco Javier Cervantes Bello (Mexico City: Universidad Nacional Autónoma de México, Instituto de Investigaciones Históricas/Benemérita Universidad Autónoma de Puebla, 2014), 131.

[42] On the relationship between the two provinces, see: Jessica Ramírez Méndez and Alba Sofía Espinosa Leal, "Las provincias franciscanas descalzas en Nueva España y Filipinas," *La iglesia y sus territorios, siglos XVI–XVIII*, eds. María del Pilar Martínez López-Cano and Francisco Javier Cervantes Bello (Mexico City: Universidad Nacional Autónoma de México, Instituto de Investigaciones Históricas, 2020), 166–77.

[43] Alfonso Martínez, "Hospicios de Nueva España para misioneros del Oriente," *Estudios* 6, no. 4 (1986): 35–49; Arturo Guevara Sánchez, *Los agustinos descalzos: breves noticias de su vida y logros en México y Filipinas* (Mexico City: Instituto Nacional de Antropología e Historia, 2006).

[44] Dionisio Victoria Moreno, *Los Carmelitas Descalzos y la conquista espiritual de México, 1585–1612* (Mexico City: Editorial Porrúa, 1966).

[45] Viceroy Monterrey to King, Jun 11, 1596, AGI, México, 24, N.21; Antonio Rubial García, *El convento agustino y la sociedad novohispana (1533–1630)* (Mexico City: Universidad Nacional Autónoma de México, 1989), 16–17.

their plans. At the same time, in New Spain they also encountered plenty of opportunities to provide, in relative personal comfort, spiritual guidance to the Spanish population and others.[46] Residents of New Spain became increasingly frustrated about these many traveling friars who wanted to abide in New Spain, which at times found expression in open hostility. In 1605, for example, the Dominican friar Diego Aduarte, the future prior of the convent of Santo Domingo in Manila, wrote about the malice he faced in a report detailing his experiences along the religious itinerary.[47] Aduarte revealed that, in spite of his holy mission, many of the ordeals the missionaries suffered were actually caused by people they encountered along the route. He lamented the arduous conditions his group had had to endure, due to insufficient funds being provided by the Crown and the royal officials who were supposed to pay for their supplies, housing, transport, and duties.[48] He also found troubling the interrogations to which the friars were subjected, first in Spain and later in New Spain, which revealed a lack of trust in the friars and their intentions.[49] To make things worse, he and his companions suffered hunger and humiliation as a result of efforts by locals to prevent them from leaving two friars in New Spain as, after he had informed officials in Mexico City about this intention, they cut off the provisions of the entire company for more than twenty days.

That such a hostile response to Aduarte's request was no exception but a calculated political move is revealed by a 1606 report in which the Marquis of Montesclaros responded to Aduarte's complaints.[50] The viceroy explained that, too often, friars stayed in New Spain or arrived there without royal permission, some even dressing up "as friars even if they

[46] In 1586, one of the reasons for the General Junta of Manila to recommend the Crown to send ships through the Strait of Magellan was that clergymen had been running off during the overland crossing. See Memorandum of the Various Points Presented by the General Junta of Manila to the Council, Blair and Robertson, *The Philippine Islands*, 6: 206–7. On the difficulties the friars faced when leaving New Spain, see also: Diego de Aduarte, O. P., *Historia de la Provincia del Santo Rosario de Filipinas, Japón y China del Sagrado Orden de Predicadores*, ed. Manuel Ferrero. Madrid: Consejo Superior de Investigaciones Científicas; Departamento de Misionología Española, 1962 [1640], 37.

[47] Report Diego Aduarte, Jan 20, 1606, AGI, Filipinas, 79, N.75.

[48] Aduarte repeats similar complaints about lack of funds being provided in a letter he sent from the Philippines two years later. Letter from Diego Aduarte, ca. 1608, AGI, Filipinas, 79, N.78.

[49] Procedures that subjects of the Spanish Crown had to go through before getting permission to embark on a ship to the Indies are described in Siegert, *Passagiere und Papiere*, 27–72.

[50] Letter from Viceroy Montesclaros, Feb 17, 1606, AGI, México, 26, N.82.

were not friars at all." He noted how costly it was to the Crown to maintain so many of these travelers. Obviously, such expenses were justified when they helped clergy get to those places where their work was needed. But bringing more of them to stay in the viceroyalty was not a priority.[51] For this reason, the Marquis tried to see to it that each mission left New Spain with the same number of friars as had been stipulated in the royal orders the commissary had received. Because the friars and prelates of the Orders still refused to comply with this rule, he had begun to impose fines on them, which were to be paid out of their alms and possessions.

Yet, maintenance of the traveling clergy was not the only issue that bothered residents of New Spain. Complaints about *filipinos*, *chinos*, or *dieguinos* – as the traveling clergy was named after their destination or the Convent of San Diego – were also a result of the growing tensions between Peninsular and creole factions within the Mendicant Orders.[52] Some priors were happy to welcome the travelers in their convents, expecting them to counterbalance the influence of the creoles. The English Dominican friar Thomas Gage commented on this dynamic in an account of his years-long stay in New Spain. Gage, who himself deserted his mission while on route to the Philippines, described how the Dominican provincial in Chiapas rejoiced upon the arrival of his band of traveling Dominicans, because there were insufficient Spanish friars to oppose the creoles and natives of the land. He also observed how their having abandoned their mission to the Philippines – Gage referred to himself and his brothers as "refugitives [sic] from Philippinas" – was not taken well by the creoles whom he met, who shot him some unfriendly gazes.[53]

On other occasions, tensions between the two groups did not remain limited to mistrustful looks. In the Augustinian Province of Michoacán, for example, a conflict rose in 1611 over the many chinos that were roaming the province.[54] What occasioned these disputes was a mission led by the custodian Fray Diego de Águila, who would end up being the

---

[51] Compare also: Letter from Count of Monterrey, Jun 11, 1599, AGI, México, 24, R.2, doc. 21.

[52] Rubial García, *El convento agustino*, 74–75.

[53] Thomas Gage, *A New Survey of the West-Indias: Or, the English American His Travail by Sea and Land* (London: E. Cotes and sold by John Sweeting, 1655), 209, 212–16.

[54] Rubial García, *El convento agustino*, 16–17. Nicolás Navarrete, *Historia de la provincia agustiniana de San Nicolás de Tolentino de Michoacán* (Mexico City: Editorial Porrúa, 1978), 1: 59–63.

only one of his party who actually crossed the Pacific. In response to such a dramatic breach of the rules, the Augustinian provincial, Fray Juan Caballero, prepared for the Superior General and the viceroy a list with the names of all the friars whom he believed should be forced to travel on to China – a name that by now was used synonymously for the Asian mission. In the following years, many friars whose names were on this list were ordered to the viceregal capital to prove they had legitimate reasons to be in New Spain. Such a procedure sparked much discontent, as more than one of the friars who should not have been allowed to remain in New Spain ended up receiving an office from the viceroy, which they were now forced to give up.[55] In this context, the Augustinians also bickered among themselves and with the viceroy over the right of the *chinos* to vote on the election of officials, confirming once more how closely linked the arrival of these friars was to questions over the distribution of responsibilities among the factions in the orders.

As we have seen, New Spain's position as a way station on the long religious itinerary between Spain and the Philippines clearly changed the ecclesiastical landscape in New Spain. Such rearrangements prompted conflicts that shaped the perceptions regarding the religious itinerary of both the clergymen who traveled through New Spain and those who resided there. Indeed, by 1636, locals had become so fed up with the constant arrival of new friars that Mexico's cabildo petitioned the viceroy to prohibit any friar from traveling to the viceroyalty, even if their ultimate destination was the Philippines.[56] Although these movements pitted peninsular Spaniards and creoles against one another, views of the significance of this route and New Spain's place in the world are hard to divide along strict lines of place of origin. More relevant in determining positions toward the religious itinerary among those involved were their political agendas. While creole friars in New Spanish convents without any link to Asia might oppose the mobility of friars along the religious itinerary, others who joined the Discalced Orders and supported their evangelizing endeavors in Asia would likely favor transpacific connections. For the same reasons, Peninsular friars at times assumed positions that, when looked at through the lens of the paradigm of creole patriotism, we would tend to associate with a creole point of view. Let us explore

---

[55] Heriberto Moreno Garcia, ed., *Los agustinos, aquellos misioneros hacendados. Historia de la provincia de San Nicolás de Tolentino de Michoacán, escrito por fray Diego de Basalenque* (Mexico City: Cien de México, 1985), 230.

[56] Proposal by don Fernando de Carrillo, Jul 26, 1636, in *Actas*, XXIII, Bk. 30, 212.

this argument in more detail by shifting attention toward the figure of the creole along with the various assessments of the qualities of the land in which they were born that began to spread along the itinerary.

ASSESSING NEW SPAIN'S QUALITIES

When Fray Rodrigo Aganduru Moriz described New Spain during the second half of the 1620s, the Discalced Augustinian painted a highly positive image of the lands situated halfway on the route to Asia. After explaining that the viceroyalty owed its name to sharing many qualities with Spain, he asserted that those of New Spain actually exceeded those of the Old. According to the friar, the land was quite fertile, providing a great variety of plants and fruits, copious harvests of grain, and an abundance of excellent cattle.[57] It also was rich in silver and gold, so much so that it was easier to find the mines than the capital required to exploit them. The part of New Spain the heavens favored the most was the kingdom of Mexico and its capital, Mexico City, which was, in his opinion, "one of the best in the world." Aganduru Moriz praised the city's "universally famous" buildings, its viceregal palace, and cathedral. He also eulogized the convents of the three Mendicant Orders and the university, from which more doctors graduated than from the largest in Europe, including that of Salamanca. Indeed, he noted:

Some of those sons of the land, whom they call criollos, have turned out to be magnificent subjects and solemn prelates. I have met some no less famous in sanctity nor learning [than, those studying in Salamanca], and it is without doubt (we relate and profess the truth) that those minds of the Indies (generally speaking) are better than those of Europe due to the influence of the heavens as well as the fineness of their food.[58]

Even though he recognized that the memory and ability to reason of some criollos decreased in their later years, as a result of them overindulging in food, overall, Aganduru Moriz's assessments of the creoles and the land in which they were born were nonetheless positive.

Fray Rodrigo's descriptions of New Spain closely resembled those in the *Itinerario*, the text that likely served as the model for his descriptions of all the islands and lands that clergymen encountered as they journeyed from Spain to Japan. The *Itinerario* provided an equally positive image of New Spain and its inhabitants. It noted, for example, that the land

---

[57] BP, R480/004, f. 102v.   [58] Ibid.

stretching out from Panama to New Mexico was blessed with a temperate climate. Although the sun produced great heat, the heavy rains and refreshing winds constantly cooled the air, causing favorable conditions for natural and human beings.[59] It also mentioned that the land provided an abundance of cattle, and crops were sown and harvested year-round, including some of the best corn known to mankind. Having described the viceroys, audiencia, Inquisition, religious Orders, and Mexico's university, the text also classified the viceroyalty's capital as "one of the great [cities] of the world."[60] In fact, it stated that the entire kingdom of Mexico compared positively "to any of the best and richest known in the world, except for China."[61]

Similarities also exist in terms of the ways in which Aganduru Moriz's text and the *Itinerario* thematized how the land and its inhabitants impacted those passing through. In the introduction to this chapter, we already saw how the Augustinian friar discussed the way the bond between heaven and terrain helped travelers to complete their daily distance.[62] The *Itinerario*, too, made an effort to set potential missionaries' minds at ease. First, it reassured readers that, even though these lands were situated in the Torrid Zone, they were not as hot as one would expect when reading the classical authorities. Second, plenty of food was available at prices lower than in Spain. And, third, medical care was offered in one of the many hospitals or by the Natives, who had cures for almost any disease. Finally, Indigenous people would also facilitate the journey, as they were so devoted and generous that the friars could "walk from sea to sea, which is over five hundred leagues, without spending a single *real* on food or anything else."[63]

Despite these obvious similarities, an important difference nonetheless exists between the two texts. Whereas the *Itinerario* focused on the Native inhabitants of North America, Aganduru Moriz discussed the Spanish population and how they compared to people in Spain. What may explain these differences are the authors' diverging missionary projects. We know that, when González de Mendoza returned from Mexico City in 1582, he wanted to present to the authorities at the court a plan for the evangelization of the Natives of New Spain and New Mexico.[64] Although this

---

[59] González de Mendoza, *Historia de las cosas más notables*, 351–53.　　[60] Ibid., 352.
[61] Ibid., 360.　　[62] BP, R480/004, f. 102r.
[63] González de Mendoza, *Historia de las cosas más notables*, 357.
[64] Francisco de Ortega wrote from Mexico that González de Mendoza returned to Spain with plans unrelated to the mission to China. Sola, *El cronista de China*, 106.

initiative failed, and Pope Gregory XIII's interest in China led him to focus rather on that part of the world, González de Mendoza did not forget about his project. On the contrary, when he revised the *Historia* in 1585, he added to the *Itinerario* parts of Antonio de Espejo's account of his journey to New Mexico (1582–83).[65] In his efforts to present North America as a valuable alternative to the mission in Asia, Mendoza had good reasons for positively assessing the Natives' qualities and their readiness to assist the friars.

Meanwhile, Aganduru Moriz's evangelizing projects were focused on Asia and he was, therefore, less interested in praising the Natives of New Spain. He only spoke about them in passing, observing that they had a dark complexion and were living in peace and order.[66] His interest in the creoles, on the other hand, mirrored his Order's positive attitude toward Spanish natives of the Indies. At the same time, it speaks to a preoccupation related to the involvement of these men in the Asian mission. Since the 1550s, high-ranking clergymen and priors in different part of the Indies had begun to complain that the sons of the land (*hijos de la tierra*), natives of the province (*naturales de la provincia*), or creoles (*criollos*) were more unruly and less inclined to live according to strict Christian rules.[67] They believed these young men to lack the capacities required to administer doctrine among the Indigenous and actually considered the lack of suitable novices a threat to the future of the evangelization of the Natives of the Americas.[68] Because the Discalced Augustinians engaged creoles in their mission, such ideas could have rubbed off on the standing of their missionary work, affecting their success in acquiring patronage from the Spanish Crown, the papacy, or private parties. To protect their reputation, Augustinians produced alternative assessments of the creoles' qualities.

To better understand why for someone like Aganduru Moriz it was important to provide these alternative appraisals, it is worth looking at the significance that assessment of the qualities of place of birth acquired in the distributive disputes in New Spain from the late sixteenth century. When Spanish clergymen first began to complain about the differences

---

[65] Nancy Vogeley, "China and the American Indies: A Sixteenth-Century 'History,'" *Colonial Latin American Review* 6, no. 2 (1997): 172–76.

[66] BP, R480/004, f. 102v.

[67] Lavallé, *Las promesas ambiguas*, 15–16. See also the first-ever descriptions of the criollos in Spain, in Juan López de Velasco, *Geografía y descripción universal de las Indias*, ed. Justo Zaragoza (Madrid: Real academia de la historia, 1894), 37–38.

[68] Morales Valerio, "Criollización de la orden Franciscana," 668–70.

between Spanish and American-born novices, they often did so due to generational differences (the old and experienced bewailing the young's inclinations toward idleness and vice),[69] cultural distinctions (peninsulars noting a general tendency in the Indies to observe eschatological rules less strictly), and a general belief in the relationship between place and the human body.[70] But as they began to use the term criollos, a category first used in Spanish in relation to the unruly behavior of the descendants of the conquistadores, it appears that they were using assessments of the qualities of people's place of birth to invert the viceregal hierarchy of merit, now positioning newcomers above the Spanish natives.[71]

That people in New Spain were keenly aware of this risk can be observed in the context of a public scandal that shook Mexico City at the beginning of the seventeenth century. In 1602, prelates of the Franciscan Order implemented new measures to make it more difficult for creole novices to receive the habit and, almost at the same time, petitioned the monarch to send up to a hundred friars from Spain. These decisions prompted fierce protests from creole Franciscans. In an account of the events, the Count of Monterrey noted that the protestors suspected the prelates of ignoring them "because of the mistrust they harbor for those who are born in the land and because they stepped up their efforts to exclude them from everything."[72]

What started out as an internal conflict within the Franciscan Order developed into a public scandal after the arrival of Viceroy Montesclaros in New Spain in October 1603. In the context of the political transition, rumors began circulating that the Franciscan prelates were composing a report for the Crown to demonstrate that creoles were "naturally insufficient and incapable of governing."[73] This afront caused outcries from Mexico's city council, the cathedral chapter, the university, as well as almost all convents and religious colleges in the

---

[69] Joaquín G. Icazbalceta, *Cartas de religiosas de Nueva España, 1539–1594* (Mexico City: Editorial Chávez Chávez Hayhoe, 1941), 33.

[70] For an introduction to these discussions, see Jorge Cañizares-Esguerra, "New World, New Stars: Patriotic Astrology and the Invention of Indian and Creole Bodies in Colonial Spanish America, 1600–1650," *American Historical Review* 104, no. 1 (1999): 33–68; Rebecca Earle, *The Body of the Conquistador: Food, Race and the Colonial Experience in Spanish America, 1492–1700* (Cambridge: Cambridge University Press, 2012), 19–50.

[71] On the first uses of the term criollo, see: Lavallé, *Las promesas ambiguas*, 15–19.

[72] Letter from Count of Monterrey, Apr 30, 1604, in Hanke, *Los virreyes españoles*, 2: 225.

[73] Ibid., 226

capital.[74] Although the prelates denied having written such reports, the old and the new viceroys had great difficulty defusing the situation. Representatives of Mexico's corporations asked them for assistance in producing alternative reports "in favor of the nature and sufficiency of the creoles, so as to qualify for His Majesty and the Council their talents for any kind of dignitaries and offices."[75] Monterrey outright refused these requests and advised the monarch and the Council of the Indies to discard any such report that made it to the Spanish court. Instead, he urged the Crown to demonstrate its confidence in the creoles and order the Mendicant prelates to favor the sons of the land whenever possible.[76]

Preoccupation with the effects that these negative assessments could have on creoles' chances of acquiring royal favor further increased the following year. An *Interrogatorio* sent around the Indies to gather information about these territories and their populations distinguished for the first time between peninsulars and criollos.[77] The 1604 questionnaire suggests that assessment of the qualities of the land and its native inhabitants had arrived at the center of the empire, providing an additional incentive to layman and the clergy involved in discussions about who deserved the king's favor to produce their own alternative assessments of both.[78] Such conversations were closely interrelated as well to the debates we have already come across in previous chapters regarding the claims of those rooted to the land to be favored in the distribution of benefits and offices. Creole clergymen could bolster such claims with a set of canonical and royal rules shaped by the idea that it would be preferable for priests to preach in the lands from which they were themselves natives.[79]

---

[74] For the emotional response of Mexico's cabildo from Oct 31, 1605, in name of all the citizens and residents of the city, including the "women and children affected by such great offenses," and all persons born in the kingdom, see: *Actas*, XIV, Bk. 16, 188–91.

[75] Letter from Count of Monterrey, Apr 30, 1604, in Hanke, *Los virreyes españoles*, 2: 226.

[76] Ibid., 227   [77] Solano, *Cuestionarios*, 97–111, esp. question 102.

[78] Illustrative of such alternative assessments are Baltsar Dorantes de Carranza's descriptions of the American continent and its inhabitants in the *Sumaria relación de las cosas de la Nueva España* (1604). For a more detailed study of his assessment of the nature of the Indies, see: Vallen, "The Self and the World," 150–56.

[79] Morales Valerio, "Criollización de la orden Franciscana," 670–71. The Spanish Crown did put such a principle into practice in the rules it set for distribution of benefices (*beneficios*) in the *Ordenanza del patronazgo*, promulgated on Jun 1, 1574, which required candidates to demonstrate their knowledge of relevant Native languages in competitive exams or *oposiciones*. Encinas, *Cedulario indiano*, 1: 83–86. See also: John F. Schwaller, "The Ordenanza del Patronazgo in New Spain, 1574–1600," *The Americas* 42, no. 3 (1986): 253–74.

An elaborate defense of the rights of the natives came from the hand of Juan Zapata y Sandoval, who was a descendant of two conquistadores and, at the time, rector of the Colegio de San Gabriel in Valladolid, Spain. In 1609, the creole Augustinian wrote a treatise in which he sought to prove that the principle of distributive justice, which assumed that candidates for an ecclesiastical office ought to be assessed solely based on their own dignity and merits, could be combined with a practice that favored the natives of the land.[80] While Zapata y Sandoval had no use for the notion criollo, others in subsequent years would. They began to refer to the criollo because of the establishment of new rotation systems that ought to ensure that administrative positions alternated between peninsular and criollo factions within the Mendicant Orders.[81] The *alternativa* (rotation system), which started to function for the first time in the Discalced Province of Michoacan in 1612, gave a positive reason to identify as criollo.

Aganduru Moriz's descriptions of New Spain and his assessment of both the qualities of the land and its inhabitants were clearly impacted by these developments. Just like Loyola and González de Mendoza, he borrowed from local panegyric writing and choreographies that appraised the qualities of the heavenly bodies above Mexico City, the greatness of its built environments, and the feats of past inhabitants to explain the kinds of virtuous talents and forms of behavior those living there were inclined toward.[82] Exemplary of such borrowing is his comment that, "if in streets, horses, houses, carriages, knights and nobility" Mexico City does not outdo, "it can at least compete with the best of the

---

[80] Juan Zapata y Sandoval, *De iustitia distributiva et acceptione personarum ei opposita disceptatio*, ed. Carlos Baciero et al. (Madrid: Editorial CSIC Consejo Superior de Investigaciones Científicas, 2008), 107, 301. Zapata y Sandoval also applied this rule to Indigenous clergymen, see: Roberto Heredia Correa, "Fray Juan Zapata y Sandoval: un paso más allá del criollismo," *Nova Tellus* 29, no. 2 (2011): 215–34.

[81] Bernard Lavallé, *Las promesas ambiguas*, 159–66; Carmen de Luna Moreno, "Gobierno interno: la alternativa tripartita en el siglo XVII," in *Franciscanos y mundo religioso en México*, ed. Francisco Morales (Mexico City: Universidad Nacional Autónoma de México, 1993); Antonio Rubial García, "Votos pactados. Las prácticas políticas entre los mendicantes novohispanos," *Estudios de historia novohispana* 26 (2002): 51–83.

[82] For an introduction to the chorographical genre in early modern Spain and the Americas, see for example: Richard L. Kagan, "La corografía en la castilla moderna. Género, historia, nación," *Stvdia Historica. Historia Moderna* XIII (1995): 47–59; Richard L. Kagan and Fernando Marías, *Urban Images of the Hispanic World, 1493–1793* (New Haven, CT: Yale University Press, 2000); Julio Alonso Asenjo, "Sin par loor de Córdoba por Góngora," *Quaderns de filologia. Estudis literaris*, no. 10 (2005): 133–54.

world."[83] As Stephanie Merrim has noted, such enumeration of excellent and beautiful things that begin with *c* became a trope in urban panegyrics celebrating the greatness of Mexico City.[84] Aganduru Moriz also stressed that many nobles and knights had migrated from Old Spain to the New, thus refuting the theory that the bad inclinations of creoles were the result of so many "restless and lost spirits" having populated the Indies.[85] Such ideas about the nobility of Mexico City's community at large reinforced his assessment of the excellent qualities he had encountered in the creoles who had graduated from the local university and were active in the church. Moriz's appraisals also helped him to defend the honor of the Augustinian Order by enthusiastically describing the four Augustinian convents built in Mexico City, highlighting the greatness of the Monastery of San Pablo, which he believed stood out even "among the many that the Order has in Europe."[86]

Aganduru Moriz was not the only one who wrote about connections between the religious itinerary and the figure of the creole. Around the time he wrote his text, Pope Urban VIII beatified six Discalced Franciscans who had been martyred in Nagasaki in 1597, one of whom was Fray Felipe de Jesús. The beatification of this young friar, supposedly born in Mexico City, inspired reassessment of the creoles from members of Mexico's clerical elite. Before we look in more detail into the development of this cult, let us consider how this martyrdom came about and how these events affected people along the religious itinerary.

DESTINATION JAPAN

During the first three decades of the seventeenth century, Japan became the destination on the Spanish religious itinerary that attracted more attention than any other part of East Asia. Christians had been active in Japan since 1549. Under the privilege of the Portuguese *Padroado*, the Jesuits had established a successful mission, acting as intermediaries between the warring *daimyō* (baronial overlords) and the Portuguese traders from Macao. Although the success of their missionary efforts had attracted the attention of the Mendicants in the Philippines, they had jealously guarded their monopoly.[87] This situation began to change

---

[83] BP, R480/004, f. 102r.   [84] Merrim, *The Spectacular City*, 81–83.
[85] López de Velasco, *Geografía*, 37–38.   [86] BP, R480/004, f. 102v.
[87] C.R. Boxer, *The Christian Century in Japan, 1549–1650* (Los Angeles: University of California Press, 1967), 137–54.

from the late 1580s. As a long era of civil wars was coming to an end, with Toyotomi Hideyoshi becoming Japan's new de facto ruler, the position of the Jesuits gradually weakened. In 1587, Hideyoshi ordered the Jesuits to leave Japan and forbade them from evangelizing in public. This decree was not actively enforced, however, and Jesuits remained active, but they did move their activities behind closed doors. In 1592, Hideyoshi further undermined their monopoly by inviting Spanish Mendicants to come to Japan and fulfill a similar role as the Jesuits did, acting as mediators with Spanish traders in Manila.[88] In July 1593, a group of Discalced Franciscans, led by Fray Pedro Bautista, arrived and began seeking to convert the Japanese.

Although the Jesuits had welcomed the Franciscans courteously, their friendly relationship ended when it became clear that the latter had come to stay.[89] The creation of a convent and church in Kyoto, as well as the establishment of friaries in Nagasaki and Osaka, prompted fierce protests. The Jesuit provincial and bishop of Japan wrote to Rome and the Spanish authorities in El Escorial and Madrid that the Discalced friars had no right to be in Japan and that their actions were only damaging the evangelization process.[90] Franciscans, in turn, ridiculed the elitism of the Jesuits and argued that the Franciscans attention to the poor and needy would inspire a more honest faith. Initially, the papacy sided with the Jesuits in this conflict, with Pope Clement VIII (1592–1606) reaffirming their exclusive rights in Japan in 1597. Yet, under pressure of the Spanish Crown, the papacy's position gradually shifted. At first, it allowed other religious orders to become active in Japan, so long as they traveled via the Portuguese route, but by 1608 it even abandoned this restriction.[91]

Competition over the right to evangelize was one reason why Japan attracted so much attention. Events taking place in Nagasaki at the beginning of 1597 became another. Several months earlier, in October 1596, authorities in the port of Urado on the island of Shikoku (modern-day Kōchi) had confiscated the Spanish galleon *San Felipe*, which had to seek harbor during its voyage from Manila to Acapulco.[92] Frustrated about the loss of their ship and trade, a group of Spaniards, including

---

[88] Tremml-Werner, *Spain, China, and Japan in Manila*, 195–97.

[89] Conover, *Pious Imperialism*, 24.

[90] Boxer, *The Christian Century*, 154–71; Conover, *Pious Imperialism*, 24–26.

[91] Dauril Alden, *The Making of an Enterprise: The Society of Jesus in Portugal, Its Empire, and Beyond, 1540–1750* (Stanford, CA: Stanford University Press, 1996), 132.

[92] An account of the journey of the *San Felipe* can be found in Report about the arrival of the *San Felipe* to Japan, undated, AGI, Filipinas, 79, N.28. For a modern account of the

several Franciscan friars, traveled to Osaka to ask Fray Pedro Bautista for diplomatic assistance. The arrival of the friars angered Hideyoshi and, in December 1596, he ordered all Franciscans in Japan and some of their followers to be apprehended.[93] The daimyō accused the friars of having come to Japan to "explore the land so as to take it afterwards just like they did in Peru, New Spain, and the Philippines."[94] Following these orders, six Franciscans and twenty converted Japanese were arrested and, after having been tortured and paraded from city to city, crucified in Nagasaki on February 5, 1597.[95]

Stories about these dramatic events spread quickly along the religious itinerary. After the Japanese authorities released the *San Pedro*, news about the martyrs of Nagasaki reached Manila, where, in addition to anger about the Japanese cruelty, strong anti-Portuguese and anti-Jesuits sentiments were aroused.[96] From the Philippines, news traveled onward to New Spain, Spain, and Italy through written and oral accounts. An important role in this process was reserved for don Francisco Tello de Guzmán, the governor of the Philippines, who wrote a report detailing what had happened in Nagasaki that was printed in Seville in 1598 and later reprinted in cities across Europe.[97] Another protagonist in this process was Fray Marcelo de Ribadeneira, a Discalced Franciscan who

---

events leading up to the crucifixion of the twenty-six martyrs of Nagasaki, see: Conover, *Pious Imperialism*, 15–35.

[93] The question of who was to blame for Hideyoshi's sudden change of heart became the subject of a series of polemical works written by Franciscans as well as Jesuits. Starting with fray Marcelo de Ribadeneira, Franciscans and Spaniards tended to blame the Jesuits for plotting to have their Order expelled. Compare: Boxer, *The Christian Century*, 154–71; Richmond Ellis, *They Need Nothing: Hispanic-Asian Encounters of the Colonial* Period (Toronto: University of Toronto Press, 2012), 39–46.

[94] Emilio Sola Castaño, *Libro de las maravillas del Oriente Lejano* (Madrid: Editora nacional, 1980), 117.

[95] The Jesuits did not escape Hideyoshi's wrath either. Several of their churches were destroyed, and it was only thanks to their role as negotiators with the Portuguese that they were able to reestablish an armed peace. Hélène Vu Thanh, "The Glorious Martyrdom of the Cross. The Franciscans and the Japanese Persecutions of 1597," *Culture & History Digital Journal* 6, no. 1 (2017): 6.

[96] Conover, *Pious Imperialism*, 38–40.

[97] Francisco Tello de Guzmán, *Relación que don Francisco Tello, gobernador: y capitán general de las Philippinas embió de seys frayles españoles de la Orden de San Francisco, que crucificaron los del Japón, este año próximo passado de 1597. Con otras veynte personas Japones, que murieron juntamente con ellos animados por los santos frayles y convertidos a su predicación* (Seville, 1598). Compare also: Rady Roldán-Figueroa, *The Martyrs of Japan: Publication History and Catholic Missions in the Spanish World (Spain, New Spain, and the Philippines, 1597–1700)* (Brill: Leiden, 2021), 81–82.

had been exiled from Japan to Macao, where he wrote a lengthy account of the martyrdom of the Nagasaki martyrs. Upon returning to Manila, Ribadeneira was elected by his order to lobby on behalf of the Franciscan martyrs and the Japanese mission at the court and in Rome. During his journey to Europe, Ribadeneira told his story again and again, initiating the lasting process of remembering the events in Nagasaki. After he passed through New Spain, Franciscans in Cuernavaca had the story of the Nagasaki martyrs painted on the walls of their convent.[98] And in Spain he inspired Juan de Santa María, superior of the Discalced Province of San José, to write his own account of the martyrdom, published in Madrid in 1601.[99] King Philip III was profoundly moved by the two Franciscans and, in following years, he not only expanded his financial aid for the Franciscan mission in Asia but also came to support Franciscan efforts to get the martyrs canonized.[100]

News about the Nagaski martyrs also reached Europe via the Portuguese route. Franciscans who were active under the Portuguese Padroado circulated reports, as did the Jesuits. Although the latter had experienced violence against Japanese neophytes and their churches on earlier occasions, their struggle with the Franciscans gave new urgency to reporting on the state of their mission in Japan.[101] They were well aware that the Franciscans were using the events to complain about the Jesuits' role in inciting the deadly violence and worried about future effects this could have for their Japanese mission.[102] In 1599, Luís Fróis's *Relatione della gloriosa morte di ventisei posti in croce* (Account of the Glorious Death of the Twenty-Six Placed on the Cross) became the first Jesuit account to be published in Europe, appearing almost simultaneously in Italian, Latin, and German and, later, was translated to Spanish as well. With the publication of this account, an information war commenced between the Jesuits and the Franciscans that raised interest in Japan not only across Europe but also in the places along the religious itinerary.

---

[98] María Celia Fontana Calvo, *Las pinturas murales del antiguo convento franciscano de Cuernavaca* (Cuernavaca: Universidad Autónoma del Estado de Morelos, 2011), 111–134.

[99] Juan de Santa María, *Relación de martirio que seis padres descalzos Franciscanos, y veinte japones cristianos padecieron en Japón* (Madrid: Imprenta del licenciado Varez de Castro, 1599).

[100] Ribadeneira, *Historia*, 507.

[101] A description of the Japanese who were martyred prior to 1597 can be found in Juan Ruiz-de-Medina, *El martirologio del Japón, 1558–1873* (Rome: Institutum Historicum S.I, 1999), 275–87.

[102] Vu Thanh, "The Glorious Martyrdom of the Cross," 3–6.

Interest would grow even further in the following decades, as violence against Christians continued and affected not only the Jesuits, who wrote extensively about the crisis of Japanese Christianity, but members of the Franciscan, Dominican, and Augustinian Orders as well. As Japan continued to produce more martyrs, it also continued to give clergymen a reason to celebrate the feats of the members of their orders.[103]

Interest in the martyrs acquired a new dimension in New Spain after 1627. After three decades of negotiating and a long bureaucratic trial, on September 14, Pope Urban VIII declared the six martyred Discalced Franciscans and seventeen of the Japanese Christians to be *beatos*, or blessed, of the Church.[104] When news of this decision reached Mexico City, two Discalced Franciscans addressed the local cabildo, asking it to organize a public celebration on the day that one of its own sons had been crucified.[105] They were talking about the aforementioned Felipe de Jesús. Born as Felipe de las Casas to Spanish immigrants Alonso de las Casas and Antonia Ruíz Martínez on May 1, 1572, Felipe had attended the Jesuit San Pedro y San Pablo College in Mexico City, and in 1589, he joined the Franciscan friary of Santa Bárbara de los Descalzos in Puebla.[106] Sometime later he left the convent and, by 1591, he was in the Philippines, probably to act as an agent for his father's business. In Manila, he returned to ecclesiastical life, taking his temporary vows in the Franciscan convent of Santa María in 1594. On his journey back to New Spain, where he was supposed to take his definite vows, fate struck and he became one of the martyrs beatified by the Church. According to the two Franciscan friars pleading before the cabildo, the city had a

---

[103] Rady Roldán-Figueroa has reckoned that forty-nine martyrological books were published between 1598 and 1609 alone. This number doubled during the 1620s and 1630s, with more than 100 publications on the topic appearing each decade – mostly in Europe but also important ones coming out of places along the religious itinerary, such as Mexico City and Manila. Roldán-Figueroa, *The Martyrs of Japan*, 67. One of the martyrological books printed in Mexico City was Pedro Morejón's *Relación de la persecución que [h]vuo en la yglesia de Iapon: y de los insignes marytres, que gloriosamente dieron su vida en defensa de n[uest]ra San Fè, el año de 1614 y 615* (Mexico City: Por Iuan Ruyz, 1616).

[104] The long trajectory leading up to Felipe de Jesús's beatification is described in more detail in Conover, *Pious Imperialism*, 37–57.

[105] Protocol Sept 4, 1628, *Actas*, XXII, Bk. 26, 341.

[106] To this day, Felipe de las Casas's place of birth remains unclear. While his hagiographers claimed that he was born in Mexico City, contemporary critics already questioned such an idea. It is possible that Felipe was born during the voyage from Spain. This discussion is traced in more detail in Ronald J. Morgan, *Spanish American Saints and the Rhetoric of Identity, 1600–1810* (Tucson: The University of Arizona Press, 2002), 144–47.

responsibility to "thank Our Lord for blessing it so much as to give it a native saint."[107]

The city council agreed. Planning for the festivities got underway, and the decision was made to financially support Felipe's mother, his sisters, and his brothers to acknowledge what the city owed to their brother for "ennobling our patria by his glorious martyrdom."[108] The celebrations on February 5, 1629, were a success and, at the beginning of the following year, San Felipe de Jesús was voted Mexico's patron saint, with the city pledging to organize an annual celebration.[109] Still, in spite of this positive start, the cult of the Blessed Felipe de Jesus lost momentum when rains flooded the city in August 1629, bringing public life almost entirely to a halt. Only when the floodwaters receded in the course of 1634, were efforts made to revive the public celebration of the city's patron. This time, however, the driving force behind these initiatives was the *maestrescuela* (schoolmaster) of Mexico's cathedral chapter, Dr. Luis Herrera, who turned Felipe de Jesús into a central figure of his own self-fashioning.

THE CREOLE SELF AND CELEBRATION OF A LOCAL MARTYR

On January 18, 1636, Luis Herrera and his colleague, Dr. Antonio de Esquivel y Castañeda, presented Mexico City's cabildo with a plan to revive the cult of the blessed Felipe. They proposed that the annual celebration of Felipe's crucifixion on February 5 could take place in the cathedral and suggested that the two cabildos could collaborate in turning the house in which the martyr was born into a parish church, while also retrieving his body or some parts that could serve as relics.[110] The cabildo agreed to a public celebration but explained that this could not take place in the cathedral, as it had already promised to commemorate the day of the crucifixion in the monastery of San Francisco.[111] The plan to construct a new parish church was rejected due to economic considerations, but the council members did commit to cooperating with the cathedral chapter to either redeem the "saint's body from Japan" or locate another relic. Later that year, Herrera and Esquivel also had an audience with the new viceroy, don Lope Díez de Armendáriz, the Marquis of Cadereyta

---

[107] Protocol Sept 4, 1628, *Actas*, XXII, Bk. 26, 341.
[108] Protocol, Mar 21, 1629, *Actas*, XXII, Bk. 27, 65.
[109] Although contemporaries commonly referred to Felipe as a saint, he was not officially canonized until 1862.
[110] Protocol Jan 18, 1636, *Actas*, XXIII, Bk. 30, 118.
[111] Protocol Jan 23, 1636, *Actas*, XXIII, Bk. 30, 123.

(1635–1640), and succeeded in convincing him to support their plan to create a chapel in the cathedral dedicated to the protomartyr.[112]

We do not know with certainty why Herrera and Esquivel chose this exact moment to promote the celebration of this particular saint. It is possible that once life in Mexico City had returned to normal, the clerics simply carried on with a practice that had become common across the Spanish empire of celebrating homegrown saints.[113] Indeed, the celebrations that took place in the metropolitan cathedral in 1638 and the two subsequent years reveal how important honoring Felipe was to enhancing Mexico City's prestige and reputation. During each of these years, a panegyric sermon that eulogized both Felipe and his patria was delivered and, later, printed. Although each of the three sermons, given by different priests, recognized that other Christians had been martyred in Nagasaki, they stressed that the city had a special obligation to celebrate Felipe. As the provincial of the Mercedarian Order in Mexico, Fray Luis Vaca Salazar, explained in his 1638 sermon, since Felipe was "the fruit of the patria" he could serve for "our embellishment, our adornment, and glory."[114] Such logic was typical of the panegyric rhetoric of the day, which used appraisal of the feats of notable members to exalt the nobility and honorable qualities of the entire community.[115]

In focusing their attention on Felipe's laudable achievements, the three sermons also established a link to the religious itinerary, showing how the workings of Divine grace became visible in the protomartyr's movements between New Spain and the Philippines. In his 1639 sermon, the Dominican friar and rector of the college of Nuestro Santo Padre de Porta Coeli, Fray Hiacinto de Caxica, considered Felipe's decision to travel across the Pacific illustrative of the "dispositions of Divine grace," moving people to traverse the world barefoot and poor, living according

---

[112] Report about cult, 1637, AHN, Diversos-Colecciones, 26, N.71; AGI, México, 33, L. 2, f. 144v.

[113] Cornelius Conover has called this the cult of saints, see *Pious Imperialism*, 7–9. Compare also: Alejandro Cañeque, "The Cabildo of Mexico City, Patron Saints, and the Making of Local and Imperial Identities," in *A Companion to Viceregal Mexico City, 1519–1821*, ed. John F. Lopez (Leiden: Brill, 2021), 166–68.

[114] Luís Vaca Salasar, *Sermón predicado en la Sancta Iglesia Cathedral Metropolitana de México, á la fiesta del Glorioso S. Felipe de Jesús, protomartyr de las Indias, y patrón de la muy noble y leal ciudad de México* (Mexico City, 1638), f. 3v.

[115] Compare, for example, the instructions that the influential Greek rhetorician Menander of Laodicea gave on how to praise a city, D. A. Russell and N. G. Wilson, *Menander Rhetor* (Oxford: Clarendon Press, 1981), 71.

to the strict rules of the Discalced Franciscans.[116] In contrast, the creole priest Miguel Sánchez in his 1640 sermon, noted that Felipe left the Franciscan Order and traveled to the Philippines under pressure from his parents, who needed his help in their trading business. Due to God's grace, however, he returned to the Franciscans in Manila – an occurrence Sánchez compared with the sprouting of a seed that had been planted earlier in "Mexican soil."[117]

All three preachers agreed that God's will was at work when Felipe returned home to his beloved patria, leaving the Philippines on the galleon that carried his name and that would bring him to Japan where, like Jesus Christ, he would spill his blood for his faith on the cross. Although Felipe's life differed from that of other clerics traveling along the religious itinerary, he did share some common experiences with them, including the hardships of oceanic traveling and his eventual martyrdom, with which he bestowed so much honor on the "Mexican nation" (*la nación mexicana*).[118]

Although Felipe was identified in the first place as a son of Mexico City, the three sermons also referred to him as a criollo. Vaca Salazar described Felipe as "a famous criollo," stressing the significance of God having chosen a criollo for this honorable death.[119] Caxica preached that, as the most accomplished of all creoles, Felipe "crowns the creole nation (*nación criolla*) with his glory."[120] Finally, Miguel Sánchez proclaimed that the Mexican territory produced men that were firm and faithful, "knowing that any one of its criollos will be a Felipe for his Felipe, a Felipe Martyr for his Felipe King."[121] In the context of the ongoing debates about the qualities of creoles, such positive usage of the term was significant. As these three sermons suggest, Felipe's life and feats provided a powerful argument against the accusations that creoles were unfit for evangelizing work. Meanwhile, public celebration of Felipe's

---

[116] Jacinto de la Cajica, *Sermón predicado en la Santa Iglesia Cathedral Metropolitana de México, a la fiesta del glorioso S. Felipe de Jesús, protomartir de las Indias, y patron de la muy noble y leal ciudad de México* (Mexico City: Bernardo Calderon, 1639), f. 421v.

[117] Miguel Sánchez, *Sermón de San Felipe de Jesús* (Mexico City: Iuan Ruiz, 1640), ff. 6v–7r.

[118] By the end of the 1630s, Japanese martyrdom was a theme that recurred again and again in the religious literature written in Europe and New Spain. According to the impressive register presented by Juan Ruiz-de-Medina, more than 1,500 Japanese, Spaniards, Portuguese, Mexicans, and Chinese were martyred after the events in Nagasaki. Ruiz-de-Medina, *El martirologio del Japón*, 297–737.

[119] Vaca Salasar, *Sermón*, f. 2v., f. 4r., f. 10r., f. 12r., and f. 12v.

[120] Cajica, *Sermón*, f. 427r.   [121] Sánchez, *Sermón*, f. 14r.

death was a way to bring such an alternative assessment under the attention of the viceroy, the members of the audiencia, the city council, and the cathedral chapter, all of whom attended the celebrations that, eventually, did take place in Mexico's cathedral. In fact, Felipe's assumed sainthood not only helped such preachers to refute negative characterizations of the qualities of the creole population but actually encouraged them to embrace the category criollo to identify a group of deserving subjects.

It was not uncommon for clergy to use the celebrations of a patron saint to reiterate specific claims of entitlement. During the annual celebration of Mexico City's oldest patron saint, San Hipólito, in 1638, the archdean of the cathedral chapter in Guadalajara, Dr. Gabriel de Ayrolo Calar, preached passionately in favor of the descendants of conquistadores and first settlers . Just like Christ rewarded his martyrs in heaven, he argued, the king should reward each of them with what they deserved, according to their status and merit.[122] It does not seem unreasonable to suspect that this type of claim-making was also what had inspired Herrera to begin promoting the cult of San Felipe in the first place. Having been born in Mexico City and being a criollo himself, he had good reasons to defend the worthiness of both. After all, as a member of both groups, he was supposed to share many qualities with others born in Mexico City or the Indies. But the role of the cult in Herrera's efforts to fashion himself as a deserving subject may have even been more complex. Indeed, when we take into consideration the exceptional circumstances the cathedral chapter was passing through, we may pose an alternative explanation of why Herrera chose this moment to begin promoting the cult of Felipe and how he used the criollo saint to improve his own tarnished public reputation.

During the previous three decades, Herrera had been battling again and again with rumors seeking to tarnish his own qualities. In 1609, he had participated in one of the competitive exams (*oposiciones*) organized to fill the position of doctoral canon (*canonjía doctoral*) on the cathedral cabildo. Herrera won the office despite accusations being raised against him of being born outside of wedlock – a social "birth defect" that would

---

[122] Gabriel de Ayrolo Calar, *Sermón que predicó el doctor don Gabriel de Ayrolo, arcediano de la Santa Iglesia de Guadalajara, y natural de la ciudad de México, el día de su patrón S. Hypólito, cuando luce reseña de su estandarte real, y se lleva a su iglesia con suntuoso acompañamiento, asistiendo en ella el excelentísimo señor Marques de Cadereyta, Virrey de esta Nueva España, Audiencia Real, y los dos Cabildos Eclesiástico y Secular* (Mexico City: Francisco Salbago, 1638).

have disqualified him for most offices.[123] These allegations resurfaced in 1623, when he landed – with the help of the Marquis of Gélves, who had positively assessed Herrera's services – the position of schoolmaster.[124] At the court, the *procurador* (legal representative) of the cathedral chapter, Dr. Diego Guerra, informed the king that the *provisor* (chief ecclesiastical judge) had concluded that Herrera was "unqualified and incapable to receive such a dignity."[125] Meanwhile in Mexico City, a significant number of people tried to prevent a perplexed Marquis of Cerralbo from appointing Herrera and, when he refused to give in to their protests, called for the cathedral cabildo to be dissolved.[126] Even the official appointment did not put an end to the protests, as Herrera's opponents continued accusing him of being an illegitimate child and having been involved in an uprising against the previous viceroy in 1624. In 1632, the Council of the Indies was still discussing a complaint brought before it by the dean and the cathedral chapter, who disagreed with current Viceroy Cerralbo's decision to appoint Herrera and wanted the position of schoolmaster to be declared vacant.[127]

It is remarkable how Herrera held on to his position in the face of such opposition. He caught an unexpected break after the installation of Dr. Diego Guerra as the cathedral chapter's new Dean on November 2, 1634. The appointment of the person who had led the cabildo's campaign against him at the court had not, at first, appeared to bode well for Herrera. But Guerra led the cathedral chapter into an unprecedent crisis that created new opportunities to renegotiate loyalties and alliances. This development was the result, on the one hand, of Guerra being out of touch with the other members of the cabildo. After having resided at the court for sixteen years, he had returned to New Spain profoundly

---

[123] Leticia Pérez Puente, "El cabildo y la universidad. Las primeras canonjías de oficio en México (1598–1616)," *Histórica* XXXVI, no. 1 (2012): 82–84.

[124] Merits of Luis de Herrera, 1641, AGI, Indiferente, 192, N.100. Leticia Pérez Puente, *Universidad de doctores: México, siglo XVII* (Mexico City: UNAM, Centro de Estudios sobre la Universidad, 2000), 160.

[125] Alberto M. Carreño, *Cedulario de los siglos XVI y XVII. El obispo don Juan de Palafox y Mendoza y el conflicto con la Compañía de Jesús* (Mexico City: Victoria, 1947), 312–13.

[126] Report from Viceroy Marquis of Cerralbo about the state in which he left New Spain, Mar 17, 1636, AGI, México, 31, N.49, f. 125v.

[127] Carreño, *Cedulario de los siglos XVI y XVII*, 334–35. See also: Information about Dr. Luis de Herrera, Edmundo O'Gorman Collection, Benson Latin American Collection, The University of Texas at Austin, M7.

Hispanized and utterly unfamiliar with the politics of the colonial metropole. On the other hand, the dean was affected by the conflicts of Mexico's Archbishop, don Francisco Manso y Zúñiga. Early in 1636, on his way to Veracruz, the prelate appointed Guerra as governor of the diocese, replacing the provisor and vicar general, Dr. Luis de Cifuentes. This decision led to a rebellion of the other members of the cabildo, who stopped voting for Guerra, thus leaving the cathedral chapter powerless.[128]

Prior to these events, Archbishop Manso's imminent return to Spain produced a power vacuum that Herrera appears to have used to rally individuals and groups around the criollo martyr Felipe. He collaborated with the city council, which at the time was involved in negotiations with the Crown and had its own reasons to boost local patriotism (more on these developments in Chapter 5). He also managed to get a positive response from Viceroy Cadereyta, who himself was a native of Quito and, despite having lived most of his life in Spain, may have felt some sympathy for the celebration of a criollo. Plus Herrera found support among the clergy, who shared with him a common interest in improving the reputation of those born in Mexico and the Indies and even actively praised him quite highly for taking on this role. For example, Luis Vaca Salazar dedicated his sermon of 1638 to Herrera and thanked him for the honor of preaching on that day. By granting this favor, the friar noted, Herrera had established a lineage of indebtedness between them. Caxica was even more flattering. Addressing Herrera as "most worthy" (*dignissimo*) in his dedication, he declared the schoolmaster his patron and expressed his wish for "God to keep Your Grace in the dignities that your merits require."[129] The promotion of the cult of Felipe thus completely changed the atmosphere around Herrera's person and, perhaps more importantly, his self-image. This is also reflected in a royal decree from August 27, 1638, through which King Philip IV responded positively to Herrera's petition to place an image of the protomartyr in a chapel of the cathedral.[130] Things turned around in such a way for the schoolmaster that he even succeeded in getting a brief but positive report about his merits filed in 1641.[131]

---

[128] Óscar Mazín Gómez, *Gestores de la Real Justicia. Procuradores y agentes de las catedrales hispanas nuevas en la corte de Madrid* (Mexico City: Colegio de México, 2007), 1: 325, 333–38.

[129] Cajica, *Sermón*, f. 418r.   [130] Carreño, *Cedulario de los siglos XVI y XVII*, 360–61.

[131] Merits Luis de Herrera, 1641, AGI, Indiferente, 192, N.100. Pérez Puente, *Universidad de doctores*, 160.

The celebrations of Felipe's feast at the end of the 1630s thus provide another glimpse into the dynamic relationship between the contested image of the criollo, the westward religious itinerary, and the struggles over benefits and offices in New Spain. As historians have long argued, local and creole patriotism were pursued on these occasions. And, yet, in a world of competing individuals and groups, not all involved parties rejoiced in such sentiments. Opposition came from the Franciscans, who felt that they had been robbed of the chance to celebrate one of their own and even protested the creation of a chapel dedicated to Felipe in the metropolitan cathedral.[132] But this chapter has shown something else as well. Thinking through the logic of assessment as it developed out of the sapiential tradition can help us to better grasp that positive assessments of a group's qualities did not necessarily exclude establishment of other hierarchies among its own members. In this respect, it is important to recognize that the notions of person- and selfhood that contemporaries held were concentric. As Timothy Reis has argued, they believed that human beings become the way they are due to interactions with different, overlapping spheres of existence that not only surrounded them but are, in fact, what they are.[133] From this perspective, someone born in Mexico City shared certain qualities with all other inhabitants of the Indies, of the kingdom of New Spain, and, ultimately, of this particular city.

Within the process of assessment in the economy of favor, such linking of an individual's worth to their place of origin could work two ways. As authors like Aganduru Moriz and Vaca Salazar demonstrate, displaying the admirable qualities of the residents of Mexico City could lead members of their audience to formulate positive assessments of the creole population in general. At the same time, this did not mean that all creoles possessed exactly the same qualities or degrees of worthiness. In fact, even when such authors addressed the qualities of all those who had been born in the Indies, they also sought to demonstrate why people born in Mexico City were thought to be even more worthy than those in, for instance, Puebla. Further distinctions were often made within particular communities by singling out specific groups or lineages. Thus, conceptualizations of the deserving self for a given category often assumed the form of a stacked pyramid of ever-smaller identifiable groups, each one above possessing qualities or having rendered services that made them more worthy than the rest of the groups, of which they also formed an inherent part.

---

[132] Protocol, Jan 22, 1641, *Actas*, XXIV, Bk. 32, 174.   [133] Reiss, *Mirages of the Selfe*, 2.

This notion of a layered assessment process will help us better understand why actors within the historical struggles presented here identified themselves with different groups. As others ascribed certain qualities by identifying them as natives of the Indies, they first needed to address these assessments before addressing others. It also encourages us to reconsider, again and again, what the exact intended meaning of the social categories they used, along with the qualities they ascribed to them, could have been. As we have seen in this chapter, instead of there being a monolithic perspective on the worthiness of creoles vis-à-vis New Spain's position along the religious itinerary to Asia, we can see that clergymen and others ascribed different values to this social category as they grappled with the new realities that the establishment of the route produced. Such a view underscores how important it is to look behind the sentiments of pride that some contemporaries expressed, including the idea that the Spanish inhabitants of New Spain were proud of the viceroyalty becoming the heart of the world. Chapter 5 continues exploring such diverse responses to another form of global integration, focusing on how debates concerning the monetization of negotiations over the distribution of royal grace factored into discussions about the desirability of transpacific trade.

5

The Merchant

Debating Transpacific Trade and the Economy of Favor

During the final two decades of the sixteenth century, New Spanish merchants increasingly began to invest in trade with Asia. Although risks were high and turnaround times on investments long, importing Asian commodities to New Spain turned out to be a highly lucrative enterprise.[1] Transpacific commerce further diversified the already varied mix of American and European products sold on New Spanish markets, adding goods from China, Japan, the Philippines, and other parts of Southeast Asia. By 1604, Bernardo de Balbuena captured this development in *La grandeza mexicana* (The Grandeur of Mexico), a city panegyric singing the praises of the viceregal capital. Revealingly, the Spanish poet enumerated an extensive inventory of commodities and luxuries that were sold in Mexico, noting how the city joined "Spain and China, Italy and Japan, and, ultimately, an entire world in trade."[2] According to Balbuena, commerce not only aggrandized this community, but the industriousness of its merchants was a sign as well of the community's "excellence" and

---

[1] A vast body of scholarship now exists examining the development of the transpacific trade and the commercial dynamics according to which this trade route functioned for two and a half centuries. See, for example, Schurz, *The Manila Galleon*; Chaunu, *Les Philippines et le Pacifique des ibériques*; Yuste López, *El comercio de la Nueva España con Filipinas*; Bonialian, *El Pacífico hispanoamericano*; Mariano A. Bonialian, *La América española: entre el Pacífico y el Atlántico: globalización mercantil y economía política, 1580–1840* (Mexico City: El Colegio de México, Centro de Estudios Históricos, 2019); Arturo Giráldez, *The Age of Trade: The Manila Galleons and the Dawn of the Global Economy* (London: Rowman & Littlefield, 2015).

[2] Balbuena, *Grandeza mexicana*, 80.

the workings within it of *"el interés,"* a force inspiring humankind's greatest achievements.[3]

In recent years, Balbuena's rendition of Mexico City's globalized marketplace has appeared regularly in studies examining impacts of the transpacific trade on New Spanish society. Scholars have found in *Grandeza mexicana* an appealing description of a city functioning as an entrepôt at the crossroads between China and Spain, one of the first places where a new culture of global consumption developed.[4] They have also argued that this position at the intersection of Atlantic and Pacific trading networks incited processes of cultural exchange and appropriation, shaping both local material cultures and perceptions of the world in which Mexico City, rather than Spain, appeared at the center of a globalizing world of trade.[5]

It is tempting to relate Balbuena's eulogizing of new patterns of global consumption to an emerging creole patriotism. Yet studies of the poem have pointed out the complex relationship between the interests of its author and those of Spaniards actually born in the colony.[6] According to Stephanie Merrim, Balbuena's "poetics of [the] marketplace" collided with epic accounts of the conquest written by the conquistadores and their descendants.[7] Jacques Joset, in turn, has argued that Balbuena's utopian descriptions of a burgeoning economic bonanza served to inspire migration from the Peninsula.[8] Meanwhile, Jorge Terukina Yamauchi has read *Grandeza mexicana* as a contribution to an "economic polemic," with Balbuena opposing the criollos' socioeconomic claims in favor of

[3] Ibid., 49. Regarding the meaning that Balbuena ascribed to the term *interés* in contributing to the community's order and well-being, see Jorge L. Terukina Yamauchi, *El imperio de la virtud: Grandeza mexicana (1604) de Bernardo de Balbuena y el discurso criollo novohispano* (Woodbridge: Tamesis, 2017), 256–68.

[4] José L. Gasch-Tomás, *The Atlantic World and the Manila Galleons: Circulation, Market, and Consumption of Asian Goods in the Spanish Empire, 1565–1650* (Leiden: Brill, 2018), 163–65.

[5] Gruzinski, *Las cuatro partes del mundo*, 50; Fuchs and Martínez-San Miguel, "La grandeza mexicana de Balbuena," 682.

[6] Georgina Sabat-Rivers, "El Barroco de la contraconquista: primicias de conciencia criolla en Balbuena y Domínguez Camargo," in *Relecturas del Barroco de Indias*, ed. Mabel Moraña (Hanover: Ediciones del Norte, 1994), 59–96.

[7] Stephanie Merrim, *The Spectacular City*, 130. Merrim has also demonstrated that, despite these tensions, the descendants of the conquistadores and first settlers, including Baltasar Dorantes de Carranza, did appropriate parts of Balbuena's panegyric language to celebrate the greatness of Mexico on their own terms.

[8] Jacques Joset, "Grandeza mexicana de Bernardo de Balbuena: ¿una corografía de propaganda económica?" *Bulletin hispanique* 116, no. 2 (2014): 855–68.

immigrants like himself.[9] Instead of simply providing a creole view onto an emerging world of trade and boundless wealth, Balbuena's poem rather opened a window onto various social conflicts that the processes of global economic integration were inciting.

Building on this literature, the present chapter examines discussions focused on how the Asian trade impacted the functioning of the economy of favor. I argue that the growing importance of conspicuous consumption in New Spain and the introduction of new venal practices raised questions about the assessment process that, according to many, was the key to a just distributive process.[10] How was the capacity to spend money on clothing or other symbols of wealth valued when a petitioner's worthiness for a position was being determined? Could judicial and fiscal offices be auctioned off without first taking into consideration an individual's social status, talents, and services? What did it mean for the relationship between the Crown and its vassals when patronage was up for sale? In the discussions of the time concerning these issues, the merchant often appeared and was sometimes pitted against other *beneméritos* (meritorious subjects), as the worthiness or unworthiness of the members of each group was debated. Yet, instead of focusing merely on the tension between these groups, I contend that what was truly at stake in these discussions were the fundamental principles of the economy of favor so crucial to keeping the Spanish empire together.

Here I explore these discussions and the role that New Spain's Pacific connections played in them from two distinct points of view. Firstly, I consider critical reflections about the ways in which consumption and trade affected ideas about worthiness, returning to Rodrigo de Vivero's *Abisos* to analyze his critique of the growing influence of commerce on New Spanish society and distributive processes in the Spanish empire. Once more taking the Chinese and Japanese as an example, the creole nobleman questioned the idea that New Spain should be the center of the world and defended a vision of the empire ruled by justice rather than money. Secondly, I examine the efforts of Mexico City's cabildo to

---

[9] Terukina Yamauchi, *El imperio de la virtud*, 243–325.

[10] The perspective I assume here differs from Elvira Vilches's study of the notion of distributive justice as it emerged in a burgeoning body of sixteenth- and seventeenth-century economic writing. While Vilches relates this concept to contemporary theorists' reflections on credit, finance, and speculation, I focus on the impact of money on the distribution of royal favor. Compare Elvira Vilches, *New World Gold: Cultural Anxiety and Monetary Disorder in Early Modern Spain* (Chicago: The University of Chicago Press, 2010), 2–3, 174–81.

fashion a particular image of a deserving community while negotiating with the Crown over financial contributions to the Armada de Barlovento.[11] During these interactions, people in New Spain and at the court weighed ideas on the relationships between worthiness, trade in the Pacific, and the influence of capital on the distributive process. By juxtaposing Vivero's reflections with those of Mexico City's cabildo, the chapter seeks once more to exhibit how, each in their own way, calls for isolationism or economic integration were crucial to the distributive struggles being fought in the viceroyalty.

ASIAN COMMODITIES IN THE ECONOMY OF LEGITIMATION

The influx of Asian goods from the 1570s onward affected New Spanish society in various ways. On the production side, New Spain's sericulture suffered severely from the import of cheap Chinese silks, and by the end of the sixteenth century, local silk production had decreased dramatically.[12] Workshops that processed raw silk, on the other hand, benefited from the arrival of cheap resources and the expansion of their markets in New Spain and Peru. Other industries saw similar developments. New Spanish pottery makers, for example, felt the impact of Chinese ceramics becoming available, but by imitating these models and selling them at lower prices they also created new markets.[13] Equally diverse were reactions on the consumer side of things. Transpacific commerce changed tastes and consumption patterns of the wealthiest and poor, who not only gained access to new kinds of commodities but also cheaper alternatives to European or locally produced ones.[14] Consequently, the galleon trade impacted what the economic historian Bartolomé Yun-Casalilla has referred to as the "economy of legitimation," an economic system

---

[11] This fleet that was to protect communication and trade routes between New Spain and Castile as well as between the viceroyalty, the Barlovento Islands, Tierra Firme, and the Gulf of Mexico (*Mar Seno Mexicano*) against Dutch, French, and English privateers. For a general history of the Armada de Barlovento, see Bibiano Torres Ramirez, *La Armada de Barlovento* (Seville: Escuela de Estudios Hispano-Americanos, 1981).

[12] Woodrow Borah, *Silk Raising in Colonial Mexico* (Berkeley: University of California Press, 1943), 87–90.

[13] Priyadarshini, *Chinese Porcelain in Colonial Mexico*, 153–59; Alberto Baena Zapatero, "Apuntes sobre la elaboración de biombos en la Nueva España," *Archivo Español de Arte* LXXXVIII, no. 350 (2015): 173–88.

[14] Gasch-Tomás, *The Atlantic World and the Manila Galleons*, 154–76.

revolving around people spending on culture, patronage, charity, pageantry, and luxury with the intent of demonstrating their social status.[15]

Displaying extravagance had been important since the times of the conquest. Spanish captains had used ostentation in dress to highlight their superiority, while the colonizers used their newly acquired wealth to distinguish themselves via their houses, goods, and apparel.[16] During the sixteenth century, this culture of conspicuous consumption became more complex due to increasing social competition.[17] As wealthy merchants began to compete with *encomenderos* and royal officials for social recognition and political positions, they used their wealth and ostentatious consumption to bolster their claims of privilege. Unwilling to fall behind, others followed their example. Residents of New Spain involved in this economy mainly relied at first on European products, dressing in fine velvets and embroidered brocades from Granada or Antwerp, decorating their houses with Italian glass, and drinking wines from Castile. With the establishment of the transpacific trade, however, they began to buy eye-catching commodities from Asia as well. Silks, velvets, satins, taffetas, gauzes, and damasks became highly popular, as did chinaware from Jingdezhen and luxuries from all over East Asia, such as desks, chairs, folding screens (*biombos*), jewelry, chests, caskets, fans, sunshades, sculptures, and religious objects.[18] Slaves from the Philippines,

[15] Bartolomé Yun-Casalilla, *Marte contra Minerva. El precio del imperio español, c. 1450–1600* (Barcelona: Crítica, 2004), 429–35.

[16] Luis Miguel Córdoba Ochoa, "Gifts, Imitation, Violence and Social Change: The Introduction of European Products in the First Decades of the American Conquest," in *American Globalization, 1492–1850: Trans-Cultural Consumption in Spanish Latin America*, eds. Bartolomé Yun-Casalilla, Ilaria Berti, and Omar Svriz-Wucherer (New York: Routledge, 2021), 123–45.

[17] Pilar Gonzalbo Aizpuru, "De la penuria y el lujo en la Nueva España. Siglos XVI-XVIII," *Revista de Indias* 56, no. 206 (1996): 49–75; Frédérique Langue, "De la munificencia a la ostentación: La nobleza de la ciudad de México y la cultura de la apariencia (siglos XVII-XVIII)," *Nuevo Mundo Mundos Nuevos* (2005), http://journals.openedition.org/nuevo mundo/642.

[18] Gasch-Tomás, *The Atlantic World and the Manila Galleons*, 56–69. Compare also: Edward R. Slack, Jr., "Orientalizing New Spain: Perspectives on Asian Influence in Colonial Mexico," *México y la Cuenca del Pacífico*, no. 43 (2012): 106–110; Antoni Picazo Muntaner, "Distribución de productos asiáticos en América en el siglo XVII: una aproximación," *Temas americanistas* 31 (2013): 87–109. Kuwayama, *Chinese Ceramics in Colonial Mexico*; Curiel, "Perception of the Other," 19–33.

China, and India also came to play a role in the households of the urban elite, adding further to a family's prestige.[19]

The transpacific trade was, however, not only limited to expensive luxuries. On the contrary, Mexican merchants hauled commodities of a wide-ranging array of prices and levels of quality, including cheaper alternatives for goods that were in high demand. This resulted in some residents gaining access to products that they traditionally had not been able to afford, which, as a result, gave them a higher value in the economy of legitimation. One of these products was chinaware. Chinese blue and white was highly appreciated in European and American societies. Often it formed the center piece of a family's property, serving as a means of self-representation through which messages about a family's wealth, sophistication, and social standing were conveyed.[20] While the wealthiest members of society were the first to buy these new objects, others followed their example by investing in crockery of lesser quality. Even Native residents of the region participated in this pattern of consumption. As Gustavo Curiel has shown, by the early seventeenth century, a chieftain named Tonati of the Cora people, in the current state of Nayarit, had bought chinaware to place himself on equal footing with the European elite.[21]

Even more impactful was the introduction of Chinese silk. Silk had been a coveted material whose use, in accordance with Spanish sumptuary laws, had been reserved for the rich. Due to the import of Chinese silks, prices for this commodity halved or at times decreased even more, allowing people of lesser means to get their hands on silk cloth or garments.[22] Contemporaries often commented on this development. For example, in 1602, Mexico City's cabildo and Viceroy Monterrey

---

[19] Seijas, *Asian Slaves in Colonial Mexico*, 119–20; Déborah Oropeza Keresey, "La esclavitud asiática en el virreinato de la Nueva España, 1565–1673," *Historia Mexicana* LXI, no. 1 (2011): 38–39.

[20] Verónica Velasquez Sánchez-Hidalgo, "Maiolica and the Doctrine of Blood Purity in New Spain, Mexico" (Doctoral thesis, University of Sheffield, 2014).

[21] Gustavo Curiel, "Customs, Conventions, and Daily Rituals among the Elites of New Spain: The Evidence from Material Culture," in *The Grandeur of Viceregal Mexico: Treasures from the Museo Franz Mayer*, eds. Héctor Rivero Borrell and Peter C. Marzio (Houston: The Museum of Fine Arts, Houston; Museo Franz Mayer Mexico, 2002), 30.

[22] Roberto Junco and Patricia Fournier, "Del Celeste Imperio a la Nueva España: importación, distribución y consumo de la loza de la China del periodo Ming Tardío en el México virreinal," in *La nueva Nao: de Formosa a América Latina. Intercambios culturales, ecpnómicos y políticos entre vecinos distantes*, eds. Lucía Chen et al. (Taipei: Kaun Tang International Publication, 2008), 3–21; Mariano A. Bonialian, *China en la América colonial: bienes, mercados, comercio y cultura del consumo desde*

disagreed about the necessity of the transpacific trade. The former recommended terminating trading relations with the Philippines and closing the Port of Acapulco, as during the past five years a total of 12 million pesos had been shipped out but, in return, only brought back "false merchandise full of shams of so little service that they are very detrimental to the public good."[23] The viceroy, on the contrary, requested the Crown to refrain from intervening in the transpacific trade, precisely because he intended to provide the needy with these cheap and low-quality Asian textiles.[24]

While the cabildo and the viceroy bickered about the worth of cheap and low-quality silks, others commented more explicitly about the impact of cheap silks on the economy of legitimation. In 1608, for example, the Portuguese merchant Pedro de Baeza did so in a report concerning the future of transpacific commerce requested by the Council of the Indies. Due to his stays in East Asia and India, the Council considered Baeza an authority on the global flows of cloth who could help in formulating their response to the unceasing complaints of Seville's *consulado* (merchant guild) and peninsular producers.[25] In his report, Baeza focused mostly on the damage that the introduction of cheap Asian products into New Spain was doing to Spanish commerce. But he also noted that silk had become so easily available to mestizos, mulattos, Natives, and vagabonds that it was no longer compelling respect for knights, who had used expensive Spanish silk to distinguish themselves from commoners.[26] To reduce the number of people that could buy silks, he proposed imposing higher taxes

---

México hasta Buenos Aires (Mexico City: Instituto de Investigaciones Dr. José María Luis Mora, 2014), 89–105.

[23] *Actas*, XIII, Bk. 15, 47.

[24] Copy of letter Count of Monterrey, May 15, 1602, AGI, Filipinas, 35, N.47, f. 820r.

[25] On Pedro de Baeza, see: José Antonio Martínez Tórrese, "Imperio y arbitrismo. Los memoriales de Pedro de Baeza sobre las Indias Orientales (1607–1609)," *Historia Social*, no. 98 (2020): 151–61. On los conflicts between the consulados de Sevilla y Mexico, see also: Yuste López, *El comercio de la Nueva España con Filipinas*, 32–40; Guillermina de Valle Pavón, "Los mercaderes de México y la transgresiónde los límites al comercio pacífico en Nueva España, 1550–1620," *Revista de Historia Económica – Journal of Iberian and Latin American Economic History*, no. 23 (2005), 213–40; Mariano A. Bonialian, "La seda china en Nueva España a principios del siglo XVII. Una mirada imperial en el memorial de Horacio Levanto," *Revista de Historia Económica – Journal of Iberian and Latin American Economic History* 35, no. 1 (2016): 147–71.

[26] "Pedro de Baeza, vezino desta Villa de Madrid. Digo, que por V. Excel. me mandar hacer este Memorial y discurso de las Indias Orientales, y de las Islas del Maluco, y demas partes de la mar del Sur, y la Orden y manera que se tenia en el traer las especerias antiguamente a Europa, y demas partes della," BNE, R/14034(3), f. 12v.

on Asian imports to achieve a better balance between the prices of Spanish and Chinese products.

Almost two decades later, Fray Thomas Gage reaffirmed some of what Baeza had written in a typical observation regarding the excessive apparel of the residents of Mexico City. The Dominican friar noted how hard it was to distinguish persons of quality from the "baser sort of people" only on the basis of their appearance.[27] His description of the *mulatas* (women of African descent) he encountered on the streets of the viceregal capital reveal why this was the case:

Their clothing is a petticoate, of silk or cloth, with many silver or golden laces, with a very broad double ribband of some light colour with long silver or golden tags hanging down before, the whole length of their petticoat to the ground, and the like behind; their wastecoats made like bodies, with skirts, laced likewise with gold or silver, without sleeves, and a girdle about their body of great price stuck with pearls and knots of gold, (if they be any ways well esteemed of) their sleeves are broad and open at the end, of Holland or fine China linen, wrought some with coloured silks.[28]

Gage's sense of wonder was in part the result of real differences between life in Europe and Mexico City, where, according to many accounts, people were generally wealthier and more inclined to a lavish lifestyle. In part, it also originated in moral discourses questioning the desirability of such lavishness as well as a more general preoccupation with what Christina Lee has described as the "anxiety of sameness," that is, the Spanish elite's fixation with socially mobile lowborns passing as members of the nobility or the privileged classes.[29]

Such fretting about the blurring of social distinctions also came to play a role in discourses about the distributive process. As we will see shortly, in a context in which personal appearance and lifestyle were being assessed by authorities and members of the community to determine a person's qualities, the rising obsession with clothing and other symbols of status prompted new critiques about self-fashioning and the effects this could have on the assessment process.[30] Before we turn to Vivero's text, however, let us first look into another question that arose and that would

---

[27] Gage, *A New Survey of the West-Indies*, 42.   [28] Ibid., 56.

[29] Christina H. Lee, *The Anxiety of Sameness in Early Modern Spain* (Manchester: Manchester University Press, 2015), 4; 55–56.

[30] The relationship between consumption and self-fashioning in the early modern world has often been studied through the lens of clothing. See, for example, Ulinka Rublack, *Dressing Up: Cultural Identity in Renaissance Europe* (Oxford: Oxford University Press, 2010); Claudia Ulbrich and Richard Wittmann, *Fashioning the Self in*

shape his treatise concerning the role of financial wealth in the process of assessing an individual's standing or status as a *benemérito*.

TRADE AND THE MERITORIOUS

As we have seen, in his *Grandeza mexicana*, Bernardo de Balbuena established an intimate link between trade and prosperity, virtue, and worthiness. He presented Mexico City's opulence and the diversity of commodities being traded and consumed there as the characteristics of "an illustrious and rich town in which one forgets about one's desire for more of the world."[31] What constituted New Spain's greatest value to the metropolis was, in his eyes, its commerce. Consequently, the main protagonist in what Barbara Fuchs and Yolanda Martínez-San Miguel have described as a "new mercantile epopee" was not the conquistador but the merchant.[32] Merchants allowed the city to render the services to the empire that Balbuena sought to showcase. The descendants of the conquistadores, in turn, became the subject of Balbuena's implicit criticism when he observed in his prologue, dedicated to the Archdeacon of New Galicia, that the poor "have to remain unworthy of all esteem and respect."[33] For a group whose members – as we have seen in their petitions for royal grace and favor – referred to their suffering being a result of their poverty, such a critique must have been hard to swallow.[34]

Balbuena's particular treatment of the relationship between trade and worthiness reflects a more general development taking place in early modern Iberian societies. Traditionally, commercial activity had been looked down upon by the elite as a vile profession.[35] Although such attitudes did not prevent members of the nobility from being involved in

Transcultural Settings: The Uses and Significance of Dress in Self-Narratives (Baden-Baden: Ergon-Verlag, 2015).

[31] Balbuena, *Grandeza mexicana*, 59.

[32] Fuchs and Martínez-San Miguel, "La grandeza mexicana de Balbuena," 677.

[33] Balbuena, *Grandeza mexicana*, 128.

[34] Merrim, *The Spectacular City*, 127–30; Terukina Yamauchi, *El imperio de la virtud*, 320–22.

[35] For example, candidates for a habit of the Orders of Santiago, Calatrava and Alcántara, always had to prove that they themselves or their ancestors had not been a merchant or involved in any other offices considered vile or mechanical. Such requirements spoke to the rejection of manual work that members of the nobility had professed since the Middle Ages. At the same time, they reflected a response to a reality in which commoners had the opportunity to realize upward social mobility, giving the nobility a chance to exercise some control over the king's decisions in granting habits as a form of reward for services rendered. On the ideal type of caballero and the exclusion of merchants, see: José

trade, it was clear that little value could be derived from this activity in the process of acquiring individual honors and recognition. Beginning in the second half of the sixteenth century, wealthy individuals were given new opportunities to make their fortunes work for them in acquiring royal favor, as a result of the Crown's efforts to raise money for its empty coffers by publicly auctioning off municipal offices.[36] This practice had an immediate impact on negotiations over the distribution of privileges. Not only did the number of offices that could be granted decrease; members of a new social group were also granted access to benefits from which they had previously been excluded. This development prompted controversies from which some of Balbuena's ideas about the virtuous qualities of trade originated.[37]

Spanish authors like the Dominican friar Tomás de Mercado or the erudite nobleman don Cristóbal Pérez de Herrera reflected extensively on the question of the worthiness of the merchant, basing themselves on classical authorities and medieval church literature to praise the laudable role that these men played in aggrandizing the body politic.[38] Through their treatises, they sought to demonstrate that trade, rather than being detrimental to the well-being of the soul, was actually an ennobling activity.[39] When merchants acted in accordance with the appropriate moral rules, their contributions to society made them worthy of, in the

---

A. Guillén Berrendero, *La Edad de la Nobleza. Identidad nobiliaria en Castilla y Portugal (1556–1621)* (Madrid, Ediciones Polifemo, 2012), 168–70; 492.

[36] Francisco Tomás y Valiente, *La venta de oficios en Indias (1492–1606)* (Madrid: Instituto de Estudios Administrativos, 1972); Francisco Andújar Castillo and María del Mar Felices de la Fuente, eds. *El poder del dinero. Ventas de cargos y honores en el Antiguo Régimen* (Madrid: Biblioteca Nueva, 2011); Antonio Jiménez Estrella, "Poder, dinero y ventas de oficios y honores en la España del Antiguo Régimen: un estado de la cuestión," *Cuadernos de historia moderna* 37 (2012): 259–71.

[37] For a study of the legal considerations that the practice of the sale of offices prompted among theologians and jurists such as Francisco Vitoria, Bartolomé de las Casas, Domigo de Soto, and Vázquez de Menchaca, see: Francisco Tomás y Valiente, "Opiniones de algunos juristas clásicos españoles sobrela venta de oficios públicos," in *Filosofía y derecho: estudios en honor del profesor José Corts Grau* (Valencia: Universidad de Valencia, 1977), 2: 627–49.

[38] On the revalorization of the merchant and his role in society during the early modern period, see also the contributions to Christoph Strosetzki, ed., *El poder de la economía: La imagen de los mercaderes y el comercio en el mundo hispánico de la Edad Moderna* (Madrid: Iberoamerican & Vervuert, 2018).

[39] Michel Cavillac, "El discurso del mercader y sus incidencias literarias," *Criticón*, 120–21 (2014): 46–51; Tomás de Mercado, *Suma de tratos y contratos*, eds. Nicolás Sánchez Albornoz and Graciela S. B. de Sánchez Albornoz (Madrid: Instituto de Estudios Fiscales, Ministerio de Hacienda, 1977 [1571]), 1: 71–72.

words of the Toledan merchant Damian de Olivares, "any dignity or honorable office."[40]

New Spanish merchants conveyed a similar message when communicating with the Crown. When the Mexican merchant Miguel Rodríguez petitioned the Crown for permission to establish a *consulado* in 1561, he argued that trade was crucial to the preservation and the aggrandizement of the newly conquered territories.[41] When the institution was finally created in 1593, its members continued to stress that trade solved poverty, created work, and, above all, created the wealth that the Crown could tax. As they saw it, the *consulado* and its members rendered a significant service to the monarch and the realm.

But not everyone in New Spain agreed with the ideas being promoted by Balbuena and the *consulado*. In line with peninsular authors such as Francisco de Quevedo y Villegas and the nobleman don Bernabé Moreno de Vargas, descendants of the first conquistadores and settlers depicted merchants as unworthy members of society who lived vile lives, were driven by greed and self-interest, and made false claims to nobility.[42] Dorantes de Carranza, for example, complained in the *Sumaria relación* that the time had "arrived in which deception and lies, and idleness and injury to one's fellow man prevail, when anyone who sells wine or spices or ordinary cloth or old iron obtains a great entailed estate."[43]

A more elaborate critique was formulated by the experienced royal official Gonzalo Gómez de Cervantes in a text known today as *La vida económica y social de Nueva España al finalizar del siglo XVI* (The Economic and Social Life of New Spain at the End of the Sixteenth Century, 1599).[44] Gómez de Cervantes explained that many of the

---

[40] Cavillac, "El discurso del mercader," 50.

[41] Request to the King by Miguel Rodríguez, in the name of the other merchants of the city of Mexico, Aug 14, 1561, AGI, Patronato, 182, R.1.

[42] Illustrative of such critical reflection on the role of wealth in obtaining nobility is Bernabé Moreno de Vargas' *Discursos de la nobleza de España* (Madrid: Por la Viuda de Alonso Martin, 1622). A regidor on the City Council of Mérida, Spain, Moreno de Vargas argued against the practice of commoners acquiring nobility through negotiations. Only by an act of distributive justice, through which the innate virtue of a person was rewarded, could a person acquire the qualities of the "political or civil nobility." Regarding the figure of the merchant in the discourses on nobility, compare also Lee, *The Anxiety of Sameness*, 34–36; 49–56.

[43] Dorantes de Carranza, *Sumaria relación de las cosas de la Nueva* España, 104.

[44] Gómez de Cervantes had been *alcalde mayor* in Tlaxcala, Tepeaca, and Huejotzingo and had served as governor of Tlaxcala. Through his mother, he was related to the conquistador don Juan de Cervantes and son of the early settler Juan de Cervantes Casaus. Gonzalo's grandfather is mentioned in the register produced during Mendoza's

problems threatening the well-being of the viceroyalty would be resolved if the Crown were to finally give all the descendants of the conquistadores the shares of the Native tributes and labor they were due (the *repartimiento general*) to close once and for all the conquest era. However, he realized that trade was threatening his plan to create a strong and wealthy nobility, dedicated to cultivation of the land, with residents of the viceroyalty, including members of low-ranking groups who acted as retailers (*recatones*), preferring to be involved in merchant activities rather than production. This preference for commercial activity not only decreased the available workforce but also led to retailers enriching themselves at the cost of those who ought to be the privileged members of society, who were now paying the price for the increasing number of intermediaries between the wholesalers and the consumers.[45]

Equally threatening to the formation of a strong American nobility was the development of a market for offices. Like Dorantes de Carranza, Gómez de Cervantes complained that "those who but yesterday served in shops, taverns, and other vile offices, today are placed on and provided with the best and most qualified offices of the land, while the knights and descendants of those who conquered it are poor, downhearted, disadvantaged, and trapped."[46] According to Gómez de Cervantes, it was a disgrace that unqualified sons of merchants were given positions on Mexico's city council. He also lamented that the sale of offices inspired abuse, as office holders sought to make up for their investments by exploiting the Natives and skimming the Crown's tributes. To alter this situation, he suggested that offices should no longer be passed from one person to the next after payment of a fee. Instead, they should be given for a lifetime to men who have the "quality, age, council, and merits."[47]

These opposing opinions rehearse arguments with which we are now quite familiar. On the one hand, some considered merchants to be a group worthy of receiving society's benefits and the king's favor, due to their contributions to the well-being of the community and the kingdom as a whole. On the other hand, those who felt threatened by new distributive practices and ideals of worthiness portrayed the merchant as an undeserving other – the opposite of what they considered the real *beneméritos* to

---

governance. Icaza, *Conquistadores y pobladores de Nueva España*, 1: 192. On the Gómez de Cervantes family, see Paul Ganster, "La familia Gómez de Cervantes. Linaje y sociedad en el México colonial," *Historia Mexicana* XXXI, no. 122 (1981): 197–232.

[45] Gonzalo Gómez de Cervantes, *La vida económica y social de Nueva España al finalizar el siglo XVI*, ed. Alberto María Carreño (Mexico City: Robreño, 1944), 100–1.

[46] Ibid., 94.   [47] Ibid., 132–33.

be. It is important to recognize, though, that in practice the ideals that some propagated about trade's social value did not simply come to replace old ones. Among Mexico City's elite, many continued to look with a certain suspicion toward trade. A testimony to the persistence of these ideas is a seemingly contradictory statement by Alonso Ortiz Arévalo – one of Mexico City's wealthiest merchants, who owed forty-one houses and shops and was publicly known to trade with Europe and Asia – that he "did not have a company, nor business nor trade in this city or outside of it."[48] When, as in this case, merchants had the opportunity to marry into the landed elite, they were more than happy to fashion themselves in ways that conformed to traditional aristocratic ideals.

AN OLD *BENEMÉRITO* IN A NEW WORLD OF TRADE

The two fields of contention that we have explored so far were merged into don Rodrigo de Vivero's reflections on the state of the Spanish empire at the beginning of the 1630s. During his many years of service, the Count of the Valley of Orizaba had acquainted himself with various aspects of a globalizing world of trade. He gained insight into the workings of Southeast Asian trading networks during his short stint as interim governor of the Philippines.[49] This knowledge and experience came in handy in his negotiations with Tokugawa Hidetada and Tokugawa Ieyasu about the possibility of establishing trading relationships between the Philippines, Japan, and New Spain.[50] Nowhere, however, did Vivero learn more about the fluctuations of imperial trade and the actions of those involved in it as in Tierra Firme. During the seven years he served as governor and captain general, traveling between Panama and Portobelo, he observed firsthand not only the necessity of trade for the well-being of the residents of the region but also the corruptive effect it had on many.[51]

---

[48] Cited in José F. de la Peña, *Oligarquía y propiedad en Nueva España, 1550–1624* (Mexico City: Fondo de Cultura Económica, 1983), 135. As José F. Peña has observed, Ortiz may have tried to conceal his economic activities, because of the marriage between his daughter and Legazpi's grandson: Don García de Albornoz Legazpi y Acuña.

[49] Gil, "Don Rodrigo de Vivero," 73–84.

[50] On Vivero's stay in Japan and his negotiations with the Japanese, see Gil, *Hidalgos y samurais*, 140–57; 208–25.

[51] See, for example, the reports Vivero sent during his time in office: AGI, Panamá,17, R.6, N.90 (1622); AGI, Panamá, 17, R.6, N.92 (1622); AGI, Panamá, 17, R.6, N.97 (1622); AGI, Panamá, 17, R.6, N.100 (1622); AGI, Panamá, 17, R.6, N.111 (1622).

These differing experiences shaped the complaints and proposals he presented in the *Abisos*. He underlined, for instance, the necessity of mining, reflected on the different routes along which precious metals and trade moved, and proposed solutions for improving the organization and cost efficiency of the connections within the Spanish empire.[52] Yet, in stark contrast to the letters and reports he wrote during earlier stages of his life, now, at the age of seventy, Vivero assumed a much more critical position toward the transpacific trade and commercial activity in general.[53] Writing amid increasingly heated discussions concerning the desirability of the triangular trade between Manila, Acapulco, and El Callao, Vivero advocated in favor of restrictions.[54] According to him, the impact of commerce on the Iberian societies ought to be reduced by promoting autarky and intra-imperial trade. At the same time, the Crown's judicial strength ought to be reinforced to counterbalance the corrupting effects that trade and consumption were causing within New Spanish society. In his eyes, Spain, and not New Spain as Balbuena would have it, was the true center of the empire, the place where the monarch resided, who formed the heart of a spider's web that was spun out of royal laws.[55]

Vivero's objections to the transpacific trade in particular was a typical one. He complained that too much valuable American silver was being shipped across the Pacific. Such a critique was hardly a novelty. Since the 1580s, traders specialized in shipping textiles from Spain to the Indies, members of Mexico City's cabildo, and residents of Manila had been telling the Crown the same thing.[56] In the *Abisos*, Vivero noted how this silver "enriches the Chinese and Japanese and will never be useful again to Spain except as plates and bowls and low-quality silks that are only good at first glance, [and] deceive the poor and the rich buying them."[57] At the same time, transpacific trade was arousing the greed that made some

---

[52] Vivero, "Abisos y proyectos," chapters 5–7, 32–33 and 39.
[53] Copy of letter from Rodrigo de Vivero to King, May 3, 1610, AGI, Filipinas, 193, N.3, images 21–29.
[54] Bruno de la Serna Nasser, "La prohibición del comercio entre Nueva España y Perú de 1634: génesis de una real cédula a través de la coyuntura histórica de la monarquía hispánica," *Historica* XLIV, no. 1 (2020): 41–81.
[55] Ibid., 98.
[56] Complaints about loss of silver bullion in Asia came, for example, from Seville's *consulado*. Louisa Schell Hoberman, *Mexico's Merchant Elite, 1590–1660* (Durham: Duke University Press, 1991), 215. For one of the critiques coming from the Philippines, see Antonio de Morga, *Sucesos de las Islas Filipinas*, ed. Francisca Perujo (Mexico City: Fondo de Cultura Económica, 2007), 292.
[57] Vivero, "Abisos y proyectos," 104.

vassals forget their loyalty to the monarch. Blinded by avarice, officials became involved with merchants, who promised them great wealth in return for financial contributions and political support. As a result of these alliances, Vivero lamented, "everyone lives off [the] China [trade], while Your Majesty is starving."[58] For this reason, he considered it to be to the general benefit to close the Port of Acapulco and prohibit the trade that was so manifestly detrimental to the treasury and the king's authority. In case the Crown wanted to hold on to its possessions in Asia, he noted, it would be best to return to its plan of establishing direct interaction between Seville and Manila via Cape Horn, a project that had been discussed for decades but had been largely dismissed as being unfeasible after 1621.[59]

With respect to the widespread corruption he bemoaned, Vivero offered advice on how to prevent royal officials from becoming involved in trade. In a chapter dedicated to the political practices of the Chinese and Japanese, he set out to explain that in these kingdoms, those selected for an office were given the opportunity to negotiate with the emperor the salary they deemed to be sufficient. This practice was intended to ensure that a shortage of income would never excuse involvement in any kind of trade or the acceptance of a gift or bribery from anyone in government.[60] Any remaining temptation to ignore the emperor's orders would be stifled by the rigorous and merciless legal system that the Japanese maintained. To demonstrate the advantages of such a system, Vivero described how in the Japanese city of Usuki he witnessed the sentencing to death of a thief just three hours after he had robbed a Spanish sailor.[61] When he had learned about the sentence, Vivero tried to convince the presiding official to show some clemency. The latter had responded to this request that no one in the realm dared to act against the emperor's wishes, for this was considered a capital crime. According to Vivero, the Spanish monarch could learn from such severity, as the Japanese political system had ensured that "for many years no governor or viceroy had traded or been engaged in trade, nor taken more than the little that remained of their salary; something that may seem confusing, that people without God can show us [how] to maintain similar commandments."[62]

[58] Ibid., 105.

[59] For a more detailed study of discussions revolving around this project during the first two decades of the seventeenth century, see Domingo de Guzmán Centenero de Arce, "La política asiática de Felipe III: Los intereses cruzados de los socorros a Filipinas (1610–1624)," *Historia* 52, no. 2 (2019): 421–36.

[60] Vivero, "Abisos y proyectos," 79.   [61] Ibid., 79–80.   [62] Ibid., 80.

Vivero returns to this example in another chapter, explaining that it would be useful to keep this lesson in mind when creating a new armada in the Atlantic. As governor in Tierra Firme, he had already experienced firsthand the growing threat that English, French, and Dutch corsairs in the Atlantic were posing to interaction between the Indies and the metropolis. As the recently appointed general of the forces of the city of Veracruz, he was even more eager to draw attention to the Atlantic and offer his views on the plans that were being discussed for creating a new armada.[63] In addition to serving as a defense force, Vivero argued that this fleet could contribute toward preventing merchants involved in trade with the metropolis from importing merchandise without paying the appropriate taxes.[64] Just like their Japanese counterparts, Spanish, preferably American-born, men-at-arms commanding this fleet would play a key role in maintaining the justice that merchants sought to undermine.

As he reflected on the selection of appropriate candidates for the officials of this new armada, Vivero raised another issue related to global commerce: the culture of consumption and excess that he, as so many other *arbitristas* at the time, considered one of the main causes of Spain's apparent decline.[65] Once more he referred to his experiences in Japan to argue in favor of a political system that functioned according to the principle of justice. He recalled how, in a private conversation, Hideyoshi's secretary confided in him that two aspects of Spanish conduct had dissuaded his lord from doing business with them.[66] First, they had demonstrated a lack of humility in petitioning him for favors, which was not only deemed offensive but also a sign of the Spaniards' impudence. Second, the Spaniards who appeared at the imperial court had been wearing different styles of garments every two years. Such a custom worried Hideyoshi, who feared that Spanish leaders would be as capricious in their politics as their subjects were in their choice of clothing. To further highlight the differences between the two nations, Vivero recounted how the secretary had shown him histories demonstrating that Japanese clothing, like their laws, had not changed for over 1,000 years.[67]

Vivero then explained how he had tried to defend the Spanish nation against such negative assessments. At the same time, however, he made

---

[63] Vivero was appointed to the position of general of the military forces of Veracruz in 1632. See Conde y Díaz-Rubín and Sanchiz Ruiz, *Historia genealógica*, 29.

[64] Vivero, "Abisos y proyectos," 89–91.

[65] Compare, for example, Fernández Navarrete, *Conservación de Monarquías*, 108–13; 295–315; 316–21.

[66] Vivero, "Abisos y proyectos," 94–95.   [67] Ibid., 95.

clear that he did not entirely disagree with Hideyoshi's observations. Echoing the moral critiques of Fernández de Navarrette and the classical authorities to whom the monarch's chaplain referred, he criticized the excessive costs entailed by continuously changing fashions and galas where people showed off their wealth.[68] He even blamed King Philip IV for setting a poor example and reminded him that "the greatness of kings is not based on dressing rooms and silks."[69] Instead, the king should be punishing the immodest behavior of his subjects and rewarding their temperance. Vivero also urged him to follow the example of his great-grandfather, Charles V, who had spent on his court not even half of what Philip was spending, or that of his grandfather, Philip II, whom he had personally seen pass over a trusted vassal and knight of excellent descent for important positions, because the man was indebted to others. Vivero further related that, when the knight asked why he was never considered, Philip had replied: "How do you, Don Diego, want me to entrust the governance of my kingdoms and my treasury to someone who does not have the [governance] of his own household and that of his [estate] in order?"[70]

The juxtaposition of Vivero's two divergent experiences – one at the Japanese and the other at the Spanish royal court – helps us understand the double message he sought to convey about the relationship between conspicuous consumption and negotiations over royal favor. Although Hideyoshi was right to criticize the Spaniards for their mercurial customs and impudent manners, his judgments of their nature had been flawed. This was the result, opined Vivero, of this ruler's focus on outward appearance and his lack of experience with the Iberians. On the other hand, Philip II's treatment of don Diego reveals how he had not been deceived by a man's appearance. Due to his personal acquaintance with this vassal, he was able to come to a correct assessment of the latter's true qualities or, rather, lack thereof. At a time in which discussions about contact between Asia and the Indies were revolving around clothing, Vivero used this theme to reflect on a tendency to value outward appearance over an individual's true qualities. More than a mere moral critique of a culture of excessive consumption, he was defending here a core idea

---

[68] Ibid., 94–98.
[69] Ibid., 96. It is somewhat curious that in his earlier account of his visit to the imperial court, Vivero noted that the Japanese emperor sent a secretary with a gift of twelve garments decorated "with many flowers of gold and silk, and in diverse colors." See "Primera relación," in Gil, *Hidalgos y samurais*, 172.
[70] Vivero, "Abisos y proyectos," 95–96.

of the theory of distributive justice, which held that each person deserves their due in accordance with their individual virtues.[71] For a man who was pitied by Viceroy Cerralbo for being "poor after so many years of service," it was not illogical to remind the authorities that, when it comes to the distribution of royal favors, services rendered ought to be valued rather than personal wealth or appearance.[72]

Finally, Vivero's fascination with the monolithic societies of the Orient and his aversion to commerce merged in his comments on the relationship between the Spanish empire and the rest of the world. Here, he complained that too much value was being ascribed to merchandise coming from outside the realm, while much of what the Indies had to offer was not used at all. New Spain, for example, could perfectly support itself, as it was capable of producing wines, olives, textiles, and even silks that were better than those of Segovia or China.[73] Nonetheless, instead of exploiting these natural resources, Spaniards used their valuable silver to trade with others. Consequently, the number of vagabonds roaming the Indies increased and foreigners – non-Spaniards that is – were being drawn to the viceroyalty who were more loyal to their own patria than to the Spanish Crown. Venting his frustration about this situation, he asked the reader:

[A]nd if the Turk, the Moor, the Japanese, and the Chinese live in peace and realize this by not admitting strangers to their lands, why, then, would Spain not do the same? What to bring from France, from Flanders, from China but tops made of jet, whistles, spectacles, and dolls with which they tempt us like children, while bringing gold and silver to the markets that, because of the bankers' tyrannical achievements and dealings, harm the Crown and Spain. Of this attests the experience of so many millions that they have owed and paid to them, without us learning anything from seeing others enriching themselves with our blood.[74]

The isolationist tendencies of this creole nobleman dovetail with the reflections discussed in Chapter 3 about who the real *beneméritos* of New Spain were. Having served the Crown his entire life, Vivero was frustrated with the difficulties he now experienced living up to his newly acquired status as count. Being forced to leave Mexico City because of his poverty, it appears that he lashed out against those whom he considered to be responsible for shaping the culture of conspicuous consumption and

---

[71] Vallen, "What Distributive Justice Requires,'" 106–7.
[72] Letter Viceroy Cerralbo, Jan 24, 1630, AGI, México, 30, N.26, f. 8.
[73] Vivero, "Abisos y proyectos," 107–8.   [74] Ibid., 108.

were unjustly enjoying the benefits that he had been denied.[75] Moreover, in direct opposition to the contemporary tendency of merchants to move their children into political or even military offices, he propagated a state of affairs in which "everyone follows the calling of his ancestors."[76]

Vivero found in the great Asian empires the perfect model for such a static order, revealing what Ricardo Padrón has described as a form of Japanophilia.[77] Clearly, his descriptions of Japan and China were often more fictitious than real, but widespread admiration at the time of the two cultures that the Spaniards had not been able to subdue added additional value to the message he presented. That Iberian societies could not do without trade was clear, also to Vivero. But, from his perspective, such commercial interaction should take place between different parts of the empire and under the strict supervision of a military and administrative elite. External trade, on the contrary, should be limited as much as possible. His comments about the futility of trade with China served to underline the waste of maintaining the Philippines at such high costs. This was even more true now that the Crown and its vassals were fully occupied with the European privateers who were threatening the Atlantic coasts. According to Vivero, shifting the focus from the Pacific toward the Atlantic was essential to ensure proper communication between the metropolis and the Indies as well as to preserve an administrative system based on strict observance of its own laws and the principles of distributive justice.

NEGOTIATING PACIFIC TRADE

This critique concerning New Spain's commercial relations in the Pacific, as voiced by Rodrigo de Vivero in the *Abisos*, did not stand alone. His call for stricter control over merchants and their activities with the help of the judicial apparatus corresponded with a hardening stance toward fiscal fraud that emerged during King Philip IV's reign (1621–65). Not only *arbitristas* had been railing against corruption but the period also saw a sharp rise in investigations of fraud committed by individuals and institutions.[78] In 1635, the effects of these developments became noticeable in

---

[75] Gil, "Don Rodrigo de Vivero," 123.   [76] Vivero, "Abisos y proyectos," 92.

[77] Ricardo Padrón, "The Confusions of Idolatry: Rodrigo Vivero, Japan, and the Hapsburg Monarchy," *Revista de Estudios Hispánicos* 55, no. 1 (2021): 125.

[78] John H. Elliott, *The Count-Duke of Olivares: The Statesman in an Age of Decline* (London: Yale University Press, 1986), 102–3.

New Spain with the arrival on September 16 of the incoming viceroy, the Marquis of Cadereyta, and Dr. Pedro de Quiroga y Moya, a royal official with years of experience in Seville who had been appointed by the Crown as investigative judge (*visitador*) to the Port of Acapulco.[79] Both men were determined to end corruption in the Pacific trade. Yet their fight against it was affected by the Crown's need for Mexico City to contribute financially to the Armada de Barlovento. During the negotiations over the city's contribution, the relationship between trade – both in the Pacific and in general – worthiness, and the distribution of royal favor once more became an important theme.

The Crown had been trying for decades to regulate trade in the Pacific. Such efforts were mostly the result of the necessity to strike a balance between the interests of textile producers and wholesale traders on the Peninsula and those in the Indies. In 1593, the Crown had established the first limitations on the transpacific trade, allowing only 2 galleons of 300 tons each to make the long journey carrying a maximum of 500,000 pesos of pieces of 8 from Acapulco to Manila and a cargo not exceeding a value of 250,000 pesos on the return journey.[80] It also ordered that the Asian goods these galleons brought could only be consumed by residents of New Spain. In 1604, the Crown sought to curb the booming trade along the American west coast by limiting trade to the ports of Manila and Acapulco. For the same reason, during the first two decades of the seventeenth century, several royal orders were issued that set restrictions upon the number of ships allowed to sail between New Spain and Peru.[81] Little had been done, however, to enforce these rules. Galleons sailing from Acapulco regularly carried more silver than what was allowed and returned with goods with a total value far exceeding the

---

[79] Pedro de Quiroga had actually in 1634 been involved in an investigation of a shipment of silver and gold that had arrived in Seville from the fleet of which the Marquis of Cadereyta had been the general. AGI, Indiferente, 434, L.6, ff. 325v-326.

[80] Royal order regulating trade between the Philippines and New Spain, Jan 11, 1593, AGI, Filipinas, 339, l. 2, f. 70r. This order and its consequences are discussed in Luis Alonso Álvarez, "E la nave va. Economía, fiscalidad e inflación en las regulaciones de la carrera de la Mar del Sur, 1565–1604," in *Un océano de seda y plata: el universo económico del Galeón de Manila*, ed. Salvador Bernabéu Albert and Carlos Martínez Shaw (Seville: CSIC, 2013), 36, 67–72; Carmen Yuste López, "De la libre contratación a las restricciones de la permission. La andadura de los comerciantes de México en los giros iniciales con Manila, 1580-1610," in *Un océano de seda y plata*, eds. Bernabéu Albert and Martínez Shaw, 91–92.

[81] Margarita Suárez, "Sedas, rasos y damascos: Lima y el cierra del comercio triangular con México y Manila en la primera mitad del siglo XVII," *América Latina en la historia económica* 22, no. 2 (2015): 101–34.

permitted 250,000 pesos. With respect to the trade with Peru, the impact of these restrictions was even less noticeable. According to Engel Sluiter, the number of Peruvian ships arriving at the port of Acapulco actually reached its highest point between 1631 and 1634.[82]

Annoyed by reports of such flagrant disobedience, the monarch had ordered Cadereyta to tighten the reins during his tenure in New Spain.[83] After several months in office, the viceroy informed the king that he believed this was indeed the right thing to do. In a letter to the monarch, dated April 17, 1636, he noted that fraud was so common in the Pacific that "terminating the trade with the Philippines would generally benefit all vassals."[84] He had not yet formed an opinion about the trade with Peru, but he intended to find the most suitable solution through deliberation. Meanwhile, Quiroga y Moya had commenced his inquiries regarding the situation in the port of Acapulco. Just like Vivero, he considered Spain to be the heart of the Spanish monarchy and believed all the benefits of the Indies were to go there.[85] From the outset of his investigation, he revealed a resolve to end the illicit trade between New Spain and Peru and make New Spanish merchants pay for the damage they had done to the royal treasury.[86]

Mexico's powerful trading guild and city council quickly realized the danger heading toward them and sought ways to attenuate its impacts. One month after Cadereyta had taken office, the city's *corregidor* (royal representative), Fernando de Sosa Suárez, informed both institutions about Quiroga's intention to audit the Port of Acapulco. The news prompted rumors that the Crown was planning to close the port entirely. Worried about this possibility, the chief justice, Francisco de Solis y Barraza, argued in the cabildo that the viceroy and the royal *visitador* should immediately be informed about "the miserable state of the city's commerce."[87] Fernando de la Barrera, another member of the municipal council, underscored Solis y Barraza's warning and urged the council to communicate to the viceroy the problems that the city was facing as a

---

[82] Engel Sluiter Historical Documents Collection at the UC Berkeley Bancroft Library, Carton 80 and 81.

[83] Titles and appointments conceded to the Marquis of Cadereyta, Apr 19, 1635, AHN, Diversos-Colecciones, 31, N.2, f. 20v.

[84] AGI, Mexico, 31, N.42, images 26–27.

[85] Opinion of Pedro de Quiroga y Moya, undated, AGI, México, 32, L.1, f. 50r.

[86] For a study of Quiroga's audit of the Port of Acapulco, see Sales Colín, *El movimiento portuario*, 117–33.

[87] *Actas*, XXIII, Bk. 30, 66–67.

result of the loss of a fleet in 1629 and the massively destructive floods of that same year, from which the city had just recovered. Due to the decline "of the trade and commerce of this marketplace," he noted, "the city will be unable to comply with the sales taxes and service as it had done for the Unión de Armas."[88]

At the end of 1635, the viceroy and *visitador*'s mission to reform the system turned into open conflict, resulting from Quiroga's attempt to force Mexico's *consulado* to pay the Crown 600,000 pesos in return for a guarantee that the first two galleons to arrive at the Port of Acapulco would be treated in the same way as they had in preceding years, that is, without their cargos being inspected in detail by opening each shipping crate.[89] The *consulado* was furious about the way the auditor was trying to extort them.[90] Unable to send word to Manila to load the coming galleons according to the letter of the law, they had the choice between paying a hefty fine or accepting even greater losses if the entire cargo were to be confiscated. Both the *consulado* and the cabildo deduced that such a measure must be about much more than fighting corruption. They believed Quiroga to have taken the side of the *consulado* of Seville in a long-running struggle over the global textile trade, with this fine being an unjust measure to hurt Mexican traders. At the same time, all the actors involved realized that Quiroga's penalty was directly related to another of Cadereyta's principal preoccupations: raising money for the creation and the outfitting of the Armada de Barlovento.

Having overseen the protection of the Atlantic fleets, Cadereyta was a great advocate of this project and sought to transmit some of his enthusiasm to those whose financial contributions were deemed indispensable to its success.[91] In his communication with the municipal council, Cadereyta insisted again and again that funding a fleet consisting of twelve galleons and two support vessels would be of utmost interest to the inhabitants of New Spain. In a letter written on February 23, 1636, he asked the cabildo for a one-time contribution of 600,000 ducats for construction of the fleet

---

[88] Ibid., XXIII, Bk. 30, 67. Introduced in 1626, the *Unión de Armas* was an ambitious project for military cooperation between all the kingdoms and territories of the Spanish crown.

[89] Gasch-Tomás, *The Atlantic World and the Manila Galleons*, 122.

[90] Transcript of letter from consulado of Mexico, Dec 15, 1635, AGI, México, 32, L.1, ff. 165r.–174r.

[91] The negotiations between the Viceroy and Mexico's cabildo are also studied in Manuel Alvarado Morales, *La ciudad de México ante la fundación de la Armada de Barlovento, 1635–1643* (Mexico City: El Colegio de México; Universidad de Puerto Rico, 1983).

as well as an annual payment of the same amount for its maintenance, explaining that this was an ideal way for the city to show its enduring loyalty to the Spanish Crown.[92] Creating the fleet was also in the city's own interest, he advised, as it would guard the ships carrying their trade and silver. Finally, to those who were not directly involved in trade, the fleet offered opportunities for the rendering of services that would later result in benefiting from the king's generosity. By serving on the fleet, Cadereyta pointed out, the descendants of the conquistadores could distinguish themselves in war like their ancestors during the conquest, earning themselves a habit from one of the military orders that he had been authorized to reward.

Although Cadereyta made a compelling case about the benefits the city could derive from this project, the cabildo was not eager to commit itself to another expensive imperial project. In its response to the viceroy's request, the council members recognized the importance of the fleet and expressed their unfaltering desire to support the Crown. Nevertheless, the letter made no actual promises to raise any money. On the contrary, the cabildo continued to explain why it was unable to commit to new fiscal obligations.[93] Since 1624, the authors noted, the city had made several extraordinary financial contributions, including those to the Union of Arms, while its own financial situation had deteriorated due to the loss of 8 million pesos to Dutch pirates in 1628 and the costs for drainage projects and reconstruction of the city after the floods of 1629 and 1630. Adding to its problems was the decline of the Indian population. As less people were now working the land and the mines, food prices were soaring and production of bullion had plummeted. The cabildo's letter also brought up Quiroga's sanctions and the negative effects these were having on the triangular commerce between the Philippines, New Spain, and Peru. Without commercial interaction with the Southeast-Asian archipelago and the viceroyalty to the south, New Spain did not have an outlet for its merchandise. As the cabildo observed, it negatively impacted the viceroyalty's capacity to finance royal projects "if all contributions would have to come from the body of this city as the destination of all the trade of New Spain."[94]

---

[92] Propositions by Viceroy Cadereyta for the city of Mexico, Feb 23, 1636, AGI, Mexico, 31, N.42, image 18.

[93] Response from Mexico to proposals by the viceroy, Mar 11, 1636, AGI, Mexico, 31, N.42, images 19–21.

[94] Ibid., image 20.

During the following three months, the viceroy and cabildo continued their dialogues, each further elaborating their respective positions.[95] Cadereyta urged the city council to deliver on their promise to be loyal to the royal cause, while the cabildo continued to stress the difficulties with which the city was grappling. In its letters, the municipal council gradually shifted its attention to measures that could be taken to resolve these problems as well as the rewards that the Crown could grant in return for any possible contributions. At the top of this list of requests was permission to trade with Peru again. Refuting the argument of the *consulado* of Seville that the Atlantic trade would benefit from the ban, the cabildo argued that, by keeping open the triangular trade, more sales taxes could be raised that would directly benefit the royal treasury. Furthermore, the city council proposed to buy the office of the *corregidor* and replace him with two *alcaldes ordinarios* elected from among the institution's members.[96] Finally, it petitioned the viceroy to extend the city's jurisdiction to three leagues, mostly to bring the population of the towns of Tacuba, Azcapotzalco, San Cristobal Xochimilco, Mexicaltzingo, and Iztapalapa under its authority, paying their tributes directly to the city.

By the beginning of May 1636, still no agreement had been reached, and Cadereyta began to lose his patience. He wrote the cabildo that he had expected to raise the money without difficulty, as this was a project that benefited all of the city's residents, including merchants and men-at-arms.[97] The Crown had generously agreed to provide not only four galleons and a *patache* but also favors to Mexico City's residents. Rather than responding to this generosity with positive action, the viceroy grumbled, the cabildo had only set more conditions. Pressured by the departure of the annual fleet from New Spain, he promised to write the monarch and the Council of the Indies that the city intended to search for ways to contribute toward maintenance of the Armada with the largest possible contribution it could muster, without yet specifying the exact sum nor the measures that would be taken to raise the money. The cabildo did not miss the warning tone of Cadereyta's letter. In a prompt response, council members assured that they had not wanted to raise the

---

[95] Ibid., images 23–26; *Actas*, XXIII, Bk. 30, 153–54, 178, 190–93.

[96] On the cabildo's earlier attempts to get rid of the *corregidor*, see Francisco Quijano Velasco, "Los argumentos del ayuntamiento de México para destituir al corregidor en el siglo XVI. El pensamiento político novohispano visto desde una institución local," *Estudios de Historia Novohispana* 55 (2016): 46–63.

[97] Letter from Viceroy Cadereyta, May 2, 1636, AGI, Mexico, 31, N.42, images 29–34.

suggestion that the city was unwilling to serve the Crown but, rather, it had only wanted to explain why its means were limited and that all the favors it had asked for were only to help the viceregal capital and its residents to improve this situation.[98]

Now that the urgency of a quick solution had been agreed upon, Cadereyta ordered the creation of several committees tasked with finding solutions and determining what tax measures could be implemented to raise additional revenues. Various proposals were worked up by these committees, but the one the cabildo eventually selected as its favorite was written by Fernando Alfonso Carrillo. Notary of the municipal council since 1602, Carrillo provided a detailed plan on how to raise a modest sum of 200,000 pesos by means of four taxes levied on wine, playing cards, trade, and the minting of silver.[99] Although Carrillo recognized that this amount did not cover the 600,000 ducats Cadereyta had asked for, he did nonetheless expect some significant rewards for Mexico in return. He posed a list of twenty-five demands, revealing the council members' different interests as well as their common agenda for the expansion of the city's power.[100] Again, the request to revise the monarch's stance on Pacific trade was high on Carrillo's list. His proposal explained that the decision to prohibit commercial relations with Peru should be reversed and privileges should be granted to merchants in Mexico and Lima to maintain a limited trade. Assurances were also to be given to Mexico's merchants so that trade with the Philippines could continue as usual.[101] The motivations behind these requests were simple. Inhabitants of Mexico would be unable to contribute to the new fleet without reopening the Peruvian trade. Moreover, transpacific trade was essential for the survival of the Philippines and, without it, there would not be enough options for employing the vagabonds who were roaming the viceroyalty. These arguments were further elaborated in an additional letter, in which the city council refuted one by one the complaints of Seville's *consulado*.[102]

The other demands on the list touched on a wide range of issues. Carrillo petitioned for perpetual extension of encomienda rights, stricter selection criteria for notarial offices, and more flexible rules for

---

[98] AGI, México 33, L. 2, ff. 5–11. *Actas*, XXIII, Bk. 30, 172–77.

[99] *Actas*, XXIII, Bk. 30, 216–17.

[100] This proposal had been included in the minutes of a cabildo meeting that took place on Jul 21, 1636. *Actas*, XXIII, Bk. 30, 207–18.

[101] Ibid., items 2 and 3.

[102] Letter of Mexico's cabildo, Jul 4, 1636, AGI, México, 32, L.1, ff. 43–49v.

transferring them from one holder to the next. He also asked that the viceroy be given the sole right to distribute *alcadías mayores* (office of chief magistrate) and *corregimientos* among the conquistadores' descendants, that half of the positions on the audiencia should go to sons of the land, and that this same group be considered in the distribution of offices for the new Armada de Barlovento.[103] Several demands also concerned measures to prevent religious Orders from further expanding their political and economic influence in the city and a prohibition on peninsular friars traveling to New Spain and the Philippines.[104] Finally, Carrillo asked for several privileges that would increase the city's authority and prestige, including extension of its legal jurisdiction, recognition of its honorary title of "Señoría," permission for the construction of new colleges, and support for its indispensable drainage project.[105]

The cabildo's exchanges with Viceroy Cadereyta demonstrate in yet another way how the position of this city between the Atlantic and Pacific oceans impacted its residents' struggles over the distribution of royal grace and favor. Although the same institution had asked for the closure of Acapulco only three decades earlier, by now its members agreed that trade in the Pacific was crucial to the city's well-being and its capacity to contribute to the Armada. In its negotiations with Cadereyta about the amount they would donate and the favors they would receive in return, they fashioned a particular image of the city. In their letters, they underlined the difficulties with which the community was grappling, including the necessity of investing in irrigation works that would prevent the city from flooding and the dire state of trade. While pledging their commitment to rendering services to the Crown, they also sought to shape themselves as representing a community that was worthy of significant royal favors. A painting of the city from the time Cadereyta was in office presents a remarkably similar image of such a struggling but deserving community, as explored in more detail in the following section.

THE PACIFIC AND FASHIONING OF THE COLONIAL METROPOLIS

The painting in question is known as *Vista de la Plaza Mayor de la ciudad de México y laguna de Ixtacalco* (View of the Main Square of Mexico City and Ixtacalco Lagoon, Figure 5.1); it appears on what was probably

---

[103] *Actas*, XXIII, Bk. 30, 207–18, items 5–10, 19.   [104] Ibid., items 11–13, 15.
[105] Ibid., items 4, 18, 21.

FIGURE 5.1 Anonymous, view of the Central Plaza of Mexico City and the Iztacalco Promenade (ca. 1636). Colección Rodrigo Rivero Lake. Arte y Antigüedades, Mexico City

one of the first Japanese-style folding screens, or *biombo*, made in New Spain. The *biombo* is 2.3 meters high by 3 meters wide and consists of four panels, depicting three spaces in which the city's elite passed its leisure time and did its business: Lake Ixtacalco, the Alameda, and the main square, which occupies two panels.[106] Almost all recent studies date this screen to the period 1635–40, indicated by various aspects of the painted image. The coat of arms in the upper-left corner has been identified as belonging to the Marquis de Cadereyta, making it quite probable that the painting was created during his tenure.[107] Arturo Aguilar Ochoa has corroborated this idea through a detailed study of the depicted garments, which he argues correspond to the fashions of the 1630s and 1640s.[108] A final argument for more precisely placing the production of the screen within the timeframe of the Cadereyta regime is the presence of the viceroy himself, who can be seen in the carriage crossing the *Zocalo* (main square), identified with the help of a painting that is part of the preserved portraits of viceroys collected in Chapultepec Castle, Mexico City. Here the marquis can be picked out by his blond hair and Van Dyke beard, which set him apart from the other viceroys of the period, who were all dark-haired.[109]

Due to the bird's-eye perspective taken by the artist, it is not surprising that art historians and historians have read this *biombo* and others like it through chorographic and panegyrical lenses. We have already seen in the previous chapter how important paeans to the community were to people

---

[106] The *biombo* and its characteristics are discussed in more detail in Rodrigo Rivero Lake, *Namban Art in Viceregal Mexico* (Madrid: Turner, 2005), 180. Although Rivero Lake has argued that Japanese artists may have painted the screen, others have argued that there is no evidence affirming such an involvement. Alberto Baena Zapatero, "Chinese and Japanese Influence on Colonial Mexican Furniture: The Achinado Folding Screens," *Bulletin of Portuguese-Japanese Studies* 20 (2010): 107–9.

[107] Rivero Lake, *Namban Art*, 183, 196. An exception to this opinion comes from Concepción Amerlinck de Corsi, who was the first to identify the coat of arms on the *biombo* as that of the Marquis of Cadereyta. Nevertheless, Amerlinck de Corsi has rejected the possibility that the *biombo* was made during the government of the marquis, arguing instead that his daughter, who inherited the title and married don Francisco Fernández de la Cueva, viceroy of New Spain from 1653 to 1660, had it painted after Cadereyta's reign. María Concepción Amerlinck de Corsi, "Vista del palacio del virrey de México," in *Los Siglos de Oro en los virreinatos de América. 1550–1700* (Madrid: Sociedad Estatal para la Conmemoración de los Centenarios de Felipe II y Carlos V, 1999), 161–63.

[108] Arturo Aguilar Ochoa, "La indumentaria novohispana del siglo XVII y su uso para la datación de tres biombos virreinales," *Anales del Museo de América* XXV (2017): 94–108.

[109] Ibid., 96–97.

throughout the Spanish empire. Visual choreographies began to enjoy great popularity as well.[110] Of the three approaches that early modern Europeans developed toward representation of the earth – the other two being cosmographic or geographic perspectives – the chorographic perspective depicted places and their characteristic properties to reveal their unique qualities and those of the people residing in them.[111] It should not come as a surprise, then, that contemporaries used this perspective to praise their community as a whole and turn a spotlight on the most notable residents inhabiting their city.

Historians and art historians who have studied the view of Mexico City appearing on this folding screen have often focused on these characteristics, noting how the beholder is guided through the viceregal capital – its greatness reflected in the splendor of its Royal Palace and broad, clean streets that no longer exhibit any signs of the waters that had only recently covered the city. With some exceptions, most of those depicted are real members of the Spanish and Native elites. Their status, wealth, and belonging to certain groups are displayed via the attire and symbols they wear. Women are dressed in expensive, decorated garments, some carrying colorful parasols. In comparison, most of the men are somberly outfitted in black with a white ruff, which was the traditional attire of the Spanish nobility. Seen from this perspective, the *biombo* could be interpreted as an attempt by the city to self-advertise its greatness to a newly arriving viceroy, while at the same time demonstrating, as Michael Schreffler has argued with respect to a very similar screen, its loyalty and allegiance to the Spanish Crown.[112]

One feature of the screen does challenges us, however, to forge a more nuanced understanding of this celebratory attempt at collective self-fashioning. The lower-right quadrant of the screen – running across the bottom of two panels – depicts market stalls positioned on the Plaza Mayor, in sight of the Viceroy's Palace. Although it is common to find similar representations of what would become known as the Parian

---

[110] Such visual representations of Latin American cities and towns are studied in detail in Kagan and Marías, *Urban Images of the Hispanic World*.

[111] The German humanist Petrus Apianus explained the distinction between these three perspectives in a highly influential cosmographic treatise. In brief, cosmography viewed the world as a whole, in direct relation with the heavenly bodies, whereas geography focused only on the world as a whole. Pedro Apiano, *La cosmographia: corregida y añadida por Gemma Frisio, médico y matemático* (Antwerp: Juan Bellero al Aguila de Oro, 1575), ff. 1r–2v.

[112] Schreffler, *The Art of Allegiance*, 18–22.

FIGURE 5.2 Detail from view of the Central Plaza of Mexico City and the
Iztacalco. Colección Rodrigo Rivero Lake. Arte y Antigüedades, Mexico City

market, named after Manila's Chinese neighborhood, this depiction is
unique. Nothing here evokes the buzzing trade center extolled by
Balbuena and made evident in later depictions of the Plaza Mayor.[113]
Instead, the viewer of the screen only sees a marketplace that is empty and
deprived of almost any activity (Figure 5.2). While others on the plaza are
participating in the pomp of welcoming the viceroy or engaged in an
Indigenous procession or *mitote*, the merchants can be seen staring list-
lessly out of stalls that look empty but for some common tools, simple
shirts, and drinks, with the only customers that appear obviously being of
low rank.[114] The merchants' inactivity and apparent lack of tradeable
goods or customers are surprising in an image that was supposed to
celebrate the city and its residents. Yet, this striking feature makes more
sense when related to the context in which the *biombo* was painted. As we
have already learned from the letters written by the cabildo in their
negotiations with Cadereyta, trade had been suffering due to various
problems in New Spain, which were aggravated by the viceroy's and
especially Quiroga's attempt to bring order to trade in the Pacific.
Rather than being a mere celebration of the greatness and civil order of

[113] Compare, for example, Cristobal de Villalpando's *Vista del Zócalo de México* (View of
the Zócalo of Mexico City, 1695) and Diego García Conde's *Plaza Mayor de la Ciudad
de México* (Main Square of Mexico City, 1765). These images also present a procession
taking place on Mexico's main square, but in these cases the market is buzzing with
activity and trade.

[114] *Mitotes* were ritual dances that were commonplace in the festival life of Mexico City.
They were representations of a successful evangelization and seem to have played an
important role in the constituting of collective identities. Barbara E. Mundy,
"Moteuczoma reborn: biombo paintings and collective memory in colonial Mexico
City," *Winterthur Portfolio* 45, no. 2–3 (2011): 161–76.

the city, the screen painting registers a troublesome situation: one in which lack of trade would result in the city being unable to collect great amounts of tribute for the Crown's imperial projects.

I have not been able to uncover any information on who paid for this object or ordered its production. Because of the particular details included, we can almost certainly rule out Viceroy Cadereyta himself. Although the image shows various actors paying their respects to him, it was surely not a good look for the viceroy to rule a city where trade apparently had come to a halt. In fact, toward the end of his tenure, Cadereyta faced fierce criticism, both in New Spain and at the court, for not having been able to control Quiroga and the damage he did to the transpacific trade, which came to a complete halt between 1636 and 1639.[115] In 1640, a fuming King Philip IV wrote how, in the course of the three years that no galleons had crossed the Pacific, "900,000 pesos will have been lost in custom duties, which equals what don Pedro de Quiroga, against all reason and justice, extracted in fines, he being the one who with his severity has caused this irreparable damage, both to my royal treasury and to commerce."[116] Such criticism played an important role in the audit to which Caderyta was subjected in 1641, in the context of which he wrote several reports seeking to prove that the city had never actually had any supply problems and that he had done everything in his power to ensure continuation of the transpacific trade.[117]

While the viceroy would, thus, have had little incentive to have commissioned the *biombo* in question, two other actors in the city did have very good reasons to draw attention to the dire state of commerce. One of them was the *consulado*. Members of Mexico's merchant guild elite would have had access to an original Japanese *biombo*. They also had good reason for drawing the viceroy's attention to the challenges they were facing. But the screen offers a vision of the city and its surroundings that exceeds the *consulado*'s interests. Instead, we might suspect that the cabildo or one of its members may have played a leading role in ordering and designing the screen. As we have already seen in their correspondence

---

[115] Sales Colín, *El movimiento portuario de Acapulco*, 131.

[116] Letter from King Philip IV to Juan de Palafox y Mendoza, Feb 14, 1640, AGI, Filipinas, L.5, f. 50v.

[117] Account of the state of governance when Lope Diez de Armendariz, Marquis of Cadereyta, left office, Dec 6, 1641, in Hanke, *Los Virreyes españoles*, 4: 10–17.

with the viceroy, by 1636 the *regidores* (councilmen) were extremely motivated toward finding a way to effectively draw attention to the city's financial problems. Interest in doing so only further increased during the following years, as the trade with the Philippines came to a halt and internal problems led to supply shortages. On the other hand, the cabildo wanted to convey the image that Mexico was a "very noble and loyal" city, worthy of being granted special privileges reaffirming its position as the capital of the viceroyalty. Using powerful visual language, the *Vista* communicates exactly this double-sided image of a community deserving of the king's help and favor, even when its own abilities to serve the Crown had been severely limited.

Although we unfortunately do not know how Cadereyta would have responded to the *biombo*, we do know that he eventually became more sympathetic to the city's needs. On December 12, 1636, after months of deliberating with multiple committees – comprised of *regidores*, *oidores*, and other judicial officials – he signed an agreement with the city, which promised to grant the privileges the city had asked for and some more. In so doing, he followed the advice of Mexico's audiencia to maintain trade with the Philippines and grant to New Spain and Peru the favor of being allowed to annually dispatch two ships of 200 tons each.[118] The Crown's response to the list of demands Cadereyta had forwarded was somewhat skeptical. The Council of the Indies believed some of the city's demands to be excessive. It also warned Cadereyta not to make trade with Peru a condition in negotiations over the city's donations to the Armada de Barlovento.[119] Furthermore, the councilors informed him that, despite the king's inclination to bestow honors on those subjects who served him, the favors the city requested for its residents should not be considered conditions for the agreement as such, for "it would not be convenient to introduce this kind of service, as favors can never be set as a precondition but are to be confided in the benignity and the greatness of Your Majesty."[120]

The Council's observation provides a revealing insight into the tensions explored in this chapter on money intervening in the workings of the economy of favor. Whereas the cabildo sought to use its financial contributions to the Armada de Barlovento to bypass the usual distributive

---

[118] Ibid., 139–42. See also: Alvarado Morales, *La ciudad de México*, 63–68.
[119] Instructions of the Council of the Indies for Viceroy Cadereyta, 1637, AGI, México, 31, N.49, ff. 48v–49r.
[120] Ibid., f. 51r.

processes, the councilors carefully protected their and the king's roles as sole providers of offices and honors. They expressed their sympathy with the needs of the community but would not concede to basically selling the requested offices. This attempt by the cabildo to acquire guaranteed positions through financial contributions to one project exemplified the growing influence of money in the distributive process, a development that would only further intervene within the workings of the economy of favor in centuries to come. Some favored these changes and tried to gain recognition for new norms and practices that linked trade and ostentation to worthiness. Others, however, fiercely defended the ideal that royal favor ought to be distributed in accord with the principle of distributive justice and its entailed logic of assessment. As this chapter has demonstrated, such debates produced not only varying notions of a deserving self and other but also different ideas regarding the Pacific world and the trading relationships linking its component parts, revealing once more that transpacific connections did not simply boost creole self-consciousness.

Conclusion

This book has examined the ways in which New Spain's gradual integration into the Pacific Basin impacted the identities of the viceroyalty's Spanish population. Exploration and conquest, followed by the establishment of interconnections and interaction between the viceroyalty and Asia, prompted struggles over the distribution of royal favor during which New Spain's residents produced diverging notions of a deserving self and undeserving other. In whatever forms they assumed, these self-presentations were strategic responses to a changing world in which the increasing mobility of people and goods created both opportunities and fierce competition over limited benefits and resources. As this book reveals, such acts of self-fashioning were crucial for those wishing to reap the benefits of such opportunities and influence the ways in which they were distributed. In the process, I have argued, explorers, conquistadores, and their descendants, royal officials, soldiers, clergymen, and merchants not only produced different visions of the Pacific but also contributed toward emerging definitions of the components of global integration and disintegration that were shaping New Spain's place in an increasingly mobile and interconnected world.

Beginning in the early sixteenth century, conquerors, veterans, clergymen, and entrepreneurs stressing and promoting their own abilities to successfully lead exploration in the Pacific world pushed Spain's western expansion forward. Highlighting opportunities to find wealth, imperial glory, and souls to convert, they produced geopolitical imaginaries that made connections between New Spain and Southeast Asia appear desirable and easy to establish. In tying their own interests to those of the Crown, these men contributed to the realization of the Spanish dream of gaining access to the lands from which spices and other riches so highly valued by Europeans came. Scholars of Iberian expansion have long studied these geopolitical imaginaries in relation to a Spanish imperial agenda. Ricardo Padrón, for example, has recently pointed out the Spaniards' unique tendency in early modern world-making to see connection and continuity between Asia and the New World, characterizing the idea of the Indies of the Setting Sun as "a fundamental part of Spain's entire spatial experience as an imperial power."[1] With respect to such findings, the present book has underscored how competition among individual subjects of the Spanish Crown over the future of the empire produced personal variations on what often were, indeed, arguments for further territorial expansion. Such struggles further intensified with the growing number of transpacific points of interaction that turned New Spain into a pivot connecting the Atlantic and Pacific worlds. In response, descendants of the first conquistadores and settlers, clergymen, and officials whose interests were threatened by new forms of mobility in the Pacific Basin, questioned the desirability of increasing or maintaining Spain's transpacific connections, prompting less grandly conceived visions of the world that did not align with expansionist agendas.

As we have seen, these integrative processes and the reactions they incited raised a wide-ranging variety of urgent distributional questions. By studying different disputes over how benefits and opportunities ought to have been distributed between a broad spectrum of actors with their often conflicting perspectives and material interests, this book illuminates the rich and complex thoughts and realities of those who reflected upon and sought to have practical effects on the viceroyalty's integration into the Pacific world. To many, the waters and lands west of New Spain were not merely a space for realizing exotic enterprises of a military, religious, or commercial nature. Rather, this oceanic basin was an integral part of their world, which they related again and again to their activities and interests in a colonial society in the making. Hernán Cortés's conflict with Antonio de Mendoza over who was to be recognized as the discoverer of Tierra Nueva had direct legal ramifications that impacted officials in New Spain and other parts of the empire, while veterans of the Loaísa expedition used their experiences in the Pacific to navigate the hierarchy of the meritorious, or *beneméritos*, that took shape during the 1540s. By rendering visible the dynamics of the interplay between distributive

---

[1] Padrón, *The Indies of the Setting Sun*, 3.

struggles in the viceroyalty and Spanish activities of exploration, conquest, trade, and religious evangelizing in the Pacific, this book adds to a growing body of scholarship seeking to reframe the history of Spanish expansion and the formation of colonial society from a transoceanic and global perspective. The spectrum of self-fashioning narratives considered here illustrates the importance of considering the worldviews of contemporaries in their entirety. Even when developments appeared to be part of a predominantly Atlantic history, like the promulgation of the New Laws or the organization of the Armada de Barlovento, the inhabitants of New Spain linked them in one way or another to their own activities or those of others in the Pacific.

In a similar vein, the long-term analysis of these conflicts over New Spain's integration into the Pacific world carried out here has provided novel insights into the complex nature of negotiations over the distribution of royal favor. In the scholarship on colonial Latin America, the principle of reciprocity has played a significant role, as affirmed by the rich body of scholarship examining the efforts of officials, soldiers, clergymen, merchants, and Indigenous actors to petition for the rewards they felt their services deserved. We should not, however, solely rely on this single principle to guide our understanding of the workings of the economy of favor. Equally important in determining who deserved benefits, offices, or honors were each candidate's *calidades* (social standing) and *partes* (skills and capacities). Such criteria were crucial to the logic of assessment that largely shaped contemporary expectations of what constituted a just distributive process. How each of these distinct metrics of worthiness were to be weighed in the decision-making process was the subject of constant dispute. Changing circumstances and necessities inspired new norms, laws, and practices that altered the value ascribed to each of these criteria, resulting in royal favor being distributed in varying ways in different places and times. These lessons regarding the contingencies of the reward system are important takeaways for examining the social history of colonial Latin America and the distributive struggles that shaped the region.

This book has also shown that, in their efforts to influence the outcomes of distributive processes, subjects of the Spanish monarch deployed a wide array of strategies. They wrote books and reports, drew maps, sent *relaciones de méritos y servicos*, ordered and reordered the hierarchies of the meritorious, and had an allegorical representation of the plight of their city painted on a Japanese-style *biombo* screen, often moving between both formal administrative and more personal contexts.

Notwithstanding the obvious differences between these strategies, they were all involved in some way or another with the logic of assessment. Someone like Melchor de Legazpi followed the rules set by an administrative apparatus created to produce legally verifiable assessments based on the participation of a judge and known members of the community. Others produced auto-assessments that partly built on existing ideals about what constituted a worthy subject while defining their own models. Martin Fernández de Enciso used his *Suma de geografía* to present himself as an experienced navigator and learned councilor, worthy of the king's attention and a role in the exploration of the South Sea. Hernán Cortés defined the criteria for an ideal conquistador during his stay at court, while Baltasar Dorantes de Caranza developed an elaborate assessment of New Spain's *beneméritos* to convince his readers that the descendants of a small group of settlers were equally as worthy of the viceroyalty's benefits as the descendants of the conquistadores. Such forms of engagement with the logic of assessment shaped these men's views of the world and their own place within it. Indeed, as a key element of early modern Iberian political culture and world-making, this logic impacted countless institutional practices and cultural views defining social hierarchies and the opportunities that men and women of different qualities received in particular places and times, including the famous purity of blood assessments or views of the *casta* society.

Studying the changing ways in which royal favor was distributed also helps us to do more than simply trace people's movement during this period. The actors appearing in this book not only moved but also were grappling with mobility as a phenomenon that produced tensions and conflicts. During the past three decades, the booming field of global history has led to a strong focus on entanglements and circulation, which to some extent has driven attention away from local developments and less-mobile actors. By describing the roles of mobility and rootedness as competing metrics of worthiness, I have sought to bring the two together. Again and again, royal officials, conquistadores and their descendants, and clergymen had to grapple with the tension between these two criteria as they sought to find a balance that benefited either themselves, their communities, the empire as a whole, or all together. At the same time, it has become clear that conflicts over how to value both criteria incited opposing responses to the flux of people in New Spain and the Pacific Basin, resulting in competing world-making projects. Some propagated connectivity, while others sought to sever connections by closing ports and shutting down or thwarting travel along certain routes. Such developments call on us to reckon that the history of what Serge Gruzinski has called the "Iberian mundialización" or globalization should not be told as one of ever greater connectivity.[2] Instead, we have to pay attention, too, to the struggles over how mobility was valued in specific places and moments of time by actors who affected – sometimes only locally, on other occasions on a much larger scale – the dynamics of global integration and disintegration.

The preceding chapters have also demonstrated that in these disputes, a wide variety of identities came into play. The discoverer, the conquistador, and the *poblador* became legal identifiers with specific degrees of entitlement tied to the moment of mobility realized during the usurpation and incorporation of new territories into the Spanish empire. During more than half a century, these categories topped the hierarchy of the *beneméritos*, which itself served as a common denominator deployed at times to include all those who had served the king and at other times as a collective identifier describing all those who could not claim to have arrived early to New Spain.[3] Fitting within this latter category were all those who produced relatively implicit images of themselves as worthy subjects, as veterans of the search for a route to Asia did. Later, the meaning of this category changed once more, as the Crown decided to treat all who served the Crown equally. Conflicts provoked by these transformations have often been studied through the paradigm of creole patriotism, yet the dichotomy between creoles and peninsular Spaniards does not do justice to the identities petitioners for royal favor assumed at the time nor to the complex processes of identification and categorization that their distributive struggles inspired. The notion of the deserving self has turned out to be quite useful for studying these complexities, as it can be adapted to the disputes that were meaningful to historical actors without the restrictions of working only with proto-nationalist or other group identities established a priori.

That is not to say that the creole identity should be entirely discarded, as some historians and literary scholars have suggested in the past decade. As this book has shown, in negotiations over patronage – both the king's and that of others – this identity had a specific function that cannot be ignored. To the clergy, it functioned as a beneficial identifier in their competition with peninsular Spaniards, either within their own Orders or among the secular priests. This resulted from the positive significance

---

[2] Gruzinski, *Las cuatro partes del mundo.*
[3] Pinelo, *Tratado de confirmaciones reales*, ff. 50v.–53v.

that the process of creolization acquired in the process of distributing royal patronage. This development not only favored creoles but also pushed the question of their intellectual capacities to the center of the evaluation process, resulting in increasingly sophisticated assessments of their inner natures and opposing theories about the effects of the creolization process. Being a native of the Indies became relevant to these assessments because the region's climate, flora and fauna, and Indigenous inhabitants came to serve as spheres of existence by means of which the qualities and capacities of the Spaniards born in the region could be assessed. Such instrumentalization of spatial theories about person- and selfhood was certainly not unique to the Indies; yet, distance from Spain and theories legitimizing the colonization of Native populations gave particular salience to these spatial assessments. Grappling with negative assessments and the stereotyping they produced stimulated the emergence of a collective sense of self, as demonstrated by the protests that shook Mexico in the first years of the seventeenth century. Still, the forms of auto-identification with the term criollo differed strongly among both the laity and the clergy. Moreover, the increasingly felt necessity to deal with this common dimension of their selfhood should not be confused with a singular creole view of the world. As Rodrigo de Vivero's experiences illustrate, even when he sought to refute the bad reputation creoles had garnered, he had ideas about New Spain's place in the world that differed strongly from those of representatives of Mexico's cabildo and *consulado*.

Indeed, it is important to stress that, to many, this collectively shared space was but one dimension that mattered in the process of fashioning a deserving self. Often, other dimensions of the self that could play a positive role in defining worthiness were deemed more important. This could be the city of which one was a resident, one's family, or status as a descendant of the group of first conquistadores or even the first settlers, as was the case with Dorantes de Carranza. Various actors who we have encountered in the previous chapters produced elaborate self-assessments in which they discussed several spheres of existence so as to eventually place themselves at the top of a pyramid of other competitors for favor, each worthier than those below them due to certain qualities or accomplishments. The self-image that emerged in this process of self-fashioning necessarily revealed multiple loyalties and senses of belonging as well as carefully formulated distinctions within these groups. Due to the inherently relational nature of early modern notions of the self, actors' images of a deserving self also associated them with different spaces, places, and collectives – some near and familiar, others more abstract and far away, but ultimately all part of who they were and how others perceived them as either worthy or unworthy of specific benefits.

Although this book ends in the 1640s, the impact of transpacific interactions on New Spanish society certainly did not. Residents of the viceroyalty continued to talk about events occurring in Asia while reflecting on what was happening in the viceroyalty.[4] Discussions about problems related to trade resurfaced after several decades of relative stability, as the unevenly felt impact of the commercial interactions between New Spain, Peru, and the Philippines continued to occupy the minds of officials and merchants throughout the empire.[5] As transpacific interactions stabilized again, the influx of commodified objects into viceregal society picked up, resulting in further development of new patterns of consumption and self-representation. If anything, the presence of goods from Asia or inspired by Asian examples became even more visible, not only due to trade but the work of local craftsmen as well.[6] Nevertheless, by the 1640s a transformation that has been central to this study had been completed: those who expected and sought the king's favor because of the roles their ancestors played in the first phases of the discovery, conquest, and settlement of New Spain no longer received prioritized treatment or could be certain of receiving the benefits they felt they deserved. Although descending from a conquistador did not completely lose its value, over time and due to the complex struggles treated here, the Crown reduced the impact of the hierarchy of merit that had developed in the decades after the conquest of the region. Instead, attention shifted toward assessment of imperial agents serving the Crown in various and widespread parts of the realm, and distribution of shares of the royal patrimony through sale of offices became normalized.

The *biombos* depicting scenes from the conquest of Mexico that began to emerge after the 1660s illustrate this development. As the memory of the past became less controversial, less connected with contemporary social struggles, and less strictly controlled, new actors began to present the history of the conquest for their own purposes. Inspired by the work of Bernal Díaz del Castillo and Antonio de Solís, these new representations re-narrated the conquest but without the same fixation on the identification of individual conquistadores and depiction of their feats.

---

[4] See, for example, Juan de Palafox y Mendoza, *Historia de la Conquista de la China por el Tártaro* (Paris: Antonio Bertier, 1670).

[5] Bonialian, *La América española*, 155–200.

[6] Baena Zapatero, "Biombos mexicanos," 653–58.

On the contrary, on a number of these *biombos* depicting scenes from the conquest, including the one currently preserved in the Franz Mayer Museum in Mexico City, Native actors and clergymen appear prominently and are identified by name. Such representations of the conquest painted on what had once been considered a typical Asian object did play a role in distributive negotiations. They may have done so, for example, in the attempts of Viceroy José Sarmiento de Valladares (1696–1701), count of Moctezuma by right of his wife, to demonstrate his familial ties to Motecuhzoma II and his services to the Spanish Crown during the Spanish conquest.[7] But Sarmiento was not directly related to the conquistadores, nor did he defend their prominence in the distribution of royal favor. This change in the distributive process may also explain why this type of *biombo* was now converted from mainly being a bearer of sociopolitical messages into an object of consumption, reproduced for the palaces of the rich in Mexico and in Europe.

The burgeoning trade in folding screens in New Spain's capital is proof of its continuous role as a pivot in the religious and trading networks that connected the city to places around both the Atlantic and Pacific basins. While this place at the heart of the world would continue to inspire both pride and frustration among those who resided in the city, the turbulent period of exploration and conquest that had brought it to this position had come to an end.

---

[7] Vallen, "Conquista, memoria y cultura material en la Nueva España," 27–30.

Glossary

adelantado: frontier governor who possessed a commission to discover, conquer, and settle new lands. This title was inheritable

advenedizo: upstart, migrant, or newcomer

alcalde del crimen: criminal judge of the *audiencia*

alcalde mayor: chief magistrate of town or district; fulfilled a similar function as a *corregidor*

alcalde ordinario: a first-instance judge or magistrate of the town council

alférez general: lieutenant in the local militia responsible for carrying the royal banner

alternativa: rotation system for the distribution of the provincial offices of the Mendicant Orders between creole and peninsular friars

arbitrista: person who proposed projects and policy solutions to resolve political and economic problems

asiento: monopoly contract granted by the Crown

audiencia: the high or appeals court that reviewed civil and criminal cases and wielded some political authority in the district

beato: person blessed or beatified by the Catholic Church

beneficio: a guaranteed ecclesiastical income, frequently based on an investment

benemérito: person who had served the Crown and, because of their or an ancestor's merit, deserve royal favor

biombo: folding screen of Japanese origins existing of different panels that was used to adorn private and public spaces

cabildo: the governing council of an urban area and its surroundings, or of a cathedral (*cabildo eclesiástico* or *metropolitano*)

caballero: knight; during the sixteenth century, the term becomes a synonym of a hidalgo of proven nobility

cacique: chieftain or regional lord of an Indigenous community

calidad: during the sixteenth and early seventeenth century, term referring to social distinctions based on indicators such as social status, political privilege, and wealth

cámara de Castilla: chamber or committee that dispensed royal patronage

canonjía doctoral: a benefice in a cathedral or collegiate church for which a doctorate in civil law was required

capitulación: the contract between the Spanish monarch and the leader of an expedition of conquest or discovery, recording mutual prerogatives and obligations

Casa de la Contratación: House of Trade in Seville

casa de la moneda: mint

cédula: a written order, often from the king or the royal court, settling a conflict, requiring some action, or bestowing a favor

conquistador: legal category; member of the group who first subjected a specific territory

Consejo de Órdenes: Council of the Orders; responsible for the administrative processes related to the admission of candidates to one of the military orders

consulado: merchant guild

contador: accountant

corregidor: royally appointed official who administered an encomienda or other jurisdiction held directly by the Crown; akin to an *alcalde mayor*

corregimiento: an encomienda or other jurisdiction held directly by the Crown

criado: literally "servant," but more often a crony or retainer

criollo/a: man or women of Spanish decedent born in the Indies

deán: the chief officer of a cathedral chapter

descubridor: legal category; person who first saw and described land that no other subject of the Iberian Crowns had previously seen

dignidad: one of the five high-ranking members of a cathedral chapter (i.e., the *deán, arcedeán, chantre, maestre-escuela, tesorero*).

don/doña: the honorific address in the name indicated nobility

encomendero: the holder of an encomienda

encomienda: a grant of the right to collect tribute, labor, or both from an Indigenous community in return for their protection and education in the Christian faith

entrada: an expedition penetrating unconquered territory

escribano: a public notary

escribano mayor: notary of the *audiencia*

fiscal: court official, roughly equivalent to a prosecuting attorney

hidalgo: an untitled noble; the lowest rank of nobility

hidalguía: nobility; describing a group in society that enjoyed prestige and the rights and privileges of noblemen, including tax exemptions

hijos de la tierra: like *criollo*, often used to distinguish friars of the religious orders

Indio/a: legal term used during the colonial period to refer to members of the Indigenous population

informaciones de oficio y parte: an ego document that records for individuals his familiar relations and the services rendered while in office. Similar to *relación de méritos y servicios* but documenting different kind of services

interrogatorio: questionary used in almost all institutional contexts to gather information with the help of witnesses

licenciado: title given to a person with a bachelor's degree or licentiate

letrado: holder of a law degree, a person who was a professional civil servant

Mar del Sur: South Sea, Pacific Ocean

maestrescuela: dignitary on the cathedral chapter charged with supervision of schools in the diocese

mayordomo: steward or custodian of public or private property

memorial: autobiographical statement provided in the context of a bureaucratic procedure

mérito: merit earned through service or qualification to serve

mestizo/mestiza: offspring of Natives and Spaniards in the racial imaginary

merced: grant given by the king to one of his vassals or subjects that provides him with a certain office, privilege, or honor

mulato/mulata: a man or woman of presumably African and Spanish descent

natural: native of a certain territory or province (*natural de la provincia*)

oidor: judge/legislator of an *audiencia*

oposición: a competitive examination to choose the best prepared candidate for ecclesiastical offices and benefices

parecer: opinion written about a specific matter by an official or subject to advise the monarch or other royal officials on how to deal with the matter

parte: innate talents or learned skills

patronato real: royal authority in ecclesiastical affairs. *Padroado* in Portuguese

poblador: legal category; settler

policía: civilization, civilized custom; or also, administrative order

prima de cánones: chair of canon law

probanza: collection of legal proceedings, including witness responses to questionaries and opinions (*parecer*) of the preceding judge, testifying to the assessment of a person's qualities and services

procurador general: a representative of a corporation or institution

proveedor: purveyor, contractor

provisor: the chief administrative officer of a diocese under the bishop. One of six lower members on a cathedral chapter

quinto real: the royal tax levied by the Spanish treasury on mining production

racionero: one of six lower members of a cathedral chapter

real: monetary unit, one-eighth of a peso

recatón: ambulant retail traders

regidor: councilman in municipal government

relaciones de méritos y servicios: an ego document that records for an individual his familiar relations and the services that this person and his direct relatives had rendered to God and the monarch

repartimiento: literally, a distribution. Mostly used in relationship to the distribution of encomiendas

residencia: official investigations into a viceroy or governor's term of office, or into the parishes of a bishop's episcopate or diocese

ternativa: modified version of the *alternativa* that the Franciscans in Mexico followed, which included a third group, the *hijos de provincia*

tornaviaje: eastern bound route across the Pacific from the Philippines to the Americas

vendavales: trading winds

visita: extraordinary judicial review of performance of officials

visitador: investigating judge assigned to conduct a *visita*

Bibliography

PUBLISHED PRIMARY SOURCES

Aduarte, Diego de, *Historia de la Provincia del Santo Rosario de Filipinas, Japón y China del Sagrado Orden de Predicadores*. Edited by Manuel Ferrero. Madrid: Consejo Superior de Investigaciones Científicas; Departamento de Misionología Española, 1962 [1640].

Angleria, Pedro M. de. *Décadas del Nuevo Mundo*. Madrid: Polifemo, 1989.

Apiano, Pedro. *La cosmographia: corregida y añadida por Gemma Frisio, médico y matemático*. Antwerp: Juan Bellero al Aguila de Oro, 1575.

Ayrolo Calar, Gabriel de. *Sermón que predicó el doctor don Gabriel de Ayrolo, arcediano de la Santa Iglesia de Guadalajara, y natural de la ciudad de México, el día de su patrón S. Hypólito, cuando luce reseña de su estandarte real, y se lleva a su iglesia con suntuoso acompañamiento, asistiendo en ella el excelentísimo señor Marques de Cadereyta, Virrey de esta Nueva España, Audiencia Real, y los dos Cabildos Eclesiástico y Secular*. Mexico City: Francisco Salbago, 1638.

Balbuena, Bernardo de. *Grandeza mexicana*. Edited by Asima F. X. Saad Maura. Madrid: Cátedra, 2011.

Blair, Emma Helen, and James Alexander Robertson, eds. *The Philippine Islands, 1493–1803: Explorations by Early Navigators, Descriptions of the Islands and Their Peoples, Their History and Records of the Catholic Missions*. 55 vols. Cleveland: Arthur H. Clark, 1903–1909.

Cajica, Jacinto de la. *Sermón predicado en la Santa Iglesia Cathedral Metropolitana de México, a la fiesta del glorioso S. Felipe de Jesús, protomartir de las Indias, y patron de la muy nobley leal ciudad de México*. Mexico City: Bernardo Calderon, 1639.

Camos, Marco A. de. *Microcosmia, y govierno universal del hombre christiano, para todos los estados y qualquiera de ellos*. Barcelona: Monasterio de Sancto Augustin, por Pablo Malo, 1592.

Cardona, Nicolás de. *Descripciones geográficas e hidrográficas de muchas tierras y mares del norte y sur, en las Indias, en especial del descubrimiento del Reino de California.* Edited by Pilar Hernández Aparicio. Madrid: Turner, 1989 [1632].

Carreño, Alberto M. *Cedulario de los siglos XVI y XVII. El obispo don Juan de Palafox y Mendoza y el conflicto con la Compañía de Jesús.* Mexico City: Victoria, 1947.

Cartas de Indias. Madrid: Ministerio de Fomento, 1877.

Cortés, Hernán. *Cartas y relaciones de Hernán Cortés al Emperador Carlos V.* Edited by Pascual de Gayangos. Paris: Imprenta central de los ferro-carriles, 1866.

Cartas y documentos. Edited by Mario H. Sanchez-Barba. Mexico City: Editorial Porrúa, 1963.

Cuevas, Mariano, and Genaro García, eds. *Documentos inéditos del siglo XVI para la historia de México.* Mexico City: Talleres del Museo Nacional de Arqueología, Historia y Etnología, 1914.

Dahlgren, E. W. *Map of the World by Alonso de Santa Cruz, 1542.* Stockholm: P. A. Norstedt & Söner, 1892.

Dorantes Carranza, Baltazar de. *Sumaria relación de las cosas de la Nueva España: con noticia individual de los conquistadores y primeros pobladores españoles.* Edited by Ernesto de la Torre Villar. Mexico City: Biblioteca Porrúa, 1987.

Elliott, John H., José F. de la Peña, and Fernando Negredo. *Memoriales y cartas del Conde Duque de Olivares.* 2 vols. Madrid: Edición Alfaguara, 1978–1981.

Encinas, Diego de. *Cedulario indiano.* 4 vols. Edited by Alfonso García Gallo. Madrid: Ediciones Cultura Hispánica, 1945–1946.

Enciso, Martín Fernández de. *Suma de Geografía.* Edited by José Ibáñez Cerdá. Joyas bibliográficas. Madrid: Estades, Artes Gráficas, 1948 [1519].

Escalante, Bernardino de. *Discurso de la navegación que los Portugueses hacen a los Reinos y Provincias de Oriente, y de la noticia que se tiene de las grandezas del Reino de la China.* Seville: en casa de la viuda de Alonso Escriuano, 1577.

Escalante Alvarado, García de. *Viaje a las Islas del Poniente.* Edited by Carlos Martínez Shaw. Santander: Servicio de Publicaciones de la Universidad de Cantabria, 1999.

Fernández de Navarrete, Domingo. *Tratados históricos, políticos, éticos y religiosos de la monarchia de China.* Madrid: Imprenta Real, por Juan García de Infançon, 1676.

Fernández Navarrete, Pedro. *Conservación de Monarquías y discursos políticos sobre la gran consulta que el consejo hizo al señor Rey Don Felipe Tercero.* Madrid: en la Imprenta Real, 1626.

Gage, Thomas. *A New Survey of the West-Indies: or, the English American, His Travail by Sea and Land.* London: E. Cotes and sold by John Sweeting, 1655.

Garcia de Palacio, Diego. *Diálogos militares.* Madrid: Ediciones Cultura Hispanica, 1944 [1583].

Instrución nauthica para el buen uso, y regimiento de las naos, su traça, y y govierno conforme a la altura de México. Edited by Álvaro Manrique de Zúñiga and Martín López de Gaona. Madrid: Edición Cultura Hispánica, 1944 [1587].

González de Mendoza, Juan. *Historia de las cosas más notables, ritos y costumbres del gran reino de la China.* Rome: Stampa de Vicentio Accolti, 1585.

Itinerario y compendio de las cosas notables que ay desde España, hasta el Reyno de la China, y de la China à España, boluiendo por la India Oriental, despues de auer dado buelta, à casi todo el Mundo: En el qual se trata de los ritos, cerimonias, y costumbres de la gente que en todo el ay, y dela riqueza, fertilidad, y fortaleza de muchos Reynos, y la descripción de todos. Lisbon: S. Phelippe el Real, 1586.

Gómez de Cervantes, Gonzalo. *La vida económica y social de Nueva España al finalizar el siglo XVI.* Edited by Alberto María Carreño. Mexico City: Robreño, 1944.

González-Leal, Mariano. *Relación secreta de conquistadores: informes del archivo personal del emperador Carlos I que se conserva en la Biblioteca del Escorial, años de 1539–1542.* Guanajuato: Universidad de Guanajuato, Taller de Investigaciones Humanísticas, 1979.

Hanke, Lewis. *Los Virreyes españoles en America durante el Gobierno de la casa de Austria, Méxio.* 5 vols. Madrid: Ediciones Atlas, 1976–1978.

Icaza, Franciso A. de, ed. *Conquistadores y pobladores de Nueva España: diccionario autobiográfic.* 2 vols. Madrid: El adelanto de Segovia, 1923.

Icazbalceta, Joaquín G. *Colección de documentos para la historia de México.* 2 vols. Mexico City: Biblioteca Porrua, 1858–1866.

Nueva colección de documentos para la historia de México. 5 vols. Mexico City: Antigua Librería de Andrade y Morales, Sucesores, 1886–1892.

Cartas de religiosas de Nueva España, 1539–1594. Mexico City: Editorial Chávez Chávez Hayhoe, 1941.

Jesús, Luis de. *Historia general de los religiosos descalzos del orden de los hermitaños del gran Padre y Doctor de la iglesia de S. Augustin de la Congregación de España y de las Indias.* 4 vols. Madrid: por Lucas Antonio de Bedmar, 1681.

Las Siete Partidas del rey don Alfonso el Sabio, cotejadas con varios códices antiguos por la Real Academia de la Historia. Madrid: Lope de Vega, 1972.

León Pinelo, Antonio de. *Tratado de confirmaciones reales de encomiendas, oficios, i casos, en que se requieren para las Indias Occidentales.* Madrid: Juan González, 1630.

López de Gómara, Francisco. *La conquista de México.* Edited by José Luis de Rojas. Las Rozas: Dastin, 2003.

López de Velasco, Juan. *Geografía y descripción universal de las Indias.* Edited by Justo Zaragoza. Madrid: Real academia de la historia, 1894.

Mercado, Tomás de. *Suma de tratos y contratos.* 2 vols. Edited by Nicolás Sánchez Albornoz and Graciela S. B. de Sánchez Albornoz. Madrid: Instituto de Estudios Fiscales, Ministerio de Hacienda, 1977 [1571].

Morejón, Pedro. *Relacion de la persecucion que [h]vuo en la yglesia de Iapon: y de los insignes marytres, que gloriosamente dieron su vida en defensa de n[uest]ra San Fè, el año de 1614. y 615.* Mexico City: Por Iuan Ruyz, 1616.

Moreno Garcia, Heriberto, ed. *Los agustinos, aquellos misioneros hacendados. Historia de la provincia de San Nicolás de Tolentino de Michoacán, escrito por fray Diego de Basalenque.* Mexico City: Cien de México, 1985.

Morga, Antonio de. *Sucesos de las Islas Filipinas.* Edited by Francisca Perujo. Mexico City: Fondo de Cultura Económica, 2007.

Navarrete, Nicolás. *Historia de la provincia agustiniana de San Nicolás de Tolentino de Michoacán.* 2 vols. Mexico City: Editorial Porrúa, 1978.

Nuttall, Zelia, ed. *New Light on Drake: A Collection of Documents relating to His Voyage of Circumnavigation.* London: for the Hakluyt Society, 1914.

Núñez Cabeza Vaca, Álvar de. *Naufragios y comentarios.* Madrid: Calpe, 1922.

Obregón, Baltasar de. *Historia de los descubrimientos antiguos y modernos de la Nueva España, escrita por el conquistador en el año de 1584.* Edited by Mariano Cuevas. Mexico City: Editorial Porrúa, 1988.

Oviedo, Gonzalo Fernández de. *Historia general y natural de las Indias.* 4 vols. Madrid: Biblioteca de Autores Españoles, 1959.

Palafox y Mendoza, Juan de. *Historia de la Conquista de la China por el Tartaro.* Paris: Antonio Bertier, 1670.

Pedro, Maestre. *Libro del consejo e de los consejeros.* Edited by Agapito Rey. Zaragoza: Librería general, 1962.

Pérez, Antonio. *Norte de príncipes, virreyes, presidentes, consejeros, y governadores, y advertencias políticas sobre lo público y particular de una monarquía importantísimas a los tales.* Edited by Martín de Riquer. Madrid: Espasa-Calpe, 1969 [1601].

Pérez de Tudela y Bueso, Juan, et al. *Colección documental del descubrimiento (1470–1506).* 3 vols. Madrid: Real Academia de la Historia, Consejo Superior de Investigaciones Científicas, 1994.

Priestley, Herbert Ingram. *The Luna Papers: Documents relating to the Expedition of Don Tristan de Luna y Arellano for the Conquest of la Florida in 1559–1561,* Vols. 1 & 2. Tuscaloosa: The University of Alabama Press, 2010 [1928].

Pseudo-Aristóteles. *Secreto de los secretos, poridat de las poridades: Versiones castellanas del Pseudo-Aristóteles Secretum Secretorum.* Edited by Hugo O. Bizzarri. Valencia: Publicaciones de la Universitat de València, 2010.

Rea, Alonso de la. *Crónica de la orden de N. Seráfico P.S. Francisco, Provincia de S. Pedro y S. Pablo de Mechoacan en la Nueva España.* Edited by Patricia Escandón. Zamora: El Colegio de Michoacán, 1996 [1643].

Recopilación de Leyes de los Reinos de las Indias, mandadas imprimir y publicar por la Magestad Católica del Rey don Carlos II. Nuestro Señor. Va dividida en Quatro Tomos. En Madrid: Por Iulian de Paredes, Año de 1681. [Edición Facsímil] Madrid: Ediciones de Cultura Hispánica, 1973.

Ribadeneira, Marcelo de. *Historia de las islas del archipiélago filipino y reinos de la Gran China, Tartaria, Cochinchina, Malaca, Siam, Cambodge y Japón.* Edited by Juan R. de Legísima. Madrid: La editorial católica, 1947.

Russell, D. A., and N. G. Wilson, *Menander Rhetor*. Oxford: Clarendon Press, 1981.

San Agustín, Gaspar de, O. S. A. *Conquistas de las Islas Filipinas (1565–1615)*. Edited by Manuel Merino. Madrid: Consejo Superio de Investigaciones Científicas, 1975.

Sánchez, Miguel. *Sermón de San Felipe de Jesús*. Mexico City: Iuan Ruiz, 1640.

Santa Cruz, Alonso de. *Libro de las longitudines y manera que hasta agora se ha tenido en el arte de navegar, con sus demostraciones y ejemplos, dirigido al muy alto y muy poderoso señor don Philipe II de este nombre rey de España*, ed. Delgado Aguilera and Antonio Blázquez. Seville: Centro oficial de estudios americanistas, 1921.

Santa María, Juan de. *Relación de martirio que seis padres descalzos Franciscanos, y veinte japones cristianos padecieron en Japón*. Madrid: Imprenta del licenciado Varez de Castro, 1599.

Tratado de república y policía christiana para reyes y príncipes, y para los que el gobierno tienen sus veces. Barcelona: Por Sebastian de Cormellas, 1616.

Sola Castaño, Emilio. *Libro de las maravillas del Oriente Lejano*. Madrid: Editora nacional, 1980.

Solano, Francisco de, ed. *Cuestionarios para la formación de las relaciones geográficas de Indias, siglos XVI / XIX*. Madrid: Consejo Superior de Investigaciones Científicas, 1988.

Suárez de Peralta, Juan. *Tratado del descubrimiento de las Indias*. Edited by Teresa Silva Tena. Mexico City: Consejo Nacional para la Cultura y las Artes, 1990.

Tello de Guzmán, Francisco. *Relación que don Francisco Tello, gobernador: y capitán general de las Philippinas embió de seys frayles españoles de la Orden de San Francisco, que crucificaron los del Japón, este año próximo passado de 1597. Con otras veynte personas Japones, que murieron juntamente con ellos animados por los santos frayles y convertidos a su predicación*. Seville, 1598.

Terrazas, Francisco de. *Poesías*. Edited by Antonio Castro. Mexico City: Porrúa, 1941.

Vaca Salasar, Luís. *Sermon predicado en la Sancta Iglesia Cathedral Metropolitana de Mexico, á la fiesta del Glorioso S. Felipe de Iesvs, protomartyr de la Indias, y patrón de la mvy noble y leal ciudad de México*. Mexico City, 1638.

Vargas, Bernabé Moreno. *Discursos de la nobleza de España*. Madrid: Por la Viuda de Alonso Martin, 1622.

Vivero, Rodrigo de. *Du Japon et du bon gouvernement de l'Espagne et des Indes*. Edited by Juliette Monbeig. Paris: SEVPEN, 1972.

Walsh, John K. *El libro de los doze sabios o Tractado de la nobleza y lealtad (ca. 1237): estudio y edición*. Madrid: Aguire, 1975.

Zapata y Sandoval, Juan. *De iustitia distributiva et acceptione personarum ei opposita disceptatio*. Edited by Carlos Baciero, Jesús María García Añoveros, and José María Soto Rábanos. Madrid: Editorial CSIC Consejo Superior de Investigaciones Científicas, 2004.

Zorita, Alonso de. *Relación de la Nueva España: relación de algunas de las muchas cosas notables que hay en la Nueva España y de su conquista y pacificación y de la conversión de los naturales de ella*. Edited by Ethelia Ruiz Medrano, Wiebke Ahrndt, and José M. Leyva. 2 vols. Mexico City: CONACULTA, 1999.

SECONDARY LITERATURE

Ahern, Maureen. "Mapping, Measuring, and Naming Cultural Spaces in Castañeda's *Relación de la jornada de Cíbola*," in *The Coronado Expedition from the Distance of 460 years*. Edited by Richard Flint and Shirley Cushing Flint. Albuquerque: University of New Mexico Press, 2003, 265–89.

Aiton, Arthur Scott. *Antonio de Mendoza, First Viceroy of New Spain*. Durham, NC: Duke University Press, 1927.

Aguilar Ochoa, Arturo. "La indumentaria novohispana del siglo XVII y su uso para la datación de tres biombos virreinales." *Anales del Museo de América* XXV (2017): 94–108.

Alberro, Solange. *Del gachupín al criollo o de cómo los españoles de México dejaron de serlo*. Mexico City: El Colegio de México, 1992.

El águila y la cruz: orígenes religiosos de la conciencia criolla, México, Siglos XVI–XVII. Mexico City: El Colegio de México, 1999.

Alden, Dauril. *The Making of an Enterprise: The Society of Jesus in Portugal, Its Empire, and Beyond, 1540–1750*. Stanford, CA: Stanford University Press, 1996.

Alonso Álvarez, Luis. "E la nave va. Economía, fiscalidad e inflación en las regulaciones de la carrera de la Mar del Sur, 1565–1604," in *Un océano de seda y plata: el universo económico del Galeón de Manila*. Edited by Salvador Bernabéu Albert and Carlos Martínez Shaw. Seville: Consejo Superior de Investigaciones Científicas, 2013, 25–84.

Alvarado Morales, Manuel. *La ciudad de México ante la fundación de la Armada de Barlovento, 1635–1643*. Mexico City: El Colegio de México; Universidad de Puerto Rico, 1983.

Alvárez, Salvador. "Cortés, Tenochtitlan y la otra mar: geografías y cartografías de la Conquista." *Historia y Grafía* 24, no. 47 (2016): 49–90.

Amerlinck de Corsi, María Concepción. "Vista del palacio del virrey de México," in *Los Siglos de Oro en los virreinatos de América. 1550–1700*. Madrid: Sociedad Estatal para la Conmemoración de los Centenarios de Felipe II y Carlos V, 1999, 158–63.

Andrade, Tonio. *How Taiwan Became Chinese: Dutch, Spanish, and Han Colonization in the Seventeenth Century*. New York: Columbia University Press, 2008.

Andújar Castillo, Francisco, and María del Mar Felices de la Fuente, eds. *El poder del dinero. Ventas de cargos y honores en el Antiguo Régimen*. Madrid: Biblioteca Nueva, 2011.

Aram, Bethany. *Leyenda negra y leyendas doradas en la conquista de América: Pedrarias y Balboa*, translated by Antonio J. Carasco Alvarez. Madrid: Marcial Pons Historia, 2008.

Arróniz, Othón. *El despertar científico en América: la vida de Diego García de Palacio*. Mexico City: Universidad Autónoma Metropolitana, 1980.

Asenjo, Julio Alonso. "Sin par loor de Córdoba por Góngora." *Quaderns de filologia. Estudis literaris* no. 10 (2005): 133–54.

Babcock, William H. "The Island of the Seven Cities." *Geographical Review* 7, no. 2 (1919): 98–106.

Bacigalupo, Martin H. *A Changing Perspective: Attitudes towards Creole Society in New Spain (1521–1610)*. London: Tamesis, 1981.

Baena Zapatero, Alberto. *Mujeres novohispanas e identidad criolla (siglos XVI y XVII)*. Madrid: Ayuntamiento Alcalá de Henares, 2009.

"Chinese and Japanese Influence on Colonial Mexican Furniture: The Achinado Folding Screens." *Bulletin of Portuguese-Japanese Studies* 20 (2010): 95–123.

"Apuntes sobre la elaboración de biombos en la Nueva España." *Archivo Español de Arte* LXXXVIII, no. 350 (2015): 173–88.

"Biombos mexicanos e identidad criolla." *Revista De Indias* 80, no. 280 (2020): 651–86.

Barandica Martínez, Luis A. "Andrés de Urdaneta en la Nueva España (1538–1568)," in *Urdaneta novohispano*. Edited by María Cristina E. Barrón Soto. Mexico City: Universidad Iberoamericana, 2012, 35–65.

Barrón, Soto, and María Cristina E., eds. *Urdaneta novohispano: la inserción del mundo hispano en Asia*. Mexico City: Universidad Iberoamericana, 2012.

Bauer, Ralph, ed. *Creole Subjects in the Colonial Americas: Empires, Texts, Identities*. Chapel Hill: University of North Carolina Press, 2009.

Bauer, Ralph, and José A. Mazzotti. "Introduction," in *Creole Subjects in the Colonial Americas*. Edited by Ralph Bauer. Chapel Hill: University of North Carolina Press, 2009, 1–60.

Bawlf, Samuel. *The Secret Voyage of Sir Francis Drake, 1577–1580*. Vancouver: Douglas & McIntyre, 2003.

Bernal, Rafael. *México en Filipinas: estudio de un transculturación*. Mexico City: UNAM: Instituto de Investigaciones Histróricas, 1965.

Bizzarri, Hugo O. "Las colecciones sapienciales castellanas en el proceso de reafirmación del poder monárquico (siglos XII y XIV)." *Cahiers de linguistique hispanique médiévale* 20 (1995): 35–73

Bjork, Katharine. "The Link That Kept the Philippines Spanish: Mexican Merchant Interests and the Manila Trade, 1571–1815." *Journal of World History* 9, no. 1 (1998): 25–50

Bonialian, Mariano Ardash. *El Pacífico hispanoamericano: política y comercio asiático en el Imperio Español (1680–1784)*. Mexico City: El Colegio de México, 2012.

China en la América colonial: bienes, mercados, comercio y cultura del consumo desde México hasta Buenos Aires. Mexico City: Instituto de Investigaciones Dr. José María Luis Mora, 2014.

"La seda china en Nueva España a principios del siglo XVII. Una mirada imperial en el memorial de Horacio Levanto." *Revista de Historia Económica – Journal of Iberian and Latin American Economic History* 35, no. 1 (2016): 147–71.

La América española: entre el Pacífico y el Atlántico: globalización mercantil y economía política, 1580–1840. Mexico City: El Colegio de México, Centro de Estudios Históricos, 2019.

Borah, Woodrow. *Silk Raising in Colonial Mexico.* Berkeley: University of California Press, 1943.

"Hernán Cortés y sus intereses marítimos en el Pacífico. El Perú y la Baja California." *Estudios de Historia Novohispana* 4 (1971): 7–25.

Boxer, C. R. *The Christian Century in Japan, 1549–1650.* Berkeley: University of California Press, 1951.

Brading, David A. *The First America: The Spanish Monarchy, Creole Patriots, and the Liberal State, 1492–1967.* Cambridge: Cambridge University Press, 1991.

Brendecke, Arndt. *Imperium und Empirie: Funktionen des Wissens in der spanischen Kolonialherrschaft.* Cologne: Böhlau, 2009.

Brown, Matthew. "The Global History of Latin America." *Journal of Global History* 10, no. 3 (2015): 365–86.

Brubaker, Rogers, and Frederick Cooper. "Beyond Identity." *Theory and Society* 29 (2000): 1–47.

Burkholder, Mark A. *Spaniards in the Colonial Empire: Creoles vs. Peninsulars?* Malden, MA: Wiley-Blackwell, 2013.

Byrd Simpson, Lesley. *The Encomienda in New Spain: The Beginning of Spanish Mexico.* Berkeley: University of California Press, 1950.

Calvo, Thomas, and Paulina Machuca, eds. *México y Filipinas: culturas y memorias sobre el Pacífico.* Zamora: El Colegio de Michoacán; Quezon City: Aleneo de Manila University Press, 2016.

Cañeque, Alejandro. *The King's Living Image: The Culture and Politics of Viceregal Power in Colonial Mexico.* New York: Routledge, 2004.

"The Cabildo of Mexico City, Patron Saints, and the Making of Local and Imperial Identities," in *A Companion to Viceregal Mexico City, 1519–1821.* Edited by John F. Lopez, 163–80. Leiden: Brill, 2021, 163–80.

Cañizares-Esguerra, Jorge. "New World, New Stars: Patriotic Astrology and the Invention of Indian and Creole Bodies in Colonial Spanish America, 1600–1650." *American Historical Review* 104, no. 1 (1999): 33–68.

"Racial, Religious, and Civic Creole Identity in Colonial Spanish America." *American Literary History* 17, no. 3 (2005): 420–37.

Canny, Nicholas, and Anthony Pagden, eds. *Colonial Identity in the Atlantic World, 1500–1800.* Princeton, NJ: Princeton University Press, 1987.

Cardim, Pedro, Tamar Herzog, José Javier Ruis Ibáñez, and Gaetano Sabatini, eds. *Polycentric Monarchies: How Did Early Modern Spain and Portugal Achieve and Maintain a Global Hegemony?* Eastbourne: Sussex Academic Press, 2012.

"Introduction," in *Polycentric Monarchies: How Did Early Modern Spain and Portugal Achieve and Maintain a Global Hegemony?* Edited by Pedro Cardim, Tamar Herzog, José Javier Ruis Ibáñez, and Gaetano Sabatini. Eastbourne: Sussex Academic Press, 2012, 3–8.

Carrillo Cázares, Alberto. *El debate sobre la Guerra Chichimeca, 1531–1585: derecho y política en la Nueva España.* Zamora: El Colegio de Michoacán and Colegio de San Luis, 2000.

Castañeda Delgado, Paulino. "Las exploraciones castellanas y los problemas con Portugal antes de 1492" in *El tratado de Tordesillas y su época*, Vol. 2. Edited by Luís A. Ribot García. Madrid: Sociedad V Centenario del Tratado de Tordesillas; Junta de Castilla y León Consejería de Educación y Cultura, 1995, 913–34.

Cavillac, Michel. "El discurso del mercader y sus incidencias literarias." *Criticón*, 120–21 (2014): 41–56.

Cervera Jiménez, José Antonio. "Andrés de Urdaneta y su trabajo como científico: el problema de la demarcación de Filipinas" in *Urdaneta novohispano*. *Urdaneta novohispano*. Edited by María Cristina E. Barrón Soto. Mexico City: Universidad Iberoamericana, 2012, 67–90.

Tras el sueño de China: agustinos y dominicos en Asia Oriental a finales del siglo XVI. Madrid: Plaza y Valdés Editores, 2013.

"Los planes españoles para conquistar China a través de Nueva España y Centroamérica en el siglo XVI." *Cuadernos Inter.c.a.mbio sobre Centroamérica y el Caribe* 10, no. 12 (2013): 207–34.

Chaunu, Pierre. *Les Philippines et le Pacifique des Ibériques (XVIe, XVIIe, XVIIIe siècles): Introduction méthodologique et indices d'activité.* Paris: SEVPEN, 1960.

Conde y Díaz-Rubín, José Ignacio, and Javier Sanchiz Ruiz. *Historia genealógica de los títulos y dignidades nobiliarias en Nueva España y México: Casa de Austria* (siglos XVI-XVII). 2 vols. Mexico City: Universidad Nacional Autónoma de México, Instituto de Investigaciones Históricas, 2012.

Conover, Cornelius. *Pious Imperialism: Spanish Rule and the Cult of Saints in Mexico City.* Albuquerque: University of New Mexico Press, 2019.

Córdoba Ochoa, Luis Miguel. "Movilidad geográfica, capital cosmopolita y relaciones de méritos. Las élites del imperio entre Castilla, América y el Pacífico," in *Las redes del imperio: Élites sociales en la articulación de la monarquía hispánica, 1492–1714*. Edited by Bartolomé Yun Casalilla. Madrid: Marcial Pons, 2009, 359–78.

"Gifts, Imitation, Violence and Social Change: The Introduction of European Products in the First Decades of the American Conquest," in *American Globalization, 1492–1850: Trans-Cultural Consumption in Spanish Latin America.* Edited by Bartolomé Yun-Casalilla, Ilaria Berti, and Omar Svriz-Wucherer. New York: Routledge, 2021, 123–45.

Cosgrove, Denis. *Apollo's Eye: A Cartographic Genealogy of the Earth in the Western Imagination.* London: The John Hopkins University Press, 2001.

Crailsheim, Eberhard. *The Spanish Connection: French and Flemish Merchant Networks in Seville (1570–1650).* Cologne: Böhlau, 2016.

Crawford, Michael J. *The Fight for Status and Privilege in Late Medieval and Early Modern Castile, 1465–1598*. University Park: The Pennsylvania State University Press, 2014.

Crewe, Ryan Dominic. "Connecting the Indies: The Hispano-Asian Pacific World in Early Modern Global History." *Etudos Históricos* 30, no. 60 (2017): 17–34.

The Mexican Mission: Indigenous Reconstruction and Mendicant Enterprise in New Spain, 1521–1600. New York: Cambridge University Press, 2019.

Cuesta Domingo, Mariano. "La fijación de la linea - de Tordesillas - en el Extremo Oriente," in *El tratado de Tordesillas y su época*, Vol. 3. Edited by Luís A. Ribot García. Madrid: Sociedad V Centenario del Tratado de Tordesillas; Junta de Castilla y León Consejería de Educación y Cultura, 1995, 1483–518.

"La Casa de la Contratación de La Coruña." *Mar oceana: Revista del humanismo español e iberoamericano* 16 (2004): 59–88.

Cuevas, Mariano P., S. J., *Monje y marino: la vida y los tiempos de Fray Andrés de Urdaneta*. Mexico City: Galatea, 1943.

Curiel, Gustavo. "Customs, Conventions, and Daily Rituals among the Elites of New Spain: The Evidence from Material Culture," in *The Grandeur of Viceregal Mexico: Treasures from the Museo Franz Mayer*. Edited by Héctor Rivero Borrell M. and Peter C. Marzio. Houston: The Museum of Fine Arts, Houston; Museo Franz Mayer Mexico, 2002, 23–43.

"Perception of the Other and the Language of 'Chinese Mimicry' in the Decorative Arts of New Spain," in *Asia & Spanish America: Trans-Pacific Artistic and Cultural Exchange, 1500–1850*. Edited by Donna Pierce and Ronald Y. Otsuka. Denver: Denver Art Museum, 2009, 19–36.

Cushing Flint, Shirley. "Treason or Travesty: The Martín Cortés Conspiracy Reexamined." *The Sixteenth Century Journal* 39, no. 1 (2008): 23–44.

Dalton, Heather. *Merchants and Explorers: Roger Barlow, Sebastian Cabot, and Networks of Atlantic Exchange, 1500–1560*. Oxford: Oxford University Press, 2016.

Dawa Ango, Junald. "The Cebu-Acapulco Galleon Trade." *Philippine Quarterly of Culture and Society* 38, no. 2 (2010): 147–73.

Delbrugge, Laura, ed. *Self-Fashioning and Assumptions of Identity in Medieval and Early Modern Iberia*. Leiden: Brill, 2015.

De Vos, Paula. "The Science of Spices: Empiricism and Economic Botany in the Early Spanish Empire." *Journal of World History* 17, no. 4 (2006): 399–427.

Diéz-Canedo, Aurora. *Los desventurados barrocos: sentimiento y reflexión entre los descendientes de los conquistadores: Baltasar Dorantes de Carranza, Juan Suárez Peralta y Gonzalo Gómez de Cervantes*. Mexico City: Universidad Pedagógica Nacional, 1990.

Dios, Salustino de. *Gracia, merced y patronazgo real: la Cámara de Castilla entre 1474–1530*. Madrid: Centro de estudios constitucionales, 1993.

Earle, Rebecca. *The Body of the Conquistador: Food, Race and the Colonial Experience in Spanish America, 1492–1700*. Cambridge: Cambridge University Press, 2012.

Elliott, Anthony. *Identity Troubles: An Introduction.* New York: Routledge, 2016.

Elliott, John H. *The Count-Duke of Olivares: The Statesman in an Age of Decline.* New Haven: Yale University Press, 1986.

Escudero Buendía, Francisco J. *Antonio de Mendoza: comendador de la villa de Socuéllamos y primer virrey de la Nueva España.* Perea: Pedro Muñoz, 2003.

Francisco de Mendoza, "El Indio" (1524-1563): Protomonarca de México y Perú, Comendador de Socuéllamos y Capitán General de las Galeras de España. Guadalajara: Aache Ediciones, 2006.

Ette, Ottmar. "EntreMundos o la relacionalidad transarchipiélica de Nueva España." *Iberoamericana* XII, no. 48 (2012): 157-72.

Feros, Antonio. "Clientelismo y poder monárquico en la España de los siglos XVI y XVII." *Relaciones. Estudios de Historia y Sociedad* 29, no. 73 (Winter 1998): 17-49.

Speaking of Spain: The Evolution of Race and Nation in the Hispanic World. Cambridge, MA: Harvard University Press, 2017.

Flint, Richard. *Great Cruelties Have Been Reported: The 1544 Investigation of the Coronado Epxedition.* Dallas: Southern Methodist University Press, 2002.

No Settlement, No Conquest: A History of the Coronado Entrada. Albuquerque: University of New Mexico Press, 2008.

"When East Was West: The Oriental Aim of the Coronado Expedition," in *The Latest Word from 1540: Peoples, Places, and Portrayals of the Coronado Expedition.* Edited by Richard Flint and Shirley Cushing Flint. Albuquerque: University of New Mexico Press, 2011, 105-16.

Flint, Richard, and Shirley Cushing Flint, eds. *Documents of the Coronado Expedition, 1539-1542.* Dallas: Southern Methodist University Press, 2005.

eds. *The Latest Word from 1540: Peoples, Places, and Portrayals of the Coronado Expedition.* Albuquerque: University of New Mexico Press, 2011.

A Most Splendid Company: The Coronado Expedition in Global Perspective. Albuquerque: University of New Mexico Press, 2019.

Flint, Valerie I. J. *The Imaginative Landscape of Christopher Columbus.* Princeton, NJ: Princeton University Press, 1992.

Flynn, Dennis O., and Arturo Giráldez. "Born with a 'Silver Spoon': The Origin of World Trade in 1571." *Journal of World History* 6, no. 2 (1995): 201-21.

Folch, Dolors. "Biografía de Fray Martín de Rada." *Huarte de San Juan. Geografía e historia,* nr. 15 (2008): 33-63.

Folger, Robert. *Generaciones y semblanzas: Memory and Genealogy in Medieval Iberian Historiography.* Tübingen: Gunter Narr, 2003.

Picaresque and Bureaucracy: Lazarillo de Tormes. Newark, DE: Juan de la Cuesta, 2009.

Writing as Poaching: Interpellation and Self-Fashioning in Colonial relaciones de méritos y servicios. Leiden: Brill, 2011.

Fontana Calvo, María Celia. *Las pinturas murales del antiguo convento franciscano de Cuernavaca.* Cuernavaca: Universidad Autónoma del Estado de Morelos, 2011.

Fuchs, Barbara, and Yolanda Martínez-San Miguel. "La grandeza mexicana de Balbuena y el imaginario de una "metropolis colonial." *Revista Iberoamericana* 75, no. 228 (2009): 675–95.

Ganster, Paul. "La familia Gómez de Cervantes. Linaje y sociedad en el México colonial." *Historia Mexicana* XXXI, no. 122 (1981): 197–232.

García-Abásolo, Antonio Francisco. "La expansión mexicana hacia el Pacífico: La primera colonización de Filipinas (1570–1580)." *Historia Mexicana* 32, no. 1 (1982): 55–88.

Gasch-Tómas, José L. "Asian Silk, Porcelain, and Material Culture in the Definition of Mexican and Andalusian Elites, c. 1565–1630," in *Global Goods and the Spanish Empire, 1492–1824: Circulation, Resistance and Diversity*. Edited by Bethany Aram and Bartolomé Yun-Casalilla. London: Palgrave Macmillan, 2014, 153–73.

The Atlantic World and the Manila Galleons: Circulation, Market, and Consumption of Asian Goods in the Spanish Empire, 1565–1650. Leiden: Brill, 2018.

Gaudin, Guillaume. "Parecer sobre las dudas que hay cerca de la demarcación del tratado de Zaragoza en Filipinas (1568), e Instrucción del virrey de Nueva España, don Martín Enríquez al capitán Juan de la Isla sobre lo que debe hacer para ir al descubrimiento de la China." *Relaciones Estudios de Historia y Sociedad* 40, no. 160 (2020): 102–22.

Gerhard, Peter. *Pirates of the Pacific, 1575–1742*. London: University of Nebraska Press, 1990 [1960].

Giráldez, Arturo. *The Age of Trade: The Manila Galleons and the Dawn of the Global Economy*. London: Rowman & Littlefield, 2015.

Gil Fernández, Juan. *Mitos y utopías del descubrimiento, vol. 2: El Pacífico*. Madrid: Alianza universidad, 1989.

Hidalgos y samurais: España y Japón en los siglos 16-17. Madrid: Alianza editorial, 1991.

"Don Rodrigo de Vivero. Un criollo en Filipinas y Japon," in *El Mar del Sur en la historia: ciencia, expansión, representación y poder en el Pacífico*. Edited by Rafael Sagredo Baeza and Rodrigo Moreno Jeria. Santiago de Chile: Universidad Adolfo Ibáñez, 2014, 65–158.

Legazpi. El Tornaviaje: navegantes olvidados por el Pacífico norte. Madrid: Fundación José Antonio de Castro, 2019.

Ghobrial, John-Paul A. "Moving Stories and What They Tell Us: Early Modern Mobility between Microhistory and Global History." *Past & Present* 242, Issue Supplement 14 (2019): 243–80.

González Alonso, Nuria. "Sebastián Hurtado de Corcuera: Gobernador de Panamá y de Filipinas." *Anales del Museo de América* 20 (2012): 199–218.

Gonzalbo Aizpuru, Pilar. "De la penuria y el lujo en la Nueva España. Siglos XVI-XVIII." *Revista de Indias* 56, no. 206 (1996): 49–75.

Goodman, David C. *Power and Penury: Government, Technology and Science in Philip II's Spain*. Cambridge: Cambridge University Press, 1988.

Gough, Barry M. *Juan de Fuca's Strait: Voyages in the Waterway of Forgotten Dreams*. Madeira Park, BC: Harbour Publishing, 2012.

Greenblatt, Stephen J. *Renaissance Self-Fashioning: From More to Shakespeare.* Chicago: University of Chicago Press, 1980.

Gregori Roig, Rosa María. "Representación pública del individuo. Relaciones de méritos y servicios en el Archivo General de Indias (siglos XVII-XVIII)," in *El legado de Mnemosyne: las escrituras del yo a través del tiempo.* Edited by Antonio Castillo Gómez and Verónica Sierra Blas. Gijón: Trea, 2007, 355–79.

Gruzinski, Serge. "Les élites de la monarchie catholique au carrefour des empires (fin XVIe- début XVIIe siècle)," in *L'Empire portugais face aux autres Empires.* Edited by Francisco Bethencourt and Luiz Felipe de Alencastro. Paris: Maisonneuve & Larose, 2007, 273–87.

Las cuatro partes del mundo: historia de una mundialización. Mexico City: Fondo de Cultura Económica, 2010.

L'Aigle et le Dragon: Démesure européenne et mondialisation au XVIe siècle. Paris: Editions Fayard, 2012.

Guevara Sánchez, Arturo. *Los agustinos descalzos: breves noticias de su vida y logros en México y Filipinas.* Mexico City: Instituto Nacional de Antropología e Historia, 2006.

Guillén Berrendero, José A. *La Edad de la Nobleza. Identidad nobiliaria en Castilla y Portugal (1556–1621).* Madrid: Ediciones Polifemo, 2012.

Gutiérrez, Lucio, O. P. *Domingo de Salazar, O.P.: First Bishop of the Philippines, 1512–1594.* Manila: University of Santo Tomas, 2001.

Guzmán Centenero de Arce, Domingo de. "La política asiática de Felipe III: Los intereses cruzados de los socorros a Filipinas (1610–1624)." *Historia* 52, no. 2 (2019), 409–38.

Hanke, Lewis. *The Spanish Struggle for Justice in the Conquest of America.* Boston: Little Brown, 1965.

Hartmann, William K. *Searching for Golden Empires: Epic Cultural Collisions in Sixteenth-Century America.* Tucson: The University of Arizona Press, 2014.

Hausberger, Bernd. "La guerra de los vicuñas contra los vascongados en Potosí y la etnización de los vascos a principios de la edad moderna," in *Excluir para ser: Procesos identitarios y fronteras sociales en la América hispánica (XVII-XVIII).* Edited by Christian Büschges and Frédérique Langue. Madrid: Iberoamericana/Vervuert, 2005, 23–57.

Heredia Correa, Roberto. "Fray Juan Zapata y Sandoval: un paso más allá del criollismo." *Nova Tellus* 29, no. 2 (2011): 215–34.

Herzog, Tamar. *Defining Nations: Immigrants and Citizens in Early Modern Spain and Spanish America.* New Haven, CT: Yale University Press, 2003.

Hespanha, Antonio M. "La economia de la gracia," in *La gracia del derecho. Economomia de la cultura en la Edad Moderna.* Edited by Antonio M. Hespanha. Madrid: Centro de estudios constitucionales, 1993, 151–176.

Hidalgo Nuchera, Patricio. *Encomienda, tributo y trabajo en Filipinas, 1570–1608.* Madrid: Universidad Autónoma de Madrid; Ediciones Polifemo, 1995.

"La embajada de Juan Pablo de Carrión a la Corte en 1558 y el conocimiento colectivo del tornaviaje." *Anais de história de além-mar* XV (2014): 51–78.

Hillerkuss Finn, Thomas. "Tasaciones y tributos de los pueblos de indios de la Provincia de Ávalos, 1535 hasta 1555." *Estudios de historia novohispana* 16 (1996): 15–32.

"Andrés de Urdaneta y sus años de funcionario en el occidente novohispano," in *Andrés de Urdaneta*. Edited by Susana Truchuelo García. Ordizia: Ayuntamiento de Ordizia, 2009, 391–440.

Hoffman, Paul E. *A New Andalucia and a Way to the Orient: The American Southeast during the Sixteenth Century*. Baton Rouge: Louisiana State University Press, 1990.

Huber, Vitus. *Beute und Conquista: Die politische Ökonomie der Eroberung Neuspaniens*. Frankfurt am Main: Campus Verlag, 2017.

Hunt, Lynn. *Writing History in the Global Era*. New York: W. W. Norton & Company, 2014.

Iaccarino, Ubaldo. *Comercio y diplomacia entre Japón y Filipinas en la era Keichō (1596–1615)*. Wiesbaden: Harrassowitz Verlag, 2017.

"Early Spanish Intruders in China: The 1579 Mission of Pedro de Alfaro, O.F.M., Reconsidered." *Journal of Jesuit Studies* 9 (2022): 245–62.

Jacques, Joset. "Grandeza mexicana de Bernardo de Balbuena: ¿una corografía de propaganda económica?" *Bulletin hispanique* 116, no. 2 (2014): 855–68.

Jiménez Estrella, Antonio. "Poder, dinero y ventas de oficios y honores en la España del Antiguo Régimen: un estado de la cuestión." *Cuadernos de historia moderna* 37 (2012): 259–71.

Jostmann, Christian. *Magellan, oder, Die erste Umsegelung der Erde*. Munich: C. H. Beck, 2019.

Junco, Roberto, and Patricia Fournier. "Del Celeste Imperio a la Nueva España: importación, distribución y consumo de la loza de la China del periodo Ming Tardío en el México virreinal," in *La nueva Nao: de Formosa a América Latina. Intercambios culturales, ecpnómicos y políticos entre vecinos distantes*. Edited by Lucía Chen, et al. Taipei: Kaun Tang International Publication, 2008, 3–21.

Kagan, Richard L. "La corografía en la castilla moderna. Género, historia, nación." *Studia Historica. Historia Moderna* XIII (1995): 47–59.

Kagan, Richard L., and Fernando Marías. *Urban Images of the Hispanic World, 1493–1793*. New Haven, CT: Yale University Press, 2000.

Kelsey, Harry. *Juan Rodríguez Cabrillo*. San Marino: Huntington Library, 1986.

"The Planispheres of Sebastian Cabot and Sancho Gutierrez." *Terrae Incognitae* 19 (1987): 58.

Sir Francis Drake: The Queen's Pirate. New Haven, CT: Yale University Press, 2000.

Knauth, Lothar. *Confrontación transpacífica: el Japón y el Nuevo Mundo hispánico, 1542–1639*. Mexico City: UNAM, Instituto de Investigaciones Históricas, 1972.

Krieger, Alex D. *We Came Naked and Barefoot: The Journey of Cabeza de Vaca across North America*. Austin: University of Texas Press, 2002.

Kuwayama, George. *Chinese Ceramics in Colonial Mexico*. Los Angeles: Los Angeles County Museum of Art, 1997.

Lamar Prieto, Covadonga. "La conjuración de Martín Cortés en la monarquía indiana de Fray Juan de Torquemada." *Archivum* LVII, no. 57 (2007): 91–122.

Langue, Frédérique. "De la munificencia a la ostentación: La nobleza de la ciudad de México y la cultura de la apariencia (siglos XVII–XVIII)." *Nuevo Mundo Mundos Nuevos* (2005), http://journals.openedition.org/nuevomundo/642.

Lavallé, Bernard. *Las promesas ambiguas: ensayos sobre el criollismo colonial en los Andes.* Lima: Pontificia Universidad Católica del Perú, 1993.

Lee, Christina H. *The Anxiety of Sameness in Early Modern Spain.* Manchester: Manchester University Press, 2016.

Leibsohn, Dana. "Made in China, Made in Mexico," in *At the Crossroads: The Arts of Spanish American and Early Global Trade, 1492–1850.* Edited by Donna Pierce and Ronald Otsuka. Denver: Denver Art Museum, 2012, 11–41.

León-Portilla, Miguel. "La embajada de los japoneses en México, 1614. El testimonio en Nahuatl del cronista Chimalpahin." *Estudios de asia y Africa* XVI, no. 2 (1981): 215–41.

Hernán Cortés y la Mar del Sur. Madrid: Ediciones Cultura Hispanica; Instituto de Cooperación Iberoamericana, 1985.

Cartografía y crónicas de la California. Mexico City: Universidad Nacional Autónoma de México, 1989.

Luis Salas, José, O.F.M., *Fray Martín Ignacio de Loyola: "Gran Obispo de esta tierra. Eje del desarrollo humano y cristinao del Paraguay y regiones vecinas."* Asunción: Ediciones y Arte S. R. L., 2003.

Luna Moreno, Carmen de. "Gobierno interno: la alternativa tripartita en el siglo XVII," in *Franciscanos y mundo religioso en México.* Edited by Francisco Morales. Mexico City: Universidad Nacional Autónoma de México, 1993, 55–72.

Luque Talaván, Miguel. "Al Rey la hacienda y la vida se ha de dar:' Las reclamaciones económicas de los Legazpi a la Corona," in *España y el Pacífico: Legazpi,* Vol. 1. Edited by Leoncio Cabrero. Madrid: Sociedad estatal de conmemoraciones culturales, 2004, 387–436.

Machuca, Paulina. *El vino de cocos en la Nueva España. Historia de una transculturación en el siglo XVII.* Zamora: El Colegio de Michoacán, 2018.

MacLeod, Murdo J. "Self-Promotion: The Relaciones de Méritos y Servicios and Their Historical and Political Interpretation." *Colonial Latin American Historical Review* 7, no. 1 (1998): 25–42.

Manzo-Robledo Francisco., I, *Hernán Cortés: The (Second) Trial of Residency.* New York: Peter Lang, 2013.

Martin, Georges. "Control regio de la violencia nobiliaria," in *Lucha política: condena y legitimación en la España medieval.* Edited by Isabel Alfonso, Julio Escalona, and Georges Martin. Lyon: ENS, 2004, 219–34.

Martínez, Alfonso. "Hospicios de Nueva España para misioneros del Oriente." *Estudios* 6, no. 4 (1986): 35–49.

Martínez-Loza, Abel. "Ideas geográficas de Hernán Cortés." *Anuario de Estudios Americanos* XLVII (1990): 3–26.

Martínez-San Miguel, Yolanda. *Saberes americanos: Subalternidad y epistemología en los escritos de Sor Juana.* Pittsburgh: Instituto Internacional de Literatura Iberoamericana, 1999.

Martínez Tórrese, José Antonio. "Imperio y arbitrismo. Los memoriales de Pedro de Baeza sobre las Indias Orientales (1607–1609)." *Historia Social* no. 98 (2020): 149–64.

Mathes, W. M. *Vizcaino and Spanish Expansion in the Pacific Ocean: 1580–1630.* San Francisco: California Historical Society, 1968.

——— ed. and trans. *The Conquistador in California, 1535: The Voyage of Fernando Cortés to Baja California in Chronicles and Documents.* Los Angeles: Dawson's Book Shop, 1973.

——— "Spanish Maritime Charting of the Gulf of Mexico and the California Coast," in *Mapping and Empire: Soldier-Engineers on the Southwestern Frontier.* Edited by Dennis Reinhartz and Gerald D. Saxon. Austin: University of Texas Press, 2005, 1–43.

Mawer, Granville Allen. "The Riddle of Cattigara," in *Mapping our World: Terra Incognita to Australia.* Edited by Robert and Martin Woords. Canberra: National Library of Australia, 2013, 38–39.

Mawson, Stephanie J. "Convicts or Conquistadores? Spanish Soldiers in the Seventeenth-Century Pacific." *Past & Present* 232, no. 1 (2016): 87–125.

Mayer González, Alicia. "Religious Thought in Carlos de Sigüenza y Góngora (1645–1700): A Mirror of 'criollo' Spirituality in New Spain." *Jahrbuch für Geschichte Lateinamerikas,* no. 43 (2006): 91–118.

Mayers, Kathryn M. *Visions of Empire in Colonial Spanish American Ekphrastic Writing.* Lewisburg, PA: Bucknell University Press, 2012.

Mazín Gómez, Óscar. *Gestores de la Real Justicia. Procuradores y agentes de las catedrales hispanas nuevas en la corte de Madrid,* Vol.1. *El ciclo de México: 1580–1640.* Mexico City: Colegio de México, 2007.

Mazzotti, José Antonio. "Introducción," in *Agencias criollas: la ambigüedad "colonial" en las letras hispanoamericanas.* Edited by José A. Mazzotti. Pittsburgh, PA: Instituto Internacional de Literatura Iberoamericana, 2000, 7–35.

Mazzotti, José A., ed. *Agencias criollas: la ambigüedad "colonial" en las letras hispanoamericanas.* Pittsburgh, PA: Instituto Internacional de Literatura Iberoamericana, 2000.

——— "Introducción," in *Agencias criollas: la ambigüedad "colonial" en las letras hispanoamericanas.* Edited by José A. Mazzotti. Pittsburgh, PA: Instituto Internacional de Literatura Iberoamericana, 2000, 7–35.

McCarthy, William J. "Cashiering the Last Conquistador: The Juicio de Residencia of Don Sebastián Hurtado de Corcuera, 1635–1644." *Colonial Latin American Historical Review* 18, no. 1 (2013): 35–61.

Mehl, Eva Maria. *Forced Migration in the Spanish Pacific World: From Mexico to the Philippines, 1765–1811.* Cambridge: Cambridge University Press, 2016.

Mena García, Carmen. *El oro del Darién. Entradas y cabalgadas en la onquista de Tierra Firme (1509–1526).* Madrid: Consejo Superior de Investigaciones Científicas, 2011.

Merrim, Stephanie. *The Spectacular City, Mexico, and Colonial Hispanic Literary Culture.* Austin: University of Texas Press, 2010.

Milagros del Vas Mingo, Marta. *Las capitulaciones de Indias en el siglo XVI.* Madrid: Ediciones Cultura Hispánica, 1986.

Mira Caballos, Esteban. *Hernán Cortés: el fin de una leyenda.* Trujillo: Palacio de los Barrantes-Cervantes, 2010.

Mola, Marina Alfonso, and Carlos Martínez Shaw, eds. *El Galeón de Manila.* Madrid: Aldeasa, 2000.

Moorhead, Max L. "Hernán Cortés and the Tehuantepec Passage." *The Hispanic American Historical Review* 29, no. 3 (1949): 370–79.

Morales Valerio, Francisco. "Criollización de la orden Franciscana en Nueva España, siglo XVI." *Archivo Ibero-Americano* 48 (1988): 661–84.

More, Anna. *Baroque Sovereignty: Carlos de Sigüenza y Góngora and the Creole Archive of Colonial Mexico.* Philadelphia: University of Pennsylvania Press, 2013.

Morgan, Ronald J. *Spanish American Saints and the Rhetoric of Identity, 1600–1810.* Tucson: The University of Arizona Press, 2002.

Muro, Luis F. "La expedición Legazpi-Urdaneta a las Filipinas. Organización, 1557–1564," in *Historia y sociedad en el mundo de habla española. Homenaje afosé Miranda.* Edited by Bernardo García. Mexico City: El Colegio de México, 1970, 141–216.

"Soldados de Nueva España a Filipinas, 1575." *Historia Mexicana* 19, no. 4 (1970): 479–91.

La expedición Legazpi-Urdaneta a las Filipinas. Mexico City: Secretaría de Educación Pública, 1975.

Myers, Paul A. *North to California: The Spanish Voyages of Discovery, 1533–1603.* Coral Springs, FL: Llumina Press, 2004.

Nowell, Charles E. "Arellano versus Urdaneta." *Pacific Historical Review* 31, no. 2 (1962): 111–20.

O'Gorman, Edmundo. "Nuevos datos sobre el Dr. Diego García de Palacio." *Boletín del Archivo General de la Nación* XVII, no. 1 (1946): 3–31.

Ollé, Manel. *La invención de China. Percepciones y estrategias filipinas respecto a China durante el siglo XVI.* Wiesbaden: Harrasowitz Verlag, 2000.

La empresa de china. De la Armada Invencible al Galeón de Manila. Barcelona: Acantilado, 2002.

"Portugueses y castellanos en Asia Oriental," in *Portugal na Monarquia Hispânica. Dinâmicas de integração e conflito.* Edited by Pedro Cardim, Leonor Freire Costa, and Mafalda Soares da Cunha. Lisboa: CHAM, 2013, 253–76.

Oropeza Keresey, Déborah. "La esclavitud asiática en el virreinato de la Nueva España, 1565–1673." *Historia Mexicana* LXI, no. 1 (2011): 5–57.

Ortuño Sánchez-Pedreño, José María "La expedición de Ruy López de Villalobos a las islas del Mar del Sur y de Poniente. Estudio histórico-jurídico." *Anales de derecho*, no. 23 (2005): 249–92.

Osterhammel, Jürgen. "Global History and Historical Sociology," in *The Prospect of Global History.* Edited by James Belich et al. Oxford: Oxford University Press, 2016, 23–43.

Owens, Sarah E. *Nuns Navigating the Spanish Empire*. Albuquerque: University of New Mexico Press, 2017.

Pacheco S. J., Juan Manuel. "Fray Juan González de Mendoza, obispo de Popayán." *Boletín de historia y antigüedades* LIII, nr. 618–620 (1966): 301–18.

Padrón, Ricardo. *The Spacious Word: Cartography, Literature and Empire in Early Modern Spain*. Chicago: The University of Chicago Press, 2004.

"'The Indies of the West' or the Tale of How and Imaginary Geography Circumnavigated the Globe," in *Western Visions of the Far East in a Transpacific Age, 1522–1657*. Edited by Christina Hyo Jung Lee. Farnham: Ashgate, 2012, 19–42.

"(Un)Inventing America: The Transpacific Indies in Oviedo and Gómara." *Colonial Latin American Review* 25, no. 1 (2016): 16–34.

The Indies of the Setting Sun: How Early Modern Spain Mapped the Far East as the Transpacific West. Chicago: The University of Chicago Press, 2020.

"The Confusions of Idolatry: Rodrigo Vivero, Japan, and the Hapsburg Monarchy." *Revista de Estudios Hispánicos* 55, no. 1 (2021): 117–38.

Pagden, Anthony. "Identity Formation in Spanish America," in *Colonial Identity in the Atlantic World, 1500–1800*. Edited by Nicholas Canny and Anthony Pagden. Princeton, NJ: Princeton University Press, 1987, 51–93.

Pastor, María Alba. "Criollismo y contrarreforma. Nueva España entre 1570 y 1630." *Ibero-amerikanisches Archiv* 22, no. 3/4 (1996): 247–66.

Crisis y recomposición social: Nueva España en el tránsito del siglo XVI al XVII. Mexico City: Universidad Nacional Autónoma de México; Fondo de Cultura Económica, 1999.

Peña, José F. de la. *Oligarquía y propiedad en Nueva España, 1550–1624*. Mexico City: Fondo de Cultura Económica, 1983.

Pereira Fernández, José Manuel. "Andrés de Urdaneta: In memoriam en el quinto centenario de su nacimiento." *Revista de historia naval* 26, no. 102 (2008): 7–22.

Pérez Bustamante, Ciriaco. *Los orígenes del gobierno virreinal en las Indias españolas. Don Antonio de Mendoza, primer Virrey de la Nueva España (1535–1550)*. Santiago de Compostela: Tipografía de "El Eco Franciscano," 1928.

Pérez, Lorenzo. "Origen de las misiones franciscanas en el Extremo Oriente." *Archivo Ibero-Americano* 2, no. 10 (1915): 63–82.

Pérez Puente, Leticia. *Universidad de doctores: México, siglo XVII*. Mexico City: UNAM, Centro de Estudios sobre la Universidad, 2000.

"El cabildo y la universidad. Las primeras canonjías de oficio en México (1598–1616)." *Historica* XXXVI, no. 1 (2012): 53–96.

Picazo Muntaner, Antoni. "Distribución de productos asiáticos en América en el siglo XVII: una aproximación." *Temas americanistas* 31 (2013): 87–109.

Pierce, Donna, and Ronald Y. Otsuka, eds. *Asia & Spanish America: Trans-Pacific Artistic and Cultural Exchange, 1500–1850*. Papers from the 2006 Mayer Center Symposium at the Denver Art Museum. Denver: Denver Art Museum, 2009.

Polk, Dora. *The Island of California: A History of the Myth*. Lincoln: University of Nebraska Press, 1995.

Polo y La Borda, Adolfo. "Don Mauro's Letters: The Marquis of Villagarcía and the Imperial Networks of Patronage in Spain." *The Americas* 76, no. 4 (2019): 555–83.

Postigo Castellanos, Elena. *Honor y privilegio en la Corona de Castilla. El Consejo de las Ordenes y los Caballero de hábito en el siglo XVII*. Valladolid: Junta de Castilla y León, 1988.

Prieto, Andrés, "Alexander and the Geographer's Eye: Allegories of Knowledge in Martín Fernández de Enciso's *Suma de Geographia* (1519)." *Hispanic Review* 78, no. 2 (2010): 169–88.

Priyadarshini, Meha. *Chinese Porcelain in Colonial Mexico: The Material Worlds of an Early Modern Trade*. Cham: Palgrave Macmillan, 2018.

Puente, Juan Carlos de la. *Andean Cosmopolitans: Seeking Justice and Reward at the Spanish Royal Court*. Austin: University of Texas Press, 2018.

Quijano Velasco, Francisco. "Los argumentos del ayuntamiento de México para destituir al corregidor en el siglo XVI. El pensamiento político novohispano visto desde una institución local." *Estudios de Historia Novohispana* 55 (2016): 46–63.

Rabasa, José. *Inventing America: Spanish Historiography and the Formation of Eurocentrism*. Norman: University of Oklahoma Press, 1993.

Ramachandran, Ayesha. *The Worldmakers: Global Imagining in Early Modern Europe*. Chicago: The University of Chicago Press, 2015.

Ramírez Méndez, Jessica. "La reforma filipina del clero regular y el paso de nuevos hábitos a Indias, 1566–1585," in *Reformas y resistencias en la Iglesia novohispana*. Edited by Martínez López-Cano, María del Pilar, Cervantes Bello, and Francisco Javier. Mexico City: Universidad Nacional Autónoma de México; Benemérita Universidad Autónoma de Puebla, 2014, 113–41.

Ramírez Méndez, Jessica, and Alba Sofía Espinosa Leal. "Las provincias franciscanas descalzas en Nueva España y Filipinas," in *La iglesia y sus territorios, siglos XVI-XVIII*. Edited by María del Pilar, Martínez López-Cano, and Francisco Javier Cervantes Bello. Mexico City: Universidad Nacional Autónoma de México, Instituto de Investigaciones Históricas, 2020, 151–80.

Reinhardt, Nicole. *Voices of Conscience: Royal Confessors and Political Counsel in Seventeenth-Century Spain and France*. Oxford: Oxford University Press, 2016.

Reiss, Timothy J. *Mirages of the Selfe: Patterns of Personhood in Ancient and Early Modern Europe*. Stanford, CA: Stanford University Press, 2003.

Rensink, Brenden. "'If a Passage Could Be Found': The Power of Myth (and Money) in North American Exploration." *We Proceed On* 36, no. 2 (2010): 8–17.

Reséndez, Andrés. *Un viaje distinto: la exploración de Cabeza de Vaca por América*. Barcelona: La Vanguardia Ediciones, 2008.

Ribot García, Luís A., ed. *El tratado de Tordesillas y su época*. 3 vols. Madrid: Sociedad V Centenario del Tratado de Tordesillas; Junta de Castilla y León Consejería de Educación y Cultura, 1995.

Richmond Ellis, Robert. *They Need Nothing: Hispanic-Asian Encounters of the Colonial Period.* Toronto: University of Toronto Press, 2012.

Rinke, Stefan. *Conquistadoren und Azteken: Cortés und die Eroberung Mexikos.* Munich: C. H. Beck, 2019.

Rivero Lake, Rodrigo. *Namban Art in Viceregal Mexico.* Madrid: Turner, 2005.

Rodríguez Velasco, Jesús D. "De oficio a estado. La caballería entre el Espéculo y las Siete Partidas." *Cahiers de linguistique hispanique médiévale* 17–18 (1993–94): 49–77.

——— *El debate sobre la caballería en el siglo XV. La tratadística caballeresca castellana en su marco europeo.* Salamanca: Junta de Castilla y León Consejería de Educación y Cultura, 1996.

——— *Order and Chivalry: Knighthood and Citizenship in Late Medieval Castile,* translated by Eunice Rodríguez Ferguson. Philadelphia: University of Pennsylvania Press, 2010.

Roldán-Figueroa, Rady. *The Martyrs of Japan: Publication History and Catholic Missions in the Spanish World (Spain, New Spain, and the Philippines, 1597–1700).* Brill: Leiden, 2021.

Rose, Nikolas S. *Inventing Our Selves: Psychology, Power, and Personhood.* Cambridge: Cambridge University Press, 1996.

Rosenmüller, Christoph. *Corruption and Justice in Colonial Mexico, 1650–1755.* Cambridge: Cambridge University Press, 2019.

Rubial García, Antonio. *El convento agustino y la sociedad novohispana (1533–1630).* Mexico City: Universidad Nacional Autónoma de México, 1989.

——— "Votos pactados. Las prácticas políticas entre los mendicantes novohispanos." *Estudios de historia novohispana* 26 (2002): 51–83.

——— ed. *La Iglesia en el México colonial.* Mexico City: Instituto de Investigaciones Históricas, UNAM; Instituto de ciencias sociales y humanidades "Alfonso Vélez Pliego," BUAP; Ediciones de educación y cultura, 2013.

Rubio Mañé, José Ignacio. *El virreinato.* 4 vols. Mexico City: Instituto de Investigaciones Históricas, UNAM; Fondo de Cultura Económica, 1983.

Rubio Sánchez, Manuel. *Historia del Puerto de la Santísima Trinidad de Sonsonate o Acajulta.* San Salvador: Editorial Universitaria, 1977.

Rublack, Ulinka. *Dressing Up: Cultural Identity in Renaissance Europe.* Oxford: Oxford University Press, 2010.

Rucquoi, Adeline, and Hugo O. Bizzarri, "Los espejos de príncipes en Castilla: entre Oriente y Occidente." *Cuadernos de Historia de España* 79, no. 1 (2005): 7–30.

Ruiz-de-Medina, Juan. *El martirologio del Japón, 1558–1873.* Rome: Institutum Historicum S.I., 1999.

Ruíz Medrano, Ethelia. *Gobierno y Sociedad en Nueva España: Segunda Audiencia y Antonio de Mendoza.* Zamora: El Colegio de Michoacán y el Gobierno del Estado de Michoacán, 1991.

Sabat-Rivers, Georgina. "El Barroco de la contraconquista: primicias de conciencia criolla en Balbuena y Domínguez Camargo," in *Relecturas del Barroco de Indias.* Edited by Mabel Moraña. Hanover: Ediciones del Norte, 1994, 59–96.

Sagarra Gamazo, Adelaida. "La empresa del pacífico o el sueño pimentero burgalés (1508–29)." *Revista de Estudios Colombinos* 9 (2013): 21–36.

Sales Colín, Ostwald. *El movimiento portuario de Acapulco: el protagonismo de Nueva España en la relación con Filipinas, 1587–1648*. Mexico City: Plaza y Valdés Editores, 2000.

"Intentos de fortalecimiento español allende Filipinas: Moluco, Matheo e Isla del Norte, 1605–1653." *Estudios de Asia y África* 50, no. 2 (2015): 355–94.

Sánchez, Antonio. *La espada, la cruz y el Padrón. Soberanía, fe y representación cartográfica en el mundo ibérico bajo la Monarquía hispánica, 1503–1598*. Madrid: Consejo Superior de Investigaciones Científicas, 2013.

Sandman, Alison, and Eric H. Ash. "Trading Expertise: Sebastian Cabot between Spain and England." *Renaissance Quarterly* 57, no. 3 (2004): 816–27.

Sarabia Viejo, María Justina. *Don Luis de Velasco: virrey de Nueva España, 1550–1564*. Seville: Escuela de Estudios Hispano-Americans, 1978.

Schell Hoberman, Louisa. *Mexico's Merchant Elite, 1590–1660*. Durham, NC: Duke University Press, 1991.

Schreffler, Michael J. *The Art of Allegiance: Visual Culture and Imperial Power in Baroque New Spain*. University Park: Pennsylvania State University Press, 2007.

Schwaller, John F. "The *Ordenanza del Patronazgo* in New Spain, 1574–1600." *The Americas* 42, no. 3 (1986): 253–74.

The History of the Catholic Church in Latin America: From Conquest to Revolution and Beyond. New York: New York University Press, 2011.

Schurz, William Lytle. *The Manila Galleon*. New York: E. P. Dutton, 1939.

Sebastian, Conrad. *What Is Global History?* Princeton, NJ: Princeton University Press, 2015.

Sempat Assadourian, Carlos. *Zacatecas, conquista y transformacion de la frontera en el siglo XVI: minas de plata, guerra y evangelización*. Mexico City: El Colegio de México, Centro de Estudios Históricos, 2008.

Seijas, Tatiana. *Asian Slaves in Colonial Mexico: From Chinos to Indians*. Cambridge: Cambridge University Press, 2014.

Serna Nasser, Bruno de la. "La prohibición del comercio entre Nueva España y Perú de 1634: génesis de una real cédula a través de la coyuntura histórica de la monarquía hispánica." *Historica* XLIV, no. 1 (2020): 41–81.

Siegert, Bernhard. *Passagiere und Papiere: Schreibakte auf der Schwelle zwischen Spanien und Amerika*. Munich: Fink, 2006.

Slack, Edward R. "The Chinos in New Spain: A Corrective Lens for a Distorted Image." *Journal of World History* 20, no. 1 (2009): 35–67.

"Orientalizing New Spain: Perspectives on Asian Influence in Colonial Mexico." *México y la Cuenca del Pacífico*, no. 43 (2012): 97–127.

Sola, Diego. *El cronista de China: Juan González de Mendoza, entre la misión, el imperio y la historia*. Barcelona: Universitat de Barcelona, 2018.

Solodkow, David M. "La aristocracia de los desposeídos: Baltasar Dorantes de Carranza y la primera generación de criollos novohispanos," in *Poéticas de lo criollo: la transformación del concepto "criollo" en las letras hispanoamericanas (siglos XVI al XIX)*. Edited by Juan M. Vitulli and David M. Solodkow. Buenos Aires: Ediciones Corregidor, 2009, 105–43.

Spate, O. H. K. *The Pacific Since Magellan, Vol. 1: The Spanish Lake.* Canberra: Australian National University Press, 1979.

Stern, Steve J. "Paradigms of Conquest: History, Historiography, and Politics." *Journal of Latin American Studies* 24, Supplement S1 (1992): 1–34.

Strosetzki, Cristoph, ed. *El poder de la economía: la imagen de los mercaderes y el comercio en el mundo hispánico de la Edad Moderna.* Frankfurt am Main: Iberoamericana & Vervuert, 2018.

Suárez, Margarita. "Sedas, rasos y damascos: Lima y el cierra del comercio triangular con México y Manila en la primera mitad del siglo XVII." *América Latina en la historia económica* 22, no. 2 (2015): 101–34.

Suárez, Thomas. *Early Mappings of Southeast Asia.* Singapore: Periplus Editions (HK) Ltd., 1999.

Sykes, Godfrey. "The Mythical Straits of Anian." *Bulletin of the American Geographical Society* 47, no. 3 (1915): 161–72.

Taylor, Charles. *Sources of the Self: The Making of the Modern Identity.* Cambridge: Cambridge University Press, 1989.

Tempère, Delphine. "En las fronteras del mundo iberoasiático. Discurso y vida de los agentes de la Corona española en Filipinas (Siglo XVII)," in *Distributive Struggle and the Self in the Early Modern Iberian World.* Edited by Nikolaus Böttcher, Stefan Rinke, and Nino Vallen. Stuttgart: Verlag Hans-Dieter Heinz, Akademischer Verlag, 2019, 193–218.

Terukina Yamauchi, Jorge L. *El imperio de la virtud: Grandeza mexicana (1604) de Bernardo de Balbuena y el discurso criollo novohispano.* Woodbridge: Tamesis, 2017.

Tomás y Valiente, Francisco. *La venta de oficios en Indias (1492–1606).* Madrid: Instituto de Estudios Administrativos, 1972.

——— "Opiniones de algunos juristas clásicos españoles sobrela venta de oficios públicos," in *Filosofía y derecho: estudios en honor del profesor José Corts Grau,* Vol. 2. Valencia: Universidad de Valencia, 1977, 627–49.

Torres Ramirez, Bibiano. *La Armada de Barlovento.* Seville: Escuela de Estudios Hispano-Americanos, 1981.

Tremml-Werner, Birgit. *Spain, China, and Japan in Manila, 1571–1644: Local Comparisons and Global Connections.* Amsterdam: Amsterdam University Press, 2015.

Ulbrich, Claudia, and Richard Wittmann. *Fashioning the Self in Transcultural Settings: The Uses and Significance of Dress in Self-Narratives.* Baden-Baden: Ergon-Verlag, 2015.

Valladares, Rafael. *Castilla y Portugal en Asia (1580–1680). Declive imperial y adaptación.* Louvain: Leuven University Press, 2001.

Valle Pavón, Guillermina de. "Los mercaderes de México y la transgresiónde los límites al comercio pacífico en Nueva España, 1550–1620." *Revista de Historia Económica/Journal of Iberian and Latin American Economic History,* no. 23 (2005): 213–40.

Vallen, Nino. "Healing Power: Land Surveying Politics and the Archive of Mendoza's America (1535–1552)," in *Las agencias de lo indígena en la larga era de globalización. Microperspectivas de su producción y represetación desde la época colonial temprana hasta el presente*. Edited by Romy Köhler and Anne Ebert. Berlin: Gebr. Mann Verlag, 2015, 89–93.

"Conquista, memoria y cultura material en la Nueva España, Siglos XVI y XVII." *Iberoamericana* XIX, no. 71 (2019): 13–33.

"The Self and the World in Baltasar Dorantes de Carranza's Sumaria relación de las cosas de la Nueva España," in *Distributive Struggle and the Self in the Early Modern Iberian World*. Edited by Böttcher, Rinke, and Vallen. Stuttgart: Verlag Hans-Dieter Heinz, Akademischer Verlag, 2019, 141–68.

"'What Distributive Justice Requires': Negotiating Empire and Local Orders in Sixteenth- and Seventeenth-Century New Spain." *Revista de Indias* LXXX/ 278 (2020): 101–29.

Varela, Consuelo. *El viaje de don Ruy López de Villalobos a las islas del Poniente, 1542–1548*. Milan: Cisalpini-Goliardica, 1983.

Varela Marcos, Jesús, ed. *El tratado de Tordesillas en la cartografía histórica*. Valladolid: Sociedad V Centenario de Tratado de Tordesillas, 1994.

Varese, Juan Antonio. *Los viajes de Juan Díaz de Solís y el descubrimiento del Río de la Plata*. Montevideo: Ediciones de la banda oriental, 2016.

Velasquez Sánchez-Hidalgo, Verónica. *"Maiolica and the Doctrine of Blood Purity in New Spain, Mexico."* Doctoral thesis, University of Sheffield, 2014.

Vilches, Elvira. *New World Gold: Cultural Anxiety and Monetary Disorder in Early Modern Spain*. Chicago: The University of Chicago Press, 2010.

Vitulli, Juan M., and David M. Solodkow, eds. *Poéticas de lo criollo: la transformación del concepto "criollo" en las letras hispanoamericanas (siglo XVI al XIX)*. Buenos Aires: Ediciones Corregidor, 2009.

"Ritmos diversos y secuencias plurales: hacia una periodización del concepto "criollo," in *Poéticas de lo criollo: la transformación del concepto "criollo" en las letras hispanoamericanas (siglos XVI al XIX)*. Edited by Juan M. Vitulli and David M. Solodkow. Buenos Aires: Ediciones Corregidor, 2009, 9–58.

Vogeley, Nancy. "China and the American Indies: A Sixteenth-Century 'History.'" *Colonial Latin American Review* 6, no. 2 (1997): 165–84.

Vu Thanh, Hélène. "The Glorious Martyrdom of the Cross. The Franciscans and the Japanese Persecutions of 1597." *Culture & History Digital Journal* 6, no. 1 (2017).

Wagner, Henry R. *Spanish Voyages to the Northwest Coast of America in the Sixteenth Century*. San Francisco: California Historical Society, 1929.

"Fray Marcos de Niza." *New Mexico Historical Review* 9, no. 2 (1934): 184–226.

"Francisco de Ulloa Returned." *California Historical Society Quarterly* 19, no. 3 (1940): 240–44.

Wagner, Klaus. "Guido de Lavezaris, genovés (1512–1582), de librero a gobernador de Filipinas," in *Tra Siviglia e Genova: Notaio, documento e commercio nell'età colombiana*. Edited by Vito Piergiovanni. Milan: Giuffrè, 1992, 378–91.

Wey Gómez, Nicolás. *The Tropics of Empire: Why Columbus Sailed South to the Indies*. London: The MIT Press, 2008.

Yun Casalilla, Bartolomé. *Marte contra Minerva. El precio del imperio español, c. 1450–1600.* Barcelona: Crítica, 2004.

"Introducción. Entre el imperio colonial y la monarquía compuesta. Élites y territorios en la Monarquía Hispánica (ss. XVI y XVII)," in *Las redes del imperio. Élites sociales en la articulación de la Monarquía Hispánica, 1492–1714.* Edited by Bartolomé Yun Casalilla. Seville: Marcial Pons and Universidad Pablo Olavide, 2009, 11–35.

Yuste López, María del Carmen. *El comercio de la Nueva España con Filipinas, 1590–1785.* Mexico City: Instituto Nacional de Antropología e Historia, 1984.

Emporios transpacíficos. Comerciantes mexicanos en Manila, 1710–1815. Mexico City: Universidad Nacional Autónoma de México, 2007.

"De la libre contratación a las restricciones de la permission. La andadura de los comerciantes de México en los giros iniciales con Manila, 1580–1610," in *Un océano de seda y plata: el universo económico del Galeón de Manila.* Edited by Salvador Bernabéu Albert and Carlos Martínez Shaw. Seville: Consejo Superior de Investigaciones Científicas, 2013, 85–106.

Index